No Conde

NO CONDEMNATION IN CHRIST JESUS

*

*As Unfolded in the Eighth Chapter
of the Epistle to the Romans*

*

OCTAVIUS WINSLOW

THE BANNER OF TRUTH TRUST

THE BANNER OF TRUTH TRUST
3 Murrayfield Road, Edinburgh EH12 6EL
PO Box 621, Carlisle, Pennsylvania 17013, USA

*

First published 1853
First Banner of Truth edition 1991
ISBN 0 85151 592 4

*

Printed and bound in Great Britain by
BPCC Hazell Books
Aylesbury, Bucks, England

PREFACE.

It had been no difficult task to have expanded the following pages—the substance of which was originally delivered by the Author in the course of his stated ministrations, and in his usual extemporaneous mode of address—much beyond their present limit. His dread, however, of inflicting upon the public a volume, overgrown and unreadable—precious and alluring as was its theme—constrained him greatly to curtail his work; thus, he fears, exposing himself to the charge of having swept lightly and rapidly over subjects the greatness and importance of which demanded profounder thought, and more elaborate discussion. The portion of Holy Writ he has undertaken—it may be deemed somewhat too presumptuously—to expound, must be regarded as a mine of sacred wealth, as inexhaustible in its resources, as those resources are indescribable in their beauty, and in their excellence and worth, priceless.

It would, perhaps, be impossible to select from the Bible a single chapter in which were crowded so much sublime, evangelical, and sanctifying truth as this eighth of Romans. It is not only all gospel, but it may be said to contain the whole gospel. In this brief but luminous space is embraced an epitome of all the privileges and duties, trials and consolations, discouragements and hopes of the Christian. Commencing with his elevated position of NO CON- DEMNATION FROM GOD, it conducts him along a path where flowers bloom, and honey drops, and fragrance breathes, and music floats, and light and shade blend in beautiful and exquisite harmony to the radiant point of NO SEPARATION FROM CHRIST. And amidst the beauties and sweets, the melodies and sunshine of this glorious landscape of truth, thus spread out in all its panoramic extent and magnificence before his eye, the believer in Jesus is invited to roam, to revel, and delight himself.

May the Holy and Eternal Spirit impart to the reader, and, through his prayers, increasingly to the writer, the personal possession and heart-sanctifying experience of the Divine treasures of this precious portion of God's Word. And, if this simple and imperfect outline may but supply a faint and glim- mering light, guiding the reader to a more prayerful and thorough exploration of this mine of the " deep things of God," thus leading to the discovery of new and yet richer veins, the Author will not regret that the oil which fed the lamp has been drawn from his own exhausting, yet holy and delightful studies.

And now to the Father, Son, and Holy Ghost, as unto the TRIUNE JEHOVAH, be all honour and praise for ever. Amen.

LEAMINGTON, *April*, 1852.

CONTENTS.

CHAPTER I.

PAGE

No Condemnation 1

CHAPTER II.

Freedom from the Law of Sin and Death 22

CHAPTER III.

The Impotence of the Law, and God's method of meeting it 28

CHAPTER IV.

The Righteousness of the Law accomplished in the Believer 43

CHAPTER V.

The Unregenerate and the Regenerate contrasted . . 53

CHAPTER VI.

Spiritual-Mindedness 65

CHAPTER VII.

The Enmity of the Carnal Mind 91

CHAPTER VIII.

PAGE

Pleasing God 101

CHAPTER IX.

The Indwelling of the Spirit in the Regenerate . . 113

CHAPTER X.

The Body Dead, but the Spirit Life 122

CHAPTER XI.

The Resurrection of Christ 129

CHAPTER XII.

The Resurrection of the Christian 138

CHAPTER XIII.

The Believer's Obligation to Mortify Sin . . . 146

CHAPTER XIV.

The Guidance of the Spirit 157

CHAPTER XV.

The Spirit of Adoption 168

CHAPTER XVI.

The Spirit Testifying to the Believer's Adoption . . 174

CHAPTER XVII.

The Christian's Joint Heirship 184

CHAPTER XVIII.

PAGE

Present Suffering weighed with Future Glory . . 197

CHAPTER XIX.

The Earnest Expectation of the Renewed Creature . . 205

CHAPTER XX.

A Suffering World in Sympathy with Suffering Man . . 217

CHAPTER XXI.

The First-fruits of the Spirit, an Earnest of the Full
Redemption 226

CHAPTER XXII.

Saved by Hope 235

CHAPTER XXIII.

The Sympathy of the Spirit with the Infirmity of Prayer . 242

CHAPTER XXIV.

The Intercession of the Spirit in the Saints . . . 256

CHAPTER XXV.

All Things working for Good 264

CHAPTER XXVI.

Divine Predestination 279

CHAPTER XXVII.

Effectual Calling 303

CHAPTER XXVIII.

PAGE

Free Justification 312

CHAPTER XXIX.

Eternal Glorification 323

CHAPTER XXX.

God is For Us 344

CHAPTER XXXI.

The Gift of God's Son, the Guarantee of all other Blessing 357

CHAPTER XXXII.

The Believer's Challenge 365

CHAPTER XXXIII.

The Believer's Triumph 371

CHAPTER XXXIV.

More than Conquerors 379

CHAPTER XXXV.

No Separation from Christ Jesus 386

CHAPTER I.

NO CONDEMNATION.

"There is therefore now no condemnation to them which are in
  Christ Jesus, who walk not after the flesh, but after the
  Spirit."—ROMANS viii. 1.

IN these words the inspired Apostle supplies us
with the key to the great and precious truths embodied in the chapter, upon the unfolding of which,
as guided by the Holy Spirit, we propose to enter.
They contain the leading proposition, which, thus
distinctly enunciated, he proceeds with his usual
vigour of mind, perspicuity of reasoning, and gentleness of spirit, clothing his thoughts with the most
eloquent diction, to confirm and illustrate. He had
been descanting, with much feeling and power, upon
the painful and ceaseless conflict waging between the
antagonist principles of the regenerate heart, illustrating it, as is evident from his use of the first
person, by a reference to his own personal experience
as a Christian. The question, mooted by some,
whether Paul delineated a state preceding, or subsequent to, conversion, ought not, we think, to allow

a moment's doubt.   Since, from the fourteenth verse
to the close of the chapter, he unfolds the operation
of a law which only finds scope for its exercise in the
soul of the renewed man, and with whose hidden and
mysterious workings, the experience of the saints has
in all ages coincided.   But if this argument still
leaves the mind perplexed, the opening of the present
chapter would appear sufficiently conclusive to set
the question at rest.   Having portrayed with a
master pen—himself sitting for the picture—the
spiritual struggles of the children of God, he then
proceeds, in the passage under consideration, to
apply the divine consolation and support appropriate
to a condition so distressing and humiliating. Lifting
them from the region of conflict and cloud, he places
them upon an elevation towering above the gloom
and strife of the battle-field, around whose serene,
sunlight summit gathered the first dawning of eternal
glory.   "There is therefore now no condemnation to
them which are in Christ Jesus."   The transition
from the desponding tone of the seventh chapter, to
the triumphant language of the eighth, may appear
somewhat startling and abrupt; yet it is perfectly
easy, logical, and natural.   The verse before us is an
inference fairly deducible from the whole of the
preceding discussion; and is, in fact, the grand
conclusion toward which the Apostle had throughout
the argument been aiming to arrive.   Clear is it,
then, as the sun, that if to the saints of God belong
the conflict of sin and death, over whose thraldom

they mourn; to them also equally belongs the deliverance from the curse and the condemnation, in whose victory they rejoice. Let us now address ourselves to the exposition of this sublime and solemn theme, in humble reliance upon the Divine teaching of the Spirit, pledged and vouchsafed to guide us into all truth.

'Condemnation' is a word of tremendous import; and it is well fairly to look at its meaning, that we may the better understand the wondrous grace that has delivered us from its power. Echoing through the gloomy halls of a human court, it falls with a fearful knell upon the ear of the criminal, and thrills with sympathy and horror the bosom of each spectator of the scene. But in the court of Divine Justice it is uttered with a meaning and solemnity infinitely significant and impressive. To that court every individual is cited. Before that bar each one must be arraigned. "Conceived in sin, and shapen in iniquity," man enters the world under arrest—an indicted criminal, a rebel manacled, and doomed to die. Born under the tremendous sentence originally denounced against sin: "In the day that thou eatest thereof thou shalt surely die;" or, "Thou shalt die the death," he enters life under a present, the prelude of a future condemnation. From it he can discover no avenue of escape. He lies down, and he rises up —he repairs to the mart of business, and to the haunt of pleasure, a guilty, sentenced, and condemned man. "Cursed is every one that continueth not in

all things which are written in the book of the law,
to do them," is the terrible sentence branded upon
his brow. And should the summons to eternity
arrest him amidst his dreams, his speculations, and
his revels, the adversary would deliver him to the
judge, the judge to the officer, and the officer would
consign him over to all the pangs and horrors of the
"second" and "eternal death." " He that believeth
not, is *condemned already.*" My dear reader, without
real conversion this is your present state, and must
be your future doom.

But from this woe all believers in Christ are delivered. The sentence of death under which, in
common with others, they lay, is absolved; the curse
is removed; the indictment is quashed; and "there
is, therefore, now no condemnation."

But let us, for the better understanding of this
subject, consider what this condition does *not* imply.
It does not include deliverance from the in-being of
sin, nor exemption from Divine correction, nor the
absence of self-accusation; still less does it suppose
that there is nothing for which the believer deserves
to die. All this exists where yet no condemnation
exists. The battle with indwelling evil is still waged,
and the loving chastisement of a Father is still experienced, and the self-condemnation is still felt, and
daily in the holiest life there is still transpiring, that
which, were God strict to mark iniquities, merits and
would receive eternal woe; and yet the declaration
stands untouched and unimpeached—"No condem-

nation to them which are in Christ Jesus." This is the blessed condition we are now more fully to describe.

The freedom of the believer is just what it is declared to be—entire exemption from *condemnation*. From all which that word of significant and solemn import implies, he is, by his relation to Christ, delivered. Sin does not condemn him, the law does not condemn him, the curse does not condemn him, hell does not condemn him, God does not condemn him. He is under no power from these, beneath whose accumulated and tremendous woe all others wither. A brief and simple argument will, perhaps, be sufficient to establish this fact. The *pardon of sin* necessarily includes the negation of its condemnatory power. There being no sin legally alleged, there can be no condemnation justly pronounced. Now, by the sacrifice of Christ all the sins of the Church are entirely put away. He, the sinless Lamb of God, took them up and bore them away into a land of oblivion, whence even the Divine mind fails to recall them. " How forcible are right words !" Listen to those which declare this wondrous fact : " I, even I, am He that blotteth out thy transgressions for mine own sake, and will not remember thy sins." " Thou hast cast all my sins behind thy back." " Having forgiven you all trespasses." " Their sins and iniquities will I remember no more." The *revoking of the sentence of the law* must equally annihilate its condemnatory force. The obedience and death of Christ met the claims of that law, both in its preceptive and punitive character. A single declaration of God's Word throws a flood of light upon this truth :—" Christ hath redeemed us from the curse of the law, being made a curse for us." The sentence of the law thus falling upon the Surety, who was " made under the law, that he might redeem them that were under the law," there can be no condemnation from it to those who have taken shelter in him. Thus, then, is it evident that both sin and the law are utterly powerless to condemn a believer in the Lord Jesus Christ. We have hinted, that the perfection of Christ's satisfaction supplies the meritorious and procuring cause of our non-condemnation. This truth cannot be too frequently repeated, nor too prominently kept in view. No legal obedience—no personal merit or worthiness of the sinner whatever —is taken into the account of his discharge from condemnation. This exalted position can only be reached by an expedient that harmonizes with the attributes of God, and thus upholds, in undimmed lustre, the majesty and honour of the Divine government. God will pardon sin, and justify the sinner, but it must be by a process supremely glorifying to himself. How, then, could a creature-satisfaction, the most perfect that man, or the most peerless that angels could offer, secure this result ? Impossible ! But the case, strange and difficult though it is, is met, fully, adequately met, by the satisfaction of Jesus. The Son of God became the Son of man. He presents himself to the Father in the character of the church's substitute. The Father, beholding in him the Divinity that supplies the merit, and the humanity that yields the obedience and endures the suffering, accepts the Saviour, and acquits the sinner. Hence the freedom of the believer from condemnation. "There is, therefore, *now* no condemnation." It is the existence of a *present* condition. It is the enjoyment of a present immunity. "He is now free from condemnation,—not as if the sentence of acquittal were still in dependence, but as if the sentence had already passed,—not as if he had to look, perhaps doubtfully and ambiguously, forward to some future day, when a verdict of exculpation shall be pronounced upon him; but as if he stood exculpated before God even now, and even now might rejoice in the forgiveness of all his trespasses."* It is the simple belief of this fact that brings instant peace to the bosom. A present discharge from condemnation must produce a present joy. Open the iron-bound door of the condemned cell, and by the dim light that struggles through its bars read the sovereign's free pardon to the felon, stretched, pale and emaciated, upon his pallet of straw; and the radiance you have kindled in that gloomy dungeon, and the transport you have created in that felon's heart, will be a *present* realization. You have given him back a present life; you have touched a thousand chords in his bosom, which awake a present harmony; and where, just previous,

* Chalmers

reigned in that bosom sullen, grim despair, now reigns the sun-light joyousness of a present hope. Christian ! there is *now* no condemnation for you. Be yours, then, a *present* and a full joy. "Christ has made atonement, and with it God is satisfied; and if so, well may you be satisfied—delighting yourselves greatly in the abundance of peace, and going forth even now in the light and liberty of your present enlargement."

"To them which are in Christ Jesus." We here touch a vital and profound truth. Rich and accumulative as the passages are which offer their aid in its elucidation, we despair of conveying to other than a mind experimentally acquainted with the truth itself, anything like an adequate representation of the imposing magnitude and glory of the condition. To be in Christ may really be felt, but not easily described. The first view, then, which we present, is that which illustrates the mystical in-being of the church in Christ, when he stood as its substitute. As all the nations of the world were federally and mystically in Adam when he fell; so the "holy nation," the Church of God, was federally and mystically in the Second Adam, "the Lord from heaven," when in the counsel of God he presented himself as its Surety, and when in the fulness of time he appeared, all robed for the sacrifice, to discharge the engagement. Approach that cross, and what do you behold? Is it that you see a guilty one, suffering—a criminal, worthy of death? Nay; you see the sinless Son of

God bearing the sin, and, by consequence, the condemnation of his people. And in that wondrous spectacle, you see brought to the bar of Infinite Justice—tried, sentenced, and condemned, in the person of their surety—all those who are in Christ Jesus. In Christ they were chosen—to Christ they were betrothed—with Christ they were united—by Christ they are saved,—and, sitting with Christ on his throne, they shall reign with him for ever and ever.

But, there is the open, manifest being in Christ, on which we must lay especial stress in our attempted description of this blessed state. " Preserved in Christ Jesus," the sinner is eventually "*called* in Christ Jesus." " If any man be in Christ Jesus, he is a new creature." An external and nominal profession of the Gospel may exist, and exist, too, in connexion with great knowledge, and fervent zeal, and costly sacrifice, and morality of a high order, apart from this internal change. Such a character our Lord describes in these words : " Every branch *in me* that beareth not fruit he taketh away." Such an individual is in Christ by an outward profession only. But a state of non-condemnation implies a being in Christ in a far higher sense. It includes the great truth of Christ being in us,—" I in them." " We are in him that is true, even in his Son Jesus Christ." Thus it is a mutual in-dwelling—Christ in us, and we in Christ. Here is our security. The believer is in Christ as Jacob was in the garment of

the elder brother when Isaac kissed him, and he
" smelled the smell of the raiment, and blessed him,
and said, See, the smell of my son is as the smell of
a field which the Lord hath blessed." He is in
Christ, as the poor homicide was within the city of
refuge when pursued by the avenger of blood, but
who could not overtake and slay. He is in Christ as
Noah was inclosed within the ark, with the heavens
darkening above him, and the waters heaving beneath
him, yet with not a drop of the flood penetrating his
vessel, nor a blast of the storm disturbing the serenity
of his spirit. How expressive are these scriptural emblems of the perfect security of a believer in Christ !
He is clothed with the garment of the Elder Brother,
the righteousness of the Lord Jesus Christ, " which
is unto all, and upon all them that believe." On
that garment the Father's hands are placed; in that
robe the person of the believer is accepted; it is to
God " as the smell of a field which the Lord hath
blessed :" the blessing of the heavenly birthright is
his—and for him there is *no condemnation.* Pursued
by the avenger of blood, the threatenings of a condemning law, he has reached the city of refuge, the
Lord Jesus Christ. Fearful and trembling, yet believing and hoping, he has crossed the sacred threshold,
and in an instant he is safe—and for him there is *no
condemnation.* Fleeing from the gathering storm—
" the wrath which is to come,"—he has availed himself of the open door of the sacred ark,—the crucified

Saviour—has entered, God shutting him in—and for him there is *no condemnation*. Yes, Christ Jesus is our sanctuary, beneath whose shadow we are safe. Christ Jesus is our strong tower, within whose embattlements no avenger can threaten. Christ Jesus is our hiding-place from the wind, and covert from the tempest; and not one drop of "the wrath to come" can fall upon the soul that is in him. O how completely accepted, and how perfectly secure, the sinner who is in Christ Jesus! He feels he is saved on the basis of a law, whose honour is vindicated; through the clemency of a righteous Sovereign, whose holiness is secured; and through the mercy of a gracious God, the glory of whose moral government is eternally and illustriously exhibited. And now is his head lifted up above his enemies round about him; for there is no condemnation to them which are in Christ Jesus. Reader, are you in Christ Jesus? Is this your condition? We repeat the solemn declaration—"If any man be in Christ, he is a *new creature*; old things have passed away; behold, all things are become new." Are you that new creature? Prove, examine, and ascertain. For if you are not born again of the Spirit, be well assured that you are still under the curse and sentence of the law. And while condemnation, in dark and gloomy characters, is written upon the brow of every unbelieving sinner out of Christ; Christ has said of all who have fled out of themselves to him, "He that heareth my word, and believeth on Him that sent me, hath everlasting life, and *shall not come into condemnation*, but is passed from death unto life."

"Who walk not after the flesh, but after the Spirit." We have here the character of all those who have secured, by faith in the Lord Jesus, their full discharge from the sentence of death. Thus, in the passage under consideration are clearly stated, the cause and the consequence of the believer's discharge. It has been shown, that our being in Christ is the ground of our not being in condemnation. It then follows, that as a fruit—a consequence of our immunity from condemnation—is our walking after the Spirit. Thus, while justification and sanctification are separate and distinct conditions, they yet are cognate truths, and co-exist in the experience of all the regenerate. The deduction which the Apostle here makes of holiness from acceptance; or rather, the order of sequence which he observes, is worthy of the reader's closest attention. Its want of observance has kept numbers of sincere seekers of Christ in the cold dreary region of embarrassment and doubt, who, but for thus overlooking the order observed, or perhaps rather, by reversing that order, might have fully received into their souls that "kingdom which is righteousness, and peace, and joy in the Holy Ghost." Their great error has been an attempt to shape their course, not after the flesh, but after the Spirit, *before* having ascertained their being in Christ and consequent freedom from condemnation.

In plainer language, their placing sanctification in advance of justification; in substituting the effect for the cause; in looking to the Spirit rather than to Christ. How painfully distressing is the struggle of such an one! Sincere and earnest in his desire to love God, but with his back turned upon the cross, and his face towards the "mount that burneth with fire," he can see everything in God to awaken his fear, but nothing to inspire his love. He longs to obey God; but, lacking the impelling motive to obedience, he fails in every attempt. He sighs for rest; but his incessant effort to recover the ground perpetually sliding from beneath his feet, places that rest further and further beyond his reach. He would fain be holy; but, seeking his holiness in the way of doing, and not in the way of believing, he never attains it. But let us explain the words.

"To walk after the flesh" is to regulate the life and conduct according to our fallen and depraved nature. The "flesh," which stands for the corrupt desires and propensities, is the sole guide of the unregenerate. They are in the flesh, they are of the flesh, and they live according to the flesh. "The works of the flesh are manifest," and these they do. But the converse of this is the characteristic of all true believers. They "walk after the Spirit." Possessing, in common with the unregenerate, a fleshly nature, in which there dwelleth no good thing; they also partake of a new and divine nature, of which the unregenerate do not. Renewed by the Spirit,

inhabited by the Spirit, sanctified by the Spirit, led by
the Spirit, they aim to regulate their life according
to his divine dictates, influence, and teaching. The
bent of their minds is *holiness:* this they breathe
after, pray and labour for, as the one great purpose
of their being. That they are opposed by the flesh,
and by it are often foiled, wounded, and cast down,
cannot yet destroy the divine principle of their soul,
any more than a false attraction can destroy the
magnetic power of the needle. That there should
ever be an occasional unevenness and irregularity in
the walk of any of the Lord's people, is a matter of
the profoundest humiliation; yet even in the stum-
blings and falls of a righteous man, it cannot in
truth be said that he 'walks after the flesh,' seeing
that he rises again, restored by the grace of Christ;
and his desires and breathings after the Spirit are,
perhaps, all the deeper and stronger for that fall.
An unrenewed man falls, and where he falls he lies.
"A just man falleth seven times, and riseth up again,"
and "walks," perhaps more softly than ever, "after
the Spirit." "It is the direction of that sovereign
faculty, the will, which explains the difference. If
this be enlisted on the side of the flesh, as it is with
every unconverted man, then he sinneth wilfully. If
this be enlisted on the side of the Spirit, as it is with
every man who hath truly turned him unto the Lord
Jesus Christ, then he may sin accidentally; and in
some moment of sleep or of surprise he may be over-
taken; and ere the will, as it were, had time to rally

and to recover, some outpost may have been carried, and even some advantage have been gained, to the length of a most humiliating overthrow. But deep is the grief that is thereby awakened, and strenuous is the resistance that is thereby summoned into the future warfare; and heavy is that mourning of sackcloth and of ashes wherewith the soul of the penitent offender is afflicted; and though he hath stumbled in the way of temptation, he yet utterly refuses to walk therein—so giving testimony to the mode in which the leading tendencies of his spirit have most painfully and most offensively been thwarted, by the momentary power and assault of his great adversary; and that the whole drift of his choosing, and deliberating, and purposing faculties is indeed on the side of God and on the side of holiness." * What a high and privileged walk, then, is the believer's! While the slaves of the flesh are grovelling amidst their darkness and chains, he is walking after the Spirit, soaring and exulting in holy light and liberty.

The subject is suggestive of much important practical instruction.

What a ground of *rejoicing* does it afford you who are the saints of God! You may see within and around you—in your soul, in your family, and your circumstances—much that saddens, and wounds, and discourages you; but behold the truth which more than counterbalances it all—your freedom from condemnation. What if you are poor—you are not

* Chalmers.

condemned! What if you are afflicted—you are not *condemned!* What if you are tempted—you are not *condemned!* What if you are assailed and judged by others, you yet are not forsaken and condemned by God; and ought you not, then, to rejoice? Go to the condemned cell, and assure the criminal awaiting his execution, that you bear from his sovereign a pardon; and what though he emerge from his imprisonment and his manacles, to battle with poverty, with sorrow and contempt, will he murmur and repine, that in the redemption of his forfeited life, there is no clause that exempts him from the ills to which that life is linked? No! life to him is so sweet and precious a thing, that though you return it trammelled with want, and beclouded with shame, you have yet conferred upon him a boon which creates sunshine all within and around him. And why should not we "rejoice with joy unspeakable and full of glory," for whom, "through the redemption that is in Christ Jesus," there is now no condemnation? Christ has "redeemed our life from destruction;" and although it is "through much tribulation we are to enter the kingdom," yet shall we not quicken our pace to that kingdom, rejoicing as we go, that "there is now no condemnation to them that are in Christ Jesus?" "These things have I spoken unto you, that my joy might remain in you, and that your joy might be full."

Be earnest and diligent in making sure to yourself your discharge from the sentence and penalty of the law. Sue out the great fact in the Lord's own court by fervent prayer and simple faith. Your Surety has cancelled your debt, and purchased your exemption from death. Avail yourself of the comfort and the stimulus of the blessing. You may be certain, yea, *quite* certain, of its truth. No process is more easy. It is but to look from off yourself to Christ, and to believe with all your heart that he came into the world to save sinners, and assurance is yours. The order is,— "We *believe,* and are *sure."* Oh, do not leave this matter to a bare peradventure. Make sure of your union with Christ, and you may be sure of no condemnation from Christ.

As sin is the great condemning cause, let us aim to *condemn sin,* if we would rank with those for whom there is no condemnation. Most true is it, that either sin must be condemned by us, or we must be condemned for sin. The honour of the Divine government demands that a condemnatory sentence be passed, either upon the transgression, or upon the transgressor. And shall we hesitate? Is it a matter of doubt to which our preference shall be given? Which is best, that sin should die, or that we should die? Will the question allow a moment's consideration? Surely not, unless we are so enamoured of sin as calmly and deliberately to choose death to life, hell to heaven. "The wages of sin is death." Sin unrepented, unforgiven, unpardoned, is the certain prelude to eternal death. Everlasting destruction follows in its turbid wake. There is a present hell in sin, for which the holy shun it; and there is a future hell in sin, for which all should dread it. If, then, we would be amongst "the pure in heart who shall see God," if we would lift up our faces with joy before the Judge at the last great day, if we would be freed from the final and terrible sentence of condemnation, oh, let us be holy, "denying all ungodliness and worldly lusts, and living righteously, soberly, and godly in this present world." Oh, let us condemn sin, that sin may not condemn us. And let us draw the motive that constrains us, and the power that helps us, from that cross where Jesus "condemned sin in the flesh."

In this great matter, there is an especial blessing attached to the act of *self-condemnation*. Self-condemnation averts God's condemnation. When a penitent sinner truly, humbly, graciously, sits in judgment upon himself, the Lord will never sit in judgment upon him. "If we would judge ourselves, we should not be judged of the Lord."* The penitent publican, who stood afar off, wrapped in the spirit of self-condemnation, retired from his presence a justified man. The proud, self-righteous Pharisee, who marched boldly to the altar and justified himself, went forth from God's presence a condemned man. When God sees a penitent sinner arraigning, judging, condemning, loathing himself, he exclaims, "I do not condemn thee, go and sin no more." He who judges and condemns himself upon God's footstool, shall be

* 1 Cor. xi. 31.

acquitted and absolved from God's throne. The Lord give unto us this secret spirit of self-judgment. Such was Job's, when in deep contrition he declared, "I abhor myself, and repent in dust and ashes." Such was David's, when he penitentially confessed, "Against thee, thee only have I sinned, and done this evil in thy sight." Such was Peter's, when he vehemently exclaimed, "Depart from me, O Lord, for I am a sinful man." Such was Isaiah's when he plaintively cried, "Woe is me! for I am undone; because I am a man of unclean lips." Such was the publican's, when he humbly prayed, "God be merciful to me a sinner." O lovely posture! O sacred spirit of self-abhorrence, of self-condemnation! The Holy Ghost works it in the heart, and this stamps it as so precious, so salutary, and so safe. The great day of the Lord will unveil blessings passing all thought, and glories passing all imagination, to the soul who beneath the cross lies prostrate, in the spirit of self-condemnation. The judgment day of the self-condemning soul is on this side of eternity; while the judgment day of the self-justifying soul, is on the other side of eternity. And oh, how terrible will that judgment be!

How strong the consolation flowing from this truth to the believer in Jesus! *No condemnation* is the ground of all comfort to the suffering Christian. What a mighty breakwater is this condition to the rolling surge of sorrow, which else might flow in upon and immerse the soul! Let it be your aim to improve it on every occasion of suffering and trial. God may afflict, but he will never condemn you. Chastisements are not judgments; afflictions are not condemnations. Sickness, and bereavement, and low estate, based upon a condition of non-condemnation, you can welcome and patiently bear, since they are not the fore-castings of a coming storm, but the distillings of a mercy cloud sailing athwart the azure sky of a soul in Christ. The fiery trials which purify our faith have not a spark in them of that "unquenchable fire" that will consume the condemned hereafter. Oh, what are the crosses and the discomforts of this present world, if at last we are kept out of hell? and oh, what are the riches, and honours, and comforts of this life, if at last we are shut out of heaven? At the bottom of that cup of sinful pleasure, which sparkles in the worldling's hand, and which with such zest and glee he quaffs, there lies eternal condemnation—the death-worm feeds at the root of all his good. But at the bottom of this cup of sorrow, now trembling and darkling in the hand of the suffering Christian, bitter and forbidding as it is, there is no condemnation—eternal glory is at the root of all his evil. And in this will you not rejoice? It is not only your holy duty, but it is your high privilege to rejoice. Your whole life not only may be, but ought to be a sweetly-tuned psalm, a continual anthem of thanksgiving and praise, pouring forth its swelling notes to the God of your salvation; since, beyond the cloudy scene of your present pilgrimage there unveils the light and bliss of celestial glory, on whose portal you read as you pass within— No CONDEMNATION. Unless, then, you either distrust or disparage this your joyous condition and blessed hope, you must, in the gloomiest hour, and from the innermost depths of your soul, exultingly exclaim,—"He is near that justifieth me; who will contend with me? Let us stand together. Who is mine adversary? Let him come near to me. Behold, the Lord God will help me! who is he that shall condemn me?"

CHAPTER II.

"For the law of the Spirit of life in Christ Jesus hath made me free from the law of sin and death."

ROMANS viii. 2.

THIS passage has been regarded by some sacred critics as difficult of interpretation; one of whom furnishes three different meanings of the text, and then leaves the reader to make his own selection in the case. We think, however, that a simple examination of the words, taken in their connexion, will remove the obscurity which may be supposed to veil them. The evident design of the Apostle is, to furnish an argument in support of the leading proposition he had just laid down, namely, the believer's deliverance from condemnation. There is clearly a connexion between that declaration and the passage under consideration. "*For* the law of the Spirit of life," &c. But the main difficulty seems to lie in the meaning of the terms employed in the text. By some expositors, the "law of the Spirit of life" is interpreted of the influence or control exerted by the Spirit of God over the minds of the regenerate, emancipating them from the curse and tyranny of sin, and supplying them with a new authoritative enactment for their obedience and regulation, as those whose course is guided by the Spirit. "The law of sin and death," is by the same authority interpreted of the contesting power of sin, leading to death and condemnation; having its throne in the heart, and from its governing and despotic power, maintaining a supreme and dire sway over the whole moral man. The freedom, therefore, which the law of the Spirit of life confers upon those who are bound by the law of sin and death, is just the supremacy of one principle over the force of another principle: the triumph of an opposing law over an antagonist law.

But the interpretation which we propose for the adoption of the reader, is that which regards the "law of the Spirit of life," as describing the Gospel of Christ, frequently denominated a "law"—and emphatically so in this instance—because of the emancipation which it confers from the Mosaic code, called the "law of sin and death," as by it is the knowledge of sin, and through it death is threatened as the penalty of its transgression. With this brief, but, we believe, correct explanation of the terms of the passage, we proceed to consider the exalted liberty of the believer in Jesus, of which it speaks; tracing that freedom to the instrument by whose agency it is secured. "For the law of the Spirit of life in Christ Jesus hath made us free from the law of sin and death."

In the preceding Chapter, we were led to regard all
who were out of Christ, as under a present, and as
exposed to a future condemnation. Not less awful
is the condition of the unconverted, as depicted in
the passage before us. Reverse the state of the
believer and you have the exact state of the unbeliever. Is the believer in Christ a free man?
the unbeliever is a slave. Is the believer justified?
the unbeliever is condemned. Is the believer a
living soul? the unbeliever is a lifeless soul. Is
the believer a reconciled son? the unbeliever is a
hostile rebel. Is the believer an heir of glory? the
unbeliever is an heir of hell. Between these two
conditions there is no neutral ground. You are, my
reader, either for Christ, or you are against Christ.
In this great controversy between Christ and Satan,
you are not an indifferent and unconcerned spectator.
The Prince of Light or the prince of darkness claims
your service, and presses you into the conflict. Oh,
it is a matter of the greatest moment that you decide
to which law you are bound—the "law of life," or
"the law of death."   But in what sense is the
believer "*free* from the law of sin and death?"

As a covenant he is free from it. How clear and
impressive is the reasoning of the Apostle on this
point! "Know ye not, brethren, (for I speak to
them that know the law) how that the law hath
dominion over a man as long as he liveth? For the
woman which hath an husband is bound by the law to
her husband, so long as he liveth; but if the husband

be dead, she is loosed from the law of her husband."*
The believer's union to Christ, represented under the
figure of a marriage covenant, frees him from the
condemnatory power of this law. He looks not to
it for life; he rests not in it for hope; he renounces
it as a saving covenant, and under the influence of
another and a higher obligation,—his marriage to
Christ—he brings forth fruit unto God. Was ever
liberty so glorious as this,—a liberty associated with
the most loving, cordial, and holy obedience? Not
a single precept of that law, from whose covenant
and curse he is released by this act of freedom, is
compromised. All its precepts, embodied and re-
flected in the life of Christ—whose life is the model
of our own—appear infinitely more clear and resplendent than ever they appeared before. The
obedience of the Lawgiver infinitely enhanced the
lustre of the law, presenting the most impressive
illustration of its majesty and holiness that it could
possibly receive.

The instrument to whose agency this exalted
liberty is ascribed is, the "law of the Spirit of life
in Christ Jesus." The term law is forensic; though
not unfrequently used in God's Word to designate
the Gospel of Christ. " Out of Zion shall go forth
the *law*."† " The isles shall wait for his *law*."‡
" Where is boasting then? It is excluded. By what
law? Of works? Nay; but by the *law* of faith."§

---

* Rom. vii. 1, 2.   † Isa. ii. 3.
‡ Isa. xlii. 4.   § Rom. iii. 27.

In this sense we hold that the word is used in the text, to designate the Gospel of the blessed God, as the great instrument by which the freedom of which we have spoken is obtained. A few particulars will, we think, justify this view. The Gospel is the law which reveals the way of salvation by Christ. It is the development of God's great expedient of saving man. It speaks of pardon and adoption, of acceptance and sanctification, as all flowing to the soul through faith in his dear Son. It represents God as extending his hand of mercy to the vilest sinner; welcoming the penitent wanderer back to his home, and once more taking the contrite rebel to his heart. It is also a *quickening* law—emphatically the "law of the Spirit of *life.*" What numbers are seeking sanctification from the "law of sin," and life from the "law of death!" But the *Gospel* speaks of *life.* Its doctrines,—its precepts,—its promises,—its exhortations,—its rebukes,—its hopes, are all instinct with spiritual life, and come with quickening power to the soul. "The words that I speak unto you," says Jesus, "they are spirit and they are life."* "Being born again, not of corruptible seed, but of incorruptible, by the Word of God, which liveth and abideth for ever."† Oh, there is life in the Gospel, because it is "the law of the *Spirit of life* in Christ Jesus." It testifies of "Christ, who is our life." It declares that there is no spiritual life but in him. And although "the letter killeth," working alone, yet in the

* John vi. 63. † 1 Pet. i. 23.

hands of the Spirit it giveth life. Thus clothed with the energy of the Holy Ghost, the Gospel proves a " savour of life unto life," to all who believe in it to the saving of the soul.

In concluding this Chapter, we would remind those who can appropriate to themselves the language of the text, of the exalted privilege to which they are raised. A holy, filial, joyful liberty, is your birthright. It is the liberty of a pardoned and justified sinner. It is the liberty of a reconciled, adopted child. It is the liberty of one for whom there is " now no condemnation." And yet how few of God's people walk in the full enjoyment of this liberty! How few pray, and love, and confide, as adopted children! How few labour for life! Oh, sons of God, rise to this your high and heavenly calling! Your freedom was purchased at a high price, undervalue it not. It is most holy—abuse it not. It binds you, by the strongest obligations, to yield yourselves unto God, as those that are alive from the dead. Be these the breathings of our soul :—" Lord ! my sweetest liberty is obedience to thee; my highest freedom wearing thy yoke; my greatest rest bearing thy burden. Oh, how love I thy law after the inward man ! I delight to do thy will, O my God!" The Lord grant unto us that we, " being delivered out of the hands of our enemies, might serve him without fear, in holiness and right-eousness before him, all the days of our life."

CHAPTER III.

THE IMPOTENCE OF THE LAW, AND GOD'S METHOD OF MEETING IT.

"For what the law could not do, in that it was weak through
the flesh, God sending his own Son in the likeness of
sinful flesh, and for sin, condemned sin in the flesh."

ROMANS viii. 3.

"FOR what the law could not do." It is still the
moral law of which the apostle speaks. He affirms
of that law that it is "weak." The assertion must
be received with some qualification. It cannot be
denied that the law has power. Divest it of all
strength, and of what use would it be? How could
it accomplish the design of its enactment? There
is a sense, then, and an important one, in which
the law has strength. Wherein does its potency
lie? The law has power to convict of sin. It mirrors
to a man his moral likeness; looking into this law
he sees himself to be a sinner. It has power to bring
him in guilty before God; to breathe over his head
its fearful curse, and to shut him up to its eternal
condemnation. With what a tremendous power,
then, is this law invested! It wields a mighty arm.

Let the lawless tremble at its strength. Its divinity is not to be denied—its holiness is not to be impugned—its power is not to be trifled with. No man can do violence to this law with impunity. Deem it not a light thing to fall into its iron, merciless grasp. It lays its righteous hand upon you, exclaiming, "Pay me that thou owest." And if the demand is not met—amply, fully met—it has authority and power to adjudge you to hell for ever. Such is the strength of God's holy law.

But, nevertheless, there is a sense, and a vastly important one, in which the law is impotent—utterly powerless. What is it that the law cannot do? The law has no power to place the sinner in a *justified* state. In other words, it cannot fulfil its own righteousness. "By him, all that believe are justified from all things, *from which ye could not be justified by the law of Moses.*"* "Therefore, by the deeds of the law there shall no flesh be justified in his sight."† Nor has it power to *give life*. "For if there had been a law given *which could have given life,* verily righteousness should have been by the law."‡ It pronounces the unjustified sinner dead—his religion dead—his works dead—his faith dead; but with not one breath of spiritual life has it power to inspire the soul. Oh, the infatuation which prompts men to seek spiritual life from a law, powerful only as an instrument of eternal death ! Nor has the law power to make anything whatever perfect in the great matter

* Acts xiii. 39.　　† Rom. iii. 20.　　‡ Gal. iii. 21.

of man's salvation. "For the law *made nothing perfect*, but the bringing in of a better hope did; by the which we draw nigh unto God."* These things the law fails to achieve. And herein is it weak. Holy in its nature, it is yet incapable of making the sinner holy. Righteous in its precepts, it yet cannot justify the ungodly. Reflecting the Divine image, it yet has no power to transfer that image to the soul.

But let us trace this failure to its proper cause. From whence, then, this weakness of the law of God?

We reply, not from any inherent defect in the law. "The law is holy, just and good," and of itself powerful enough to take the soul to glory. But the Apostle supplies the answer—"weak through the flesh." It was right that he should thus shield the dignity of the law, and maintain that there belonged to it a native force and capacity worthy of Him from whom it emanated, and equal to the accomplishment of the great end for which it was enacted. The weakness of the law, then, is to be traced, not to any inefficiency of the instrument, but to the sinfulness of man; not to the agent, but to the subject. What an impressive view does this give us of the deep depravity, the utter sinfulness of our nature! So great is the corruption of the flesh, that it opposes and thwarts the law in its great work of imprinting its image upon the mind of man. Oh, what must be the character and power of that sinfulness which can thus sever the locks of its strength, and divert it from its

* Heb. vii. 19.

sacred purpose! Fain would it make us holy, but our depravity foils it. Fain would it recall our alienated affections, but our heart is so utterly estranged from God, that its generous effort fails. Thus the law is weak, through the corrupt and sinful flesh. Let us be deeply humbled by this truth. How entirely it stains the pride of all our fleshly glory! Where, now, is our native holiness, and our boasted pride, and our vaunted worthiness? The law, always on the side of purity and love, yearned to bring us beneath its holy and benign influence, but our carnality interposed, and it became weak.

"God sending his own Son in the likeness of sinful flesh." Thus has God graciously provided a remedy which exactly meets the necessity of the case. The law, thwarted and impaired by the depravity of the flesh, having failed to effect the salvation of the sinner, proving itself utterly powerless to justify or sanctify the soul, God is represented as devising another, a more stupendous and effective expedient. This was nothing less than placing the work in the hands of his own Son. The source from whence this great and precious gift emanates, supplies a tender rebuke to all those defective views we are prone to entertain of the Father's love to us. What a fulness of meaning in these words—"God sending his own Son,"—sending him from the depths of his love, from the centre of his bosom. Truly, "in this was manifested the love of God towards us, because that God sent his only begotten Son into the world, that

we might live through him." Herein, indeed, is
love! Oh, what cold, suspicious thoughts we have
cherished of it! How have we lost sight of it in
deep trial, and in the bitter anguish of our spirit!
How have we forgotten that he must love us—
chastise and rebuke us as he will—who sent his own
Son to give us life! Behold the grandeur and the
fitness of God's expedient. The Father did seem to
say to the beloved One reposing in his bosom:—" My
Son, our law has failed to accomplish the salvation of
a single individual of the human race, through the
opposing depravity into which it is sunk. Go Thou
on this embassy of love, assume the likeness of the
sinner, and in Thy mightiness to save, bring my
many sons unto glory." Contemplate, too, the cost-
liness of the gift. "His *own* Son." Angels are his
sons by creation, and saints are his sons by adoption;
but Jesus is pre-eminently and emphatically his own
Son by eternal generation,—co-equal, co-essential,
and co-eternal with the Father, ineffably begotten
from all eternity in the Divine essence. From the
abundant proofs of this doctrine, with which the
Scriptures of truth are so rich, one or two citations
will suffice. Our Lord on every occasion acknow-
ledged his filial relation to God. How often and
how touchingly did the expressive words breathe
from his sacred lips—" MY FATHER."—"I and *my
Father* are one." "All things are delivered unto
me of *my Father*." "In *my Father's* house are
many mansions." Then, as it regards his being by

eternal generation the Son of the Highest, hear what the Scriptures of truth affirm. "I know him," says Christ, "for I am *from* him, and he hath *sent* me."* How was Christ from the Father? Certainly not as it related to his mission mainly, but as it respected his eternal generation by the Father. For, observe in these remarkable words the two things are different and distinct; the being *from* the Father,—and the being *sent* by the Father. Then, as it regards his *Sonship*, how conclusive are these words—"The Lord said unto me, Thou art my Son; this day have I begotten thee."† Beyond all dispute, Christ is the person spoken of here. Three times is this passage quoted in the New Testament, and on each occasion it is invariably applied to the Lord Jesus. The expression "to-day," has an obvious reference to the eternity of his generation. Eternity is with God but as one day—an *eternal now*. "Beloved, be not ignorant of this one thing, that one day is with the Lord as a thousand years, and a thousand years as one day." Thus clear is it that Christ is God's "*own* Son," having the same essence and nature with himself; and that he is God's "*only* Son" by natural and eternal generation—"The only begotten Son of God." Further into the depths of this profound truth it would not be our wisdom to descend. There is much awful mystery connected with this fundamental verity of Christian faith, which forbids a too curious and rash investigation.

* John vii. 29.   † Psa. ii. 7.

Although it transcends our reason, it does not contravene our reason. It is propounded, like all cognate mysteries of Divine revelation, for our belief. And what human reason is not able to comprehend, divine faith can meekly and unquestionly receive.

But what words are these—God sent his own Son! A person less exalted, less Divine, could not have accomplished what the divine law failed to do. And since an enactment which was a transcript of Deity, proved too feeble for the purpose, Deity itself undertakes the work. God's own eternal and essential Son embarks in the enterprise, and achieves it. What a Rock of salvation, saint of God, is this! Springing from the lowest depths of your humiliation, see how it towers above your curse—your sin —your condemnation! It is a Rock higher than you. Infinitely removed beyond the reach of condemnation is that soul whose faith is planted upon this Rock. How securely can he rest, and how sweetly can he sing, " In the time of trouble he shall hide me in His pavilion: in the secret of His tabernacle shall He hide me; He shall set me upon a rock. And now shall mine head be lifted up above mine enemies round about me."

" In the likeness of sinful flesh." These words are striking and significant, as placing before us two essential and glorious facts in the history of our Lord—facts interwoven with our holiest experience and most precious hopes. It first places in the clearest possible light the true *humanity* of the Son of God. It was not human nature in appearance that he took, as some have taught—this was the heretical doctrine of the ancient Docetæ—but human nature in reality. There are other declarations of this truth equally as strong: "God sent forth his Son made of a woman." "The Word was made flesh, and dwelt among us." Our blessed Lord has ever been "a stone of stumbling and a rock of offence" to the ungodly world. Many are offended with him. His two natures have ever been impugned, opposed, and denied. Some have refused him the glory belonging to his Godhead, while others have attempted to undermine his manhood—thus making him, had it been in the power of his enemies, neither God nor man—a very nothing. But the truth still stands unimpeached and glorious—our Lord assumed real flesh. "My flesh is meat indeed." It was, as the Apostle terms it, "the *body* of his flesh." "Wherefore, when he cometh into the world, he saith, Sacrifice and offering thou wouldest not, but a *body* hast thou prepared me." "Who his own self bare our sins in his own *body* on the tree." It was a perfectly organized body, having all the properties, affinities, and functions belonging to our own. Therefore he is styled "the *man* Christ Jesus." "Since by man came death, by *man* came also the resurrection of the dead." "He was made in the likeness of men." "The seed of the woman." "The seed of Abraham." "The seed of David." Such are the words which

inscribe this great truth as with a sunbeam—our
Lord's perfect human body and soul. The consolation, the sympathy, the strength, which spring from
this truth, how great! Bone of our bone, and flesh
of our flesh, made in all points like unto his brethren,
O how suitable a Brother is he, born for our every
adversity! Now can he, with a feeling of sympathy
the most exquisite, be touched with my infirmity; for
this nature which I drag about with me, feeble and
bruised, jaded and crushed, was the very nature
which he took into mysterious union with his Godhead—wore it here below, and wears it still in
heaven.

But, secondly, with what care and skill does the
Holy Ghost guard the perfect *sinlessness* of our
Lord's humanity! Observe, it was not the reality
of sinful flesh that the Son of God assumed, but its
'likeness' only. He took real flesh, but bearing the
resemblance only of sinfulness. He was "made *like*
unto his brethren." "Tempted *like* as we are, yet
without sin." And so in the passage before us, "In
the *likeness* of sinful flesh." The words suppose a
resemblance to our sinful nature. And, oh! how
close that resemblance was!—as like a sinner as one
could be, who yet in deed and in truth was not one,
—"who knew no sin," but was "holy, harmless,
undefiled, and separate from sinners." Man is a
sinner; our blessed Lord was man—so truly man,
that his enemies exclaimed, "We know this man is
a sinner." They could not understand how one

could be so really human, and yet be untainted with sin! And then, did there not cling to Jesus the infirmities of our fallen nature, which, though sinless in him, were not the less the *effects* of sin? He hungered—he thirsted—he wept—he was wearied—he slept—he was afflicted—he sorrowed—he trembled—he suffered—he died. And as we trace these infirmities of our humanity floating upon the transparent surface of his pure life, how forcible do we feel the words—"Made in the *likeness* of sinful flesh"! And when we see him traduced as a sinner by man, and—standing beneath his people's transgressions—dealt with as a sinner by God; by man, denounced as "a glutton," "a wine-bibber," "a friend of publicans and sinners," an "impostor," a "deceiver," a "blasphemer"—then arraigned, condemned, and executed as a criminal not worthy to live, as an accursed one;—by God, charged with all the sins of the elect church, bruised and put to grief, and at last abandoned by him on the cross, then numbered with transgressors, and making his grave with the wicked in his death,—oh! how *like* sinful flesh was the robe of meanness and suffering which he wore! And yet, "he was without sin." It was the resemblance, not the reality. The human nature of the Son of God was as free from sin as the Deity it enshrined. He was the "Lamb of God *without spot.*" The least taint of moral guilt—a shade of inherent corruption—would have proved fatal to his mission. One leak in the glorious Ark which contained the Church of

God, had sunk it to the lowest depths. Oh ! this is the glory of his work, and the solace of our hearts, that Christ our Saviour " offered himself without spot unto God." And now we may plead his sinless oblation as the ground of our pardon, and the accept-ance of our persons. " He hath made him to be sin for us *who knew no sin,* that we might be made the righteousness of God in him." The Lord bless these truths to the comfort and edification of our souls.

" And for sin condemned sin in the flesh ;" or, " by a sacrifice for sin." And what was that sacri-fice ? It was God's own Son—" who gave himself for us." " And when he had by himself purged our sins." " Christ also hath loved us, and hath given himself for us, an offering and a sacrifice to God for a sweet-smelling savour." By this sacrifice he " condemned sin in the flesh." The word never implies simply to destroy, or remove. Consequently the present and entire destruction of sin in the believer was not the condemnation secured by the sacrifice of Christ. But in two senses we may un-derstand the word. First, he bore the condemnation and punishment of sin, and thus for ever secured our pardon. Secondly, and chiefly, he actually so con-demned sin in his own material body, that it lost the power of condemning his spiritual body, the Church. So that neither sin, nor the consequence of sin, can ever lay the believer under condemnation. Thus, while sin condemned Jesus as the Surety, Jesus con-demned sin as the Judge, assigning it to its own dark and changeless doom. That, therefore, which itself is condemned, cannot condemn. Thus it is that the last song the believer sings, is his sweetest and most triumphant—"O death! where is thy sting?" Sin being condemned, pardoned, and for ever put away, death, its consequent and penalty, is but a pleasing trance into which the believer falls, to awake up perfected in God's righteousness.

In conclusion, let us, in deep adoration of soul, admire God's illustrious method of meeting the impotence of the law. How suitable to us, how honouring to himself! Relinquishing all thought of salvation by the works of the law, let us eagerly and gratefully avail ourselves of God's plan of justification. Let our humble and believing hearts cordially embrace his Son. If the law is powerless to save, Christ is "mighty to save." If the law can but terrify and condemn, it is to drive us into Christ, that we might be justified by faith in him. In him there is a full, finished, and free salvation. We have but to believe, and be saved. We have but to look, and live. We have but to come, and be accepted. Disappointed of our hope in the law, and alarmed by its threatenings pealing in our ears louder than seven thunders, let us flee to Jesus, the "Hiding-place from the wind, and the Covert from the tempest." There is no condemnation in Christ Jesus. All is peace, all is rest, all is security there. The instant that a poor trembling sinner gets into Christ, he is safe to all eternity. Nor can he be assured of safety one moment out of Christ. Repair, then, to the Saviour. His declaration is—" Him that cometh unto me I will in no wise cast out." None are rejected but those who bring a price in their hands. Salvation is by grace ; and not to him that worketh, but to him that believeth, the precious boon is given. The turpitude of your guilt, the number of your transgressions, the depth of your unworthiness, the extent of your poverty, the distance that you have wandered from God, are no valid objections, no insurmountable difficulties, to your being saved. Jesus saves sinners "to the uttermost,"—to the uttermost degree of guilt—to the uttermost limit of unworthiness—to the uttermost extent of time. And not only let us look to Christ for salvation, but also for *strength*. Is the law weak ? " Christ is the power of God." He is prepared to perfect his strength in our weakness. And the felt conviction of that weakness will be the measure of our strength. Without him we can do nothing; but strong in his might, we can do all things. "In the Lord have I righteousness and strength." And "in him shall all the seed of Israel be justified, and shall glory."

How should this subject deepen our love ! " God is love," and the expression of that love is the sending his own Son into the world, to achieve what the law, in its weakness, could not do. Was ever love like this ? " God *so* loved." And was Jesus willing to engage in the embassy ? Did he voluntarily clothe himself in our rags, stoop to our poverty, consent to be arrested and thrown into prison for us? Was he made a curse that he might deliver us from the curse? Did judgment pass upon him that we might be saved from the wrath to come? O here is infinite, boundless love! Then let him have in return our love. It is the least that he can ask, or we can make. Let it be a hearty, cordial, obedient, increasing love. Alas! it is but a drop, when it should be an ocean. It is but a faint spark, when it should be a vehement flame. O how should our best affection flow out toward him who assumed, and still wears, our nature! What an attractive, winning object is the Incarnate God,—the God-man Mediator! Fairer than the children of men, the chiefest among ten thousand, the altogether lovely, he is the wonder and admiration, the love and song, of all heaven. O why should he not be equally so of all earth? Did the Son of God take up our rude and suffering nature, and shall we be loth to take up his lowly and despised cross, and follow hard after him? Forbid it, Lord! Forbid it, thou precious Saviour! What humiliation, what abasement, can be too much for us, the sinful sons of men, when thou, the sinless Son of God, didst so abase and humble thyself! O let thy love constrain us to stand firm to thee, to thy truth, and to thy cause, when the world despises, and friends forsake, and relatives look cold, and all seem to leave and forsake us. And as thou didst condescend to be made in the likeness of our human and sinful nature, O conform us to the likeness of thy Divine and holy nature. As thou wast a partaker with us, make us partakers with thee. As thou wast made like unto us, in what was proper to man, make us like thee, in what is proper to God. And as thou didst come down to our sinful and dim earth, lift us to thy pure and bright heaven!

CHAPTER IV.

THE RIGHTEOUSNESS OF THE LAW ACCOMPLISHED IN THE BELIEVER.

"That the righteousness of the law might be fulfilled in us, who walk not after the flesh, but after the Spirit."—ROM. viii. 4.

FROM a representation of the impotence of the law, the Apostle passes to a vindication of its holiness. As if his statement affecting its inadequacy to accomplish that in failure of which God sent his Son into the world, might derogate from its dignity, and impair its rights, he hastens to delineate its true character, and to assert the actual fulfilment of its claims. We purpose, in the elucidation of this passage, to contemplate the exalted character of the law; and then show in what sense its righteousness is fulfilled in the believer.

"The righteousness of the law." It falls not within our province, at the present moment, to establish the necessity, or to prove the existence of a Divine law, for the moral government of God's intelligent creatures. In point of fact, the doctrine requires no argument. The proposition is self-evident. There is no part of God's creation, intelligent or irrational, left to self-government; or, in other words, that is *without law*. In the outer world it is manifest; in the domestic constitution still more so; and in God's providential and moral government the evidence is demonstrative. " His kingdom ruleth over all." It is, however, with the character, not the *existence*, of the Divine law which God has framed for the well-being and happiness of his moral creatures, that we have strictly now to do.

Emanating from a Being infinitely perfect in every moral perfection, it follows as a natural sequence from this truth, that the law, designed to be a transcript of what God is—a copy of himself—must be in every respect a most perfect law. " The law of the Lord is perfect." How could it be otherwise? Is it rational to suppose that a Being of infinite holiness, wisdom, and goodness, would form a rule for the government of moral creatures that would fail to place before their eye the loftiest standard of excellence, and that should not demand and secure their supreme obedience and happiness? It follows, then, that the law being essentially and perfectly holy, all its requirements must be equally so. It cannot change, nor compromise, nor soften down either the nature, or the outline, or the enforcement of a single enactment. It demands of every creature the profoundest homage, the most implicit obedience, and the most perfect love. In requiring this, the creature shall have no ground for impeaching the Divine goodness. He shall have no reason for alleging of God that he is harsh and austere. As if fearful of perplexing the mind with a multitude of enactments, our Lord has presented *one* precept of the law, the perfect keeping of which resolves itself into a virtual fulfilment of all. "Jesus said unto him, Thou shalt love the Lord thy God with all thy heart, and with all thy soul, and with all thy mind. This is the first and great commandment."*

Who but an infinitely wise Lawgiver could have embodied all the requisitions of an extended code in a single one? What an unfolding of the wisdom of God is here! In securing to himself the supreme *love* of his creatures, he wins a willing obedience to every precept of his law. Such is the all-commanding, all-constraining power of love to God! Employing no other than this gentle and persuasive motive, God asks your intellect,—your time,—your service,—your rank,—your substance,—your person, —your life,—your all. And, in demanding this complete surrender, his law stands forth, in view of all created intelligences, as a rule worthy of him from whom it emanates. O yes! it is a most righteous law.

But in what sense is the righteousness of the law accomplished in the believer? This, it will be perceived, is the declaration of the passage, "That the righteousness of the law might be fulfilled in us."

Now it is obvious that the law required obedience,

* Matt. xxii. 37.

and that that obedience is properly termed the "righteousness of the law." How is this accomplished in us? Most clearly, not in the sense in which it supposes it fulfilled in our own persons. Where, then, would be the weakness of the law? The law has never yet received a complete fulfilment in any fallen creature. Take the most perfect specimen of human obedience, and test it by the high precept we have named. If, for instance, in your love to God there is detected any truancy of affection; if every passion of your soul, if every pulse of your heart, beat not with warm, unwavering and supreme love to God, then your love is imperfect, and your obedience necessarily so. But where is the creature who can assert his plea of perfect love to God? Who can say, "I have loved the Lord my God with all my heart, with all my soul, and with all my mind?" What a solemn truth is this, that the best obedience of the best of creatures falls as infinitely below the requirements of the law, as the obedience of the incarnate God rose above it! How, then, are we to understand the holiness of the law as fulfilled in us? Undoubtedly, in that sense only in which it was fulfilled in our Surety. The Lord Jesus fulfilled the righteousness of the law in the behalf of his people. He only could do so who was himself "holy, harmless, undefiled, and separate from sinners." The first step in this wondrous achievement was his being made under the law. What a stoop of Jehovah was this! The Lawgiver placing himself under the government of his own enactment! Let astonishment, love, and praise fill our souls, while, with more than seraphs' ardour, we look into this truth. Having made himself amenable to the law, he then proceeds to its fulfilment. He enters into no negotiation,—he proposes no conditions,—he asks no compromise, —he demurs not at its stern, unbending demand; but receiving it from God just as it was—all broken, weak, and dishonoured—he yields it back to his Father, "magnified and made honourable."* Trace the outline of his obedience. Is the grand moving spring of the law, love? Where was ever seen such costly love to God as our Surety displayed? Was he not a voluntary, a self-immolated sacrifice upon the altar of Divine justice, all for the love he bore his Father's honour? Did he not offer to God a perfectly pure and undivided heart? And did not that affection constrain him to a supreme consecration to his Father's glory? In addition to supreme love, was there not the most perfect sanctity of life? Did not Satan strive to ensnare him by his subtilty, and did not man seek to catch him in his words? And yet no sin was found in him. Trace all the subsequent stages of his course, till that course closed in suffering and blood,—accompany him to the baptismal waters, and hear him exclaim, as he meekly yielded himself into the hands of the Baptist, "Thus it becometh us to fulfil all righteousness."† Then follow him to Calvary, and behold the last, the finishing act of his

* Isaiah xlii. 21.   † Matt. iii. 15.

unparalleled obedience,—his obedience unto death!
—was there ever such a law-fulfiller as the Son of
God? Such was our Lord's fulfilment of the righteousness of the law, in behalf of his people.

But the question still returns—In what way are we
to reconcile the honouring of the law by Christ, and
the fulfilment of its righteousness in us?

The difficulty is solved by a reference to the federal
union of Christ and his Church—a subject already
adverted to in the preceding pages. Standing to his
people in the relation of a Covenant Head, the law
being fulfilled by him in a legal sense, it was virtually
a fulfilment of the law by us,—his obedience being
accepted in lieu of ours. Thus it is written—" He
hath made him to be sin for us, who knew no sin;
that we might be made the righteousness of God in
him."* "By the obedience of one shall many be
made righteous."† Thus the doctrine of substitution
at once harmonizes the apparent discrepancy. The
law thus met in all its claims, fulfilled in its utmost precept, gloriously illustrated, and divinely
honoured, there can possibly be no condemnation to
those in whose behalf the Surety acted. Thus every
humble sinner who, feeling the plague of his own
heart, breaking away from his dependence upon a
covenant of works, and repairing in simple faith
beneath the righteousness of the Incarnate God,
shall never come into condemnation. In his case
the precept has been obeyed, and the punishment

* 2 Cor. v. 21.   † Rom. v. 19.

endured, and the debt discharged, and not one drop of the dark, lowering storm shall light upon his head. Jesus hath delivered him from the wrath to come. And thus by the imputation of Christ's righteousness to the·believer, the righteousness of the law is fulfilled in him.

"Who walk not after the flesh, but after the Spirit." The rightful claimants of this privileged state are thus described. In a delineation which we have already given of this character, we remarked, that those who walked not after the flesh were those who regulated not their life by the dictates of the flesh. It supposes not his exemption from the assaults and the woundings of the flesh. So far from this, a Christian is a more prominent mark for its assailings than any other man. He may be ensnared and stumble, but he walks not after the flesh. "A just man falleth seven times, and riseth up again." An unrighteous man, when he falls through the temptations of the flesh, knows nothing of holy contrition for his sin, nor the sprinkling of the atoning blood upon the conscience. He falls, but where he falls he lies. "He that is unrighteous is unrighteous *still*." He "*walks* after the flesh." But those in whom the righteousness of the law is fulfilled in their Surety, and in whom a Gospel righteousness, an evangelical obedience, is performed by themselves, "walk after the Spirit."

Behold, what an open door does this subject set before the humble, convinced sinner. It encircles

the whole future of his being with the covenant bow
of hope.   Beneath its gorgeous and expanding arch
he is safe.   The law, now honoured as it never was—
invested with a lustre before which its former glory
pales, and at the brightness of which angels veil their
faces,—the utmost honour brought to the Divine
government, think you, penitent reader, that the
Lord will reject the application of a single sinner who
humbly asks to be saved?   What! after the Son of
God had stooped so low to save the lowest, had
suffered so much to save the vilest, will the Father
refuse to enfold to his reconciled heart the penitent
who flees to its blessed asylum?   Never!   Approach,
then, bowed and broken, weary and burdened spirit.
There is hope for you in Jesus, there is forgiveness for
you in Jesus, there is acceptance for you in Jesus,
there is rest for you in Jesus, there is a heaven of
bliss and glory awaiting you—all in Jesus, the law's
great fulfiller.   O, how welcome will the heart of
Christ make you.   How full and free will be the
pardon of God extended to you.   How deep and rich
the peace, and joy, and hope, which, like a river, will
roll its gladdening waves into your soul the moment
that you receive Christ into your heart!   " Believe
in the Lord Jesus Christ, and thou shalt be saved."
" He that believeth shall not come into condemnation,
but is passed from death unto life."

Saints of God, keep the eye of your faith intently
and immoveably fixed upon Christ, your sole patter:.
Our Lord did not keep that law that his people might

be lawless. He did not honour that law that they might dishonour its precepts. His obedience provided no licence for our disobedience. His fulfilment releases us not from the obligation,—the sweet and pleasant, yet solemn obligation—to holiness of life. Our faith does not make void the law, but rather establishes the law. The "righteousness of the law is fulfilled in us" when we "walk after the Spirit," in lowly conformity to Christ's example. Was he meek and lowly in heart? Did he bless when cursed? Did he, when reviled, revile not again? Did he walk in secret with God? Did he always seek to do those things which pleased his Father? Did he live a life of faith, and prayer, and toil? So let us imitate him, that of us it may be said, "These are they who *follow the Lamb* whithersoever he goeth."

What richer comfort can flow into the hearts of the godly than that which springs from this truth? "The righteousness of the law fulfilled in us!" What wondrous, blessed words! You are often in fear that the righteousness of the law will rise against you; and when you consider your many failures and short-comings, you justly tremble. But fear not! for in Christ the law is perfectly fulfilled, and fulfilled in your stead, as much as if you had obeyed it in your own person. Is not this a sure ground of comfort? You see the imperfection of your own obedience, and you are alarmed; but have you not an eye also for the perfection of Christ's obedience, which he has made yours by imputation? "There is therefore now no condemnation to them who are in Christ Jesus," because he has fulfilled the law's righteousness in their behalf. You are cast down because of the law of sin, —but the Spirit of life has freed you from the law. You are troubled because of the law of God—but that law, by Christ's perfect obedience, is fulfilled in you. You desire a righteousness that will present you without spot before God,—you have it in him who is the "Lord our Righteousness." Christian! Christ's whole obedience is yours. What can sin, or Satan, or conscience, or the law itself allege against you now? Be humble, and mourn over the many flaws and failures in your obedience; yet withal rejoice, and glory, and make your boast in the fulness, perfection, and unchangeableness of that righteousness of the Incarnate God which will place you without fault before the throne. Sinner! if the righteousness of the law is not fulfilled in you now, that righteousness will be exhibited in your just condemnation to all eternity! Flee to Christ Jesus, the end of the law for righteousness to every one that believeth.

CHAPTER V.

THE UNREGENERATE AND THE REGENERATE
CONTRASTED.

" For they that are after the flesh do mind the things of the flesh ;
but they that are after the Spirit the things of the Spirit."
—ROMANS viii. 5.

Two different classes are here presented to our
view, in striking and solemn contrast. With regard
to the first, a more accurate, and at the same time
a more awful, portrait of the carnal state of man
exists not in any language than this. He is described
as living after the flesh. And lest it should be supposed, as by some it is, that a corrupt tree can bring
forth good fruit, or, in other words, that holiness is
the natural product of our unrenewed nature, it is
added, who "mind the things of the flesh." But
before we go more fully into the unfolding of this
subject, we should remark, that the term "flesh"
has various significations in God's word, often decidedly opposite to that which it bears in the passage
before us. For example,. it is sometimes used to
denote a softened disposition of mind: "I will give

you a heart of *flesh*."* Again, it sets forth the tender and close union subsisting between Christ and his Church: "No man ever yet hated his own *flesh*, but nourisheth and cherisheth it, even as the Lord the Church."† A yet deeper and more sublime signification it assumes when used to describe the mysterious incarnation of the Son of God: "The Word was made *flesh*."‡ But the sense in which the word is employed in the text under consideration, is totally different to any we have quoted. It designates the fallen and carnal state of the unrenewed man. He is after the flesh, and his whole life is in accordance with the dictates of the flesh. Our Lord thus describes it:—"That which is born of the flesh *is flesh*." § That is, it is nothing more than carnal and corrupt. It is originally corrupt, and corrupt it remains until it perishes. "When we were in the flesh, the motions of sin, which were by the law, did work in our members to bring forth fruit unto death."‖ We are thus taken to the very root of all the depravity and crime which afflicts and degrades our common nature. It is not so much the outbreak of sin—the wretchedness and woe which, working upwards, floats upon the surface of society— that presents to a spiritual eye the most afflicting view of man's fallen condition, as the fact, that the root of all iniquity dwells in his nature; and that, when he hates God, and opposes his government, and

* Ezek. xxxvi. 26.　　† Eph. v. 29.　　‡ John i. 14.
§ John iii. 6.　　‖ Rom. vii. 5.

violates his laws, and injures his fellow-creatures, it is not an accident of his nature, nor the effect of a surprisal into sin, like that of our first parents, as it is the working out of an original and natural principle; it is the development of an innate and deep corruption, coursing its way upward, as we have said, from the concealed depths of his nature to the surface of his life. And thus, though the ethics of a man be sound, and his life be in harmony with the morality of his creed, yet in the absence of the Spirit's regeneration, he is still emphatically " after the flesh:" he bears about with him an original principle of evil, whose existence links him to the flesh, the full development of which is only suppressed by the laws of society, a consciousness of right and wrong, a natural regard for his own well-being, and the overruling power of God.

But we shall, perhaps, form a more accurate idea of this affecting state, in the further consideration of its workings, upon the same principle by which we judge the species of a plant by its flower, or of a tree by its fruit. It is said, that " they who are of the flesh, *do mind the things of the flesh.*" The idea is, that all the objects of attraction, the desires and pursuits of the carnal mind, are corrupt and worldly. The phrase, " do mind the things of the flesh," may express two ideas. First, and primarily, the exercise of the intellect; second, and by implication, the exercise of the affections. " Set your affection upon things above:" literally, set your *mind*. But what an awful charge thus alleged against unrenewed men! Nor is this charge unsustained by adequate proof. It is impossible, in the nature of things, that a corrupt mind could give its consideration to things opposed to itself. No nature can transcend its own powers. Each act must be in harmony with the character of the principle from whence it emanates. A beast cannot act as a man, without participating in the human. A human being cannot act with the power of an angel, without partaking the nature of the angelic. How, then, can that which is after the flesh, act as that which is after the Spirit? In other words, how can a carnal mind put forth the actings of a holy mind, unless it first become holy? How can a man believe without possessing the principle of faith? or love, without the principle of love? "Israel is an empty vine, he bringeth forth fruit unto himself."*—Hebrew, "equal to himself;" that is, a fruit partaking of his own nature. Our Lord embodies the same idea in his peculiarly graphic language: "A good tree cannot bring forth evil fruit, neither can a corrupt tree bring forth good fruit." And then follows the solemn result: "Every tree that bringeth not forth good fruit, is hewn down and cast into the fire."† We have thus most distinctly placed before us this solemn truth—that a fleshly or corrupt mind must act agreeably with its own nature; and so acting, must be supremely engrossed with the things of the flesh. This, too, must be the character

* Hosea x. 1.   † Matt. vii. 18.

of its *religion*. All its conceptions and ideas must be in harmony with its unrenewed nature. " The natural man receiveth not the things of the Spirit of God, for they are foolishness unto him; neither can he know them, because they are spiritually discerned.* The product of a fallen nature, the natural and spontaneous growth of a corrupt soil, the fruit must correspond with the character of the seed sown. The religious perceptions of such a mind must be crude and obscure, for they are the perceptions of an understanding darkened. The proffered homage of such a heart must be vain and dissembled, since it is the homage of a heart alienated from God. Such, too, must be the worship offered to that Being who is a Spirit, and who requires of those who worship him, that they worship him in spirit and in truth. Its ritual may be sound, its rites may be scriptural, its forms may be solemn, its offerings may be costly, it is still the sacrifice of the *dead* offered to a *living* God! It is the worship of those who are " walking according to the flesh." And with all the apparent thirstings of a carnal mind after a knowledge of God—and in some cases we know how deep that thirst may be—there is a starting off from, nay more, there is a deadly opposition to, God the moment he approaches wearing the character revealed in his Word. Just as Adam, who eat the fruit in the vain conceit of increasing his knowledge, yet when God, the Object and the Fountain of knowledge, drew near

* 1 Cor. ii. 14.

in the pleasant Eden, at evening's cool, calm twilight, he fled the Divine presence, and hid himself amidst its bowers. Such only "know Christ *after the flesh*."* They know him intellectually, historically, speculatively, notionally, and this is the extent of their knowledge of God. They may designate him " our Saviour," and profess no other way to heaven but by him; and yet, sad to affirm, all their conceptions of his glory, and all their views of his works, and all their protestations of attachment to his person, are those of one who, living in the flesh, "knoweth Christ only after the flesh."

" Do mind the things of the flesh." What expressive words! All their pursuits are fleshly. Those pursuits may be, in the world's view, noble, daring, refined,—they may have a tendency to develop great mental powers, to call into exercise mighty energies, to elevate the taste, to soften and refine the feelings, and even, to a certain extent, advance the present well-being of society—yet is it a "minding of the things of the flesh." Contemplate the enjoyments and pursuits of the carnal mind in what light you may—the most intellectual and elevated—they yet spring from the flesh, are bounded by the flesh, and with the flesh they perish. This is your character, if not born again of the Spirit. "It is not necessary that you mind all the things of the flesh in order to constitute you a carnal man. It is enough to fasten this character upon you, that you have given yourself

* 2 Cor. v. 16.

over to the indulgence or the pursuit even so far as one of these things. A sinner may not be a debauchee, and neither the one nor the other may be an aspiring politician. But whatever the reigning passion may be, if it have the effect of attaching you to some one object that is in the world, and which with the world will terminate and perish,—then still your mind is in subjection to an idol, and the death of the carnally-minded is your inheritance and your doom. Be not deceived then, ye men, who, engrossed with the cares, and observant of all the sobrieties of business, are not addicted to the influences of dissipation; nor ye, who, heedless of wealth's accumulations, can mix an occasional generosity with the squanderings of intemperance and riot; nor ye, who, alike exempted from sordid avarice or debasing sensuality, have yet, in pursuit of an ascendancy over the mind and the measures of your fellow men, made power the reigning felicity of your existence; nor yet even ye, who, without any settled aim after one or the other of these gratifications, fluctuate in giddy unconcern from one of the world's frivolities to another. None of you mind all the things of the flesh; yet each of you mind one or the other of these things, and that to the entire practical exclusion of the things of the Spirit from the preference of your habitual regards. We do not charge you with a devotion of heart to all these things in the world which are opposite to the love of the Father, any more than we charge you with idolatrously falling in obeisance to all the divinities of a heathen polytheism. But still, if only one of these divinities be your God, there were enough to constitute you an idolater, and to convict you of a sacrilegious disavowal of the King who is eternal and immutable. And so, your one earthly appetite, though free from the tyranny of all the others; your habit of ungodliness—though it be the only one that breaks out into visible expression in the history of your life—of itself renders you a carnal man; of itself drives you from the spiritual territory; of itself proves that you are still one of the children of this world; and that you have not passed from death unto life."*

"But they that are after the Spirit the things of the Spirit." They who are after the Spirit undoubtedly are those who are the subjects of the Spirit's renewing grace. "That which is born of the Spirit is Spirit." Under his teaching—and oh, who teacheth like him?—they have renounced their own works of righteousness as dead works; feeling, to use the figurative language of the prophet, "the bed is shorter than a man can stretch himself in it, and the covering narrower than that he can wrap himself in it." † They have broken their covenant with death, and have disannulled their agreement with hell, and fleeing out of all their "refuges of lies," they have betaken themselves to the Lord Jesus Christ, and have experienced him to be their "wisdom, and righteousness, and sanctification, and redemption."

* Chalmers.   † Isaiah xxviii. 20.

What a marvellous revolution is this, effecting a total moral change in the whole spiritual and intellectual man, yet without impairing a single mental faculty or power! The mind not unbalanced, is rather strengthened and regulated by the change. The affections, not alienated and contracted, are expanded and fixed upon their lawful object. The will has not lost a particle of its liberty, but is more free than ever, since, drawn by the Spirit, it now blends harmoniously with the Divine will. The whole man is identically the same individual—yet how transformed! The prodigal alien has become a penitent child; the slave, a freeman; the man dwelling amongst the tombs now sits at the Saviour's feet, clothed, and in his right mind. Who but the Eternal Spirit could effect this wondrous revolution?

But more than this. Having dethroned the enemy, he now enthrones himself. Having swept and garnished the abode, he enters, and makes it his unchangeable dwelling. Thus living and reigning in the soul, believers are brought under the government of the Spirit. It may emphatically be said of them, that they "mind the things of the Spirit." The new and Divine nature within is exercised upon things congenial with itself. Confronted by the powerful phalanx of the flesh, with which he holds a severe and ceaseless warfare, the Christian is yet at times enabled to concentrate his attention upon the things of the Spirit. He walks with God in his temporal calling; he holds communion with heaven while yet the present life fetters him to earth; he has spiritual desires, and holy breathings, and successful contests, in the hottest battle with the law of his members. The one bent of his inclinations, the single aim of his mind, is to the "things of the Spirit." His nature being spiritual, so are his religious enjoyments. Does he sing?—it is with "spiritual songs." Does he pray?—he "prays in the Spirit." Does he call Jesus Lord?—it is "by the Spirit." Is he Christ's? —he "has the Spirit of Christ." Thus believers walk in the Spirit; they follow the dictates of the Spirit; they yield themselves to the teaching of the Spirit; and they bring forth in their due season "the fruits of the Spirit."

By this truth let us test the reality of our religious profession. In this light let us closely examine our Christian character and walk. What, reader, is the habitual and supreme bent of your mind? Is it that which is spiritual, or that which is carnal? Judge of your preparation for death, in the near view of its approaching solemnities. Decide upon your state for eternity, in the rapid progress of its deepening shadows. Ascertain the real state of your case for the judgment, in the certain arrival of its dread scrutiny. You have your mind either set upon the things of the flesh, or upon the things of the Spirit. You are either born again from above, or are grovelling in things below. You are either sanctified, or you are unholy. You are for the Lord, or you are against him. You are either Satan's slave, or Christ's freeman. Which? You inquire, "How may I know that I am of the Spirit?" We answer, by your producing the fruits of the Spirit. A broken heart for sin—a felt conviction of the hidden plague—a humble and a contrite spirit—an utter rejection of a human righteousness—a simple, believing reception of the Lord Jesus—and a breathing after Divine conformity, are evidences of a renewed and sanctified state. If these are yours in any degree, then you are of the Spirit.

But rest not here. Be exhorted to *walk* in the Spirit. Be not satisfied with having the question decided in your favour,—with just barely knowing that you have crossed the line that separates the regenerate from the unregenerate—death from life. Remain not where you are: go forward. Be not content with a low standard. Compare not your Church with other Churches, nor yourself with other Christians; nor measure yourself by yourself. But fix your eye upon Christ; copy his example, imbibe his mind, and place yourself under the government of his Spirit. Strive to go forward! Endeavour to be always sowing to the Spirit. Be satisfied with the Lord's disposal of you. Study the divine art of contentment. Be convinced that what the Lord ordains is best. Covet but little of earthly good; and, as an old divine exhorts, "sail with a low gale." Lie low. The great secret of a holy and of a happy life is contained in a small compass—*walking humbly with God.* In all failures in duty, in all shortcomings

in practice, in all transactions with God, and in all
dealings with man,—remembering the innumerable
traces of imperfection and sin found upon all you
do,—deal frequently, closely, with the atoning blood.
" Wash and be clean."

CHAPTER VI.

SPIRITUAL-MINDEDNESS.

" For to be carnally minded is death, but to be spiritually
minded is life and peace."—Romans viii. 6.

It will not be disputed that the true test of excellence is its nearest approach to perfection. To
nothing will this rule more strictly apply than to
the Christian character. Essentially considered, there
can be no difference between one believer and another.
Both are equally the objects of God's love, and alike
the subjects of his regenerating grace. Both stand
on an equal footing of acceptance, and participate the
same in the immunities which belong to the children
of God. But it cannot be denied, nor must it be concealed, that there is a great and marked difference
in the moral influence which one Christian exerts
beyond another. In the measure of his grace—in
the depth of his Christianity—in the vigour of his
faith—in the lustre of his holiness—in the glory he
brings to God, and in the consequent happiness of
which he is conscious, it may be truly said of the
Church on earth, as of the Church in heaven, " one

star differeth from another." And to what is this
variation to be traced? Undoubtedly to a difference
in the tone of spiritual-mindedness. The one is the
man of a low, the other of a high Christian standard.
Drawing their life, light, and support from one centre,
they yet seem to move in widely distant orbits. The
one seems nearer to the Sun than the other. And
thus, standing in a closer proximity to the Fountain
of all grace, he draws from its fulness the more
largely, and dispenses the more freely. His humble
walk with God, his close adherence to Christ, his following the Lord fully, imparts a charm to his piety,
a brilliance to his example, and a potency to his
influence, which place him in the highest rank of
Christian men.

In the passage before us two characters are presented to our view: the carnal mind, with its awful
consequence; the spiritual mind, with its holy and
heavenly fruit. "To be carnally minded is death,
but to be spiritually minded is life and peace."

"To be carnally minded is death." If there is
one consideration which more than another gives us
a vivid and impressive view of man's deep apostasy
from original holiness, it is the fact, that not only
the lower sentiments and feelings of his nature are
utterly and awfully debased, but that the higher and
nobler parts of his being—the rational, the intellectual, the moral—have felt the vibrations of the
shock, and share alike in the common ruin. In
the strong language of the apostle, he is "carnally

minded." Now, to be carnally minded, in the sense
of the passage, implies a condition in which the whole
soul is entirely engrossed with things correspondent
to its fallen nature. This desperate state is not re-
solvable simply into a flaw of the understanding, or
an occasional starting off of the heart from God, but
into a deep and thorough carnalization of that which
distinguishes him from the brute creation, and which
links him in the closest resemblance to God—the
MIND. The carnal mind thus describing and governing the whole man,—all his thoughts and feelings,
pursuits and pleasures, like the stream from the fountain, correspond with its nature. "Many walk of
whom I have told you often, and now tell you even
weeping (Paul had his tears of sympathy for poor
unconverted sinners: how many have we?) that they
are the enemies of the cross of Christ: whose end
is destruction, whose God is their belly, and whose
glory is in their shame, who mind earthly things." *
This is the broad seal affixed to every unregenerate
individual—"who mind earthly things." Select the
most intellectual, ennobling, and useful objects that
ever gave development to genius, and birth to
thought, or awoke the energies and enterprise of
men, and, compared with his eternal interests, what
contemptible puerilities do they appear! Survey the
whole life of an unconverted man: how unworthy
his rational being, and his deathless existence, is that
life! "Are these *men?*" we are tempted to ask.

* Phil. iii. 18, 19.

"See what low-browed bearing—what grovelling pursuits, what contemptible enjoyments! The honours
he wears, what baubles! The things he pursues,
what shadows! The pleasures he indulges, what
bubbles!" Again we ask, Are these *men?* Are
they rational? are they sane? are they soon to die?
are they on their way to eternity? do they really
believe in a God—in a hereafter—in a judgment—
in a hell?

And what is the awful consequence of this condition? It issues in death, present and eternal death.
"To be carnally minded is *death*." The nature of
the death here spoken of is defined by the tense.
It is a *present* death. To be carnally minded *is*
death,—it is death now. To the life of God—the
high spiritual life which every believer lives—the
unregenerate are dead. Bring them to the test.
Address them upon things congenial with their nature, they are all life and animation. Bring before
them some subject with which their habitudes of
thought are familiar, or with which their taste assimilates;—let it be, for example, the progress of
literature, or the discoveries of science, or the state
of the funds, or the bearings of politics, a painting,
an oratorio, or a book, and you have touched the
spring which moves all the sympathies and powers
the soul. Converse with the scholar of his Homer,
with the philosopher of his Newton, with the poet
of his muse, with the astronomer of his stars, with
the banker of his bullion, with the merchant of his

market, with the farmer of his cattle, with the sen-
sualist of his pleasures, with the husband of his bride,
with the mother of her first-born, and you have
awakened the devotion and enthusiasm of the heart
in favour of its fond and worshipped idol. To all
this the carnal mind is alive. But alas! the end
of these things is *death*. Change your theme. Meet
him in the busy hum of business, or lonely plying
his daily task, or amidst the heat and excitement of
his speculations and his pleasures, and speak to him
of Jesus; breathe that name which fills the church
below with its fragrance, and the church above with
its music, and there is no echo; no responsive chord
vibrates to your touch; it is as though you had told
your story to a senseless automaton, or had chanted
your music to the ear of a corpse. *Death* is there.

But this is not all. All? O no! it is but the
preface, the prelude to that which is to come. Men
are compelled in their calculations to look forward to
death—but the remote consequences of death they
ponder not. "After death the judgment." But this
judgment they take not into their calculations. A
simple fact may afford an impressive illustration of
this phase of the unregenerate mind. A young man,
whom he had known as a boy, came to an aged Professor of a distinguished continental University, with
a face beaming with delight, and informed him that
the long and fondly-cherished desire of his heart was
at length fulfilled,—his parents having given their
consent to his studying the profession of the law.

As the University presided over by his friend was a distinguished one, he had repaired to its law school, and was resolved to spare no labour or expense in getting through his studies as quickly and ably as possible. In this strain he continued for some time; and when he paused, the old man, who had been listening to him with great patience and kindness, gently said, "Well! and when you have finished your career of study, what do you mean to do then?" "Then I shall take my degree," answered the young man. "And then?" asked his venerable friend. "And then," continued the youth, "I shall have a number of difficult and knotty cases to manage: shall attract notice by my eloquence, and wit, and acuteness, and win a great reputation." "And then?" repeated the holy man. "And then!" replied the youth, "why then there cannot be a question I shall be promoted to some high office in the state, and I shall become rich." "And then?" "And then," pursued the young lawyer, "then I shall live comfortably and honourably in wealth and respect, and look forward to a quiet and happy old age." "And then?" repeated the old man. "And then," said the youth, "and then—and then—and then I shall die." Here his venerable listener lifted up his voice, and again asked, with solemnity and emphasis,—"And *then?*" Whereupon the aspiring student made no answer, but cast down his head, and in silence and thoughtfulness retired. This last "*And then?*" had pierced his heart like a sword—had darted like a flash of lightning into his soul, and he could not dislodge the impression. The result was, the entire change of his mind and course of his life. Abandoning the study of the law, he entered upon that of divinity, and expended the remainder of his days in the labours of a minister of Christ. O, it is the *after* consequences that make death so terrible to the worldling. There exists a strong analogy between the present and future death of the unregenerate. The spiritual death of the sinner holds its gloomy reign in the empire of a soul, all whose intellectual and moral faculties and powers are instinct with life, are girt with strength, and glow with animation. There is a vivid impression made by external objects. There is a keen sense of animal enjoyment. There is a high relish of the sublime delights and lofty exhilarations of a virtuous heart and a cultivated mind. And still it is the empire of *death*. " Death reigns." Pass in imagination to the " second death," so vividly portrayed amid the splendours of the apocalypse. Neither is that terrible death an entire cessation of consciousness, of feeling, of sensibility. Far from it. Not a faculty of the lost mind is impaired; not a power of the soul is destroyed; not a feeling of the heart is blunted. Nay, all have acquired a development, and a strength, they never experienced before. Memory will summon back each past event with all the vividness of a present transaction. And passion will struggle intensely with its unsatisfied desire. And a burning sense of shame, of loss, and of suffering, will bear down the spirit to the fathomless depths of misery. Think not, O unregenerate man, that the "second death" is an unconscious slumber, or a mesmeric trance. O no! it is a living, an eternal death. There will be nothing to alleviate but the scathing, overwhelming conviction of the perfect equity of the sentence, the strict righteousness of the doom. God will say—"I created you for my glory. I placed you in that world to live for my praise. Where are the talents with which I created you—the gifts with which I endowed you—the rank with which I distinguished you—the substance with which I intrusted you—the influence with which I clothed you—the years which I lengthened out to you? Thou wicked and slothful servant! thou hast buried my gifts in the earth, and hast lived to thyself—depart from me!" In view of a doom so tremendous and just, with what force and solemnity do the words fall upon the ear—"To be carnally minded is *death!*" Turn we now to a more pleasing theme.

"But to be spiritually minded is life and peace." There will be no difficulty in determining the origin, and in detecting the evidences of this state. It springs from the life of God in the soul. Apart from this, there cannot possibly be any real spiritual-mindedness. True spirituality is the springing up of the living water of Christ in the renewed heart. It is the "bringing forth of fruit upward"—of a root of grace in the soul of the regenerate. There is much that bears the semblance of holiness, and which, with many, passes current as such, but which we are compelled to pronounce spurious and counterfeit. Such, for example, to a vast extent, is the apparent sanctity of the Romish Church. Far be it from us to decide thus positively upon every such case found in the most corrupt anti-Christian communion on earth. This would be to claim a power, and exercise a prerogative, which belong essentially and absolutely to God alone. That within the pale of the apostate church there have lived and died true and sincere men of God, cannot be denied. Such was the heavenly-minded Blaise Pascal, and his Port-Royalist companions. Such, too, was Martin Boos, and others of equal piety in the same communion. Does not the solemn call recognise this fact, " Come out of her, *my people*, that ye be not partakers of her sins, and that ye receive not of her plagues ? " And are we not told, that when the elect are made up, and shall " stand before the throne and before the Lamb," they shall be " a great multitude, which no man can number, of all nations, and kindreds, and people, and tongues ; " and that this shall be the anthem of all, " Thou wast slain, and hast redeemed us to God by thy blood, out of every kindred, and tongue, and people, and nation ? " Thus from all communions, and from each fold, God will call out his hidden ones, who, amidst much darkness, and error, and superstition, have groped their way to the cross ; and who, sensible of the serpent's sting, have in simple faith looked alone for salvation to the crucified Saviour ; and in whose souls, beneath

the mantle of superstition and error, there dwelt
the dim but inextinguishable spark of a divine and
heavenly light. Oh! how unspeakably great the
mercy that, in a matter so momentous as our salvation, we deal with a God who searches the heart!
Oh! cheering truth, that the Shepherd knows his
sheep, in whatever fold they are found ; and that
the sheep know the Shepherd, however dim their
perception of his grace and glory. "The foundation
of God standeth sure, having this seal, *The Lord
knoweth them that are his.*"

But we repeat the truth, that all real spiritual-
mindedness is the offspring of a new and spiritual life
in the soul. The state of which we speak is the effect
of a cause, the consequent upon a certain condition of
mind. Before a man can exercise any degree of true
heavenliness, he must be heavenly. Before he can
bring forth the fruits of holiness, he must be holy.
Dear reader, is this your condition? Have you the
life of God in your soul? Have you passed from
death unto life? Is the fruit you bear the result of
your engrafting into Christ? You attend upon the
service of the sanctuary ; you visit the abodes of the
wretched : you administer to the necessities of the
poor; you are rigid in your duties, and zealous in
your charities ; but does it all spring from faith in
Christ, and from love to God? Is it from life, or for
life? Oh! remember, that the spiritual-mindedness
which the Bible recognises, of which God approves,
has its root in the life of God in the soul !

But in what does spiritual-mindedness consist? It is the setting of the mind upon spiritual objects. The heart is fixed on God. The bent of the soul—its desires and breathings, are towards him. It is a firm, growing approximation of all the renewed faculties to spiritual and heavenly realities. God in Christ is the attraction of the heart. That the needle of the soul always thus steadily points to him we do not affirm; there are false attractions which lure the affections from God, and deaden the spirituality of the mind. To be carnally minded brings a kind of death even into the renewed soul; but this is not the reigning, predominant state. Let God remove that false attraction—let the Eternal Spirit apply with his own quickening power some precious truth to the heart, and the wayward, tremulous needle returns to its centre; and the heart is again fixed on God, its exceeding joy. Oh, how holy and precious are these restorings!

Love to God is the governing motive of the spiritual mind. All desire of human admiration and applause pales before this high and holy principle of the soul. Its religion, its devotion, its zeal, its toils, its sacrifices, spring from love. Love prompts, love strengthens, love sweetens, love sanctifies all. This it is that expels from the heart the rival and false claimant of its affections, and welcomes and enthrones the true. It may, at times, like the pulse of the natural life, beat languidly, yet, unlike that pulse, it never ceases entirely to beat. The love of God in the soul never expires. Fed from the source from whence it emanates, the holy fire, dim and dying as it may appear at times, never goes out. Have you this evidence of the spiritual mind, my reader? Does the love of Christ constrain you? It is the first and the chief grace of the Spirit,—do you possess it? "Now abideth faith, hope, and love, but the *greatest* of these is *love*." It is the main-spring, the motive power, of the spiritual mechanism of the soul,—all its wheels revolve, and all its movements are governed by it. Is this the pure motive that actuates you in what you do for God? Or, do there enter into your service and your sacrifice, aught of self-seeking, of thirst for human approbation, of desire to make a fair show in the flesh, of aiming to make religion subserve your temporal interests? Oh, search your hearts, and see; sift your motives, and ascertain! Love to God— pure, unmixed, simple love—is the attribute of the spiritual mind; and, in proportion to the intensity of the power of love, as a motive, will be the elevated tone of your spirituality. Nor need there be any lack of this motive power. "God is love," and he is prepared to supply it to the mind's utmost capacity. We are straitened in ourselves, not in him. The ocean, on whose margin we doubtingly, timidly stand, is infinite, boundless, fathomless. The Lord is willing to direct our hearts into its depths, but we hesitate and draw back, awed by its infinite vastness, or stumbling at its perfect freeness. But to attain to a high standard of heavenly-mindedness, we must have more of the love of God shed abroad in our hearts by the Holy Ghost, which he hath given unto us. We must love Christ more.

It enters essentially and deeply into this state of spiritual-mindedness, that the heart be much with Jesus on the throne. "If ye then be risen with Christ, seek those things which are above, where Christ sitteth on the right hand of God. Set your affections (mind) on things above, not on things on the earth." To win heaven, the mind must become heavenly; and to be heavenly, it must habituate itself to heavenly things and heavenly pursuits. It is a law of our mental constitution, that the mind assimilates in its tone and habits of thought with the subject which most engrosses its study. Hence it is that we sometimes become men of one idea. Now the contemplation of divine and spiritual themes has a powerful tendency to spiritualize and sanctify the mind. It seems impossible to breathe a heavenly atmosphere, and not be heavenly; to study holy things, and not be holy; to admire the image of Christ, and not resemble Christ; to have frequent intercourse with Jesus upon the throne, and not catch some stray beam of his glory. And apart from Christ nothing is really pleasant and satisfying to the heavenly mind. Without him, what a dreary, lonesome wilderness were this! But with Christ in the heart, and the heart resting in Christ—he in the centre of our souls, and our affections and desires centreing in him —the desert loses it solitude and its desolateness. To

have the eye resting on Jesus—all our heart-springs
in him—the spirit in frequent excursions where he
dwells in light and glory—to lean upon him, and converse with him as though he were actually walking by
our side, sitting at our board, associated with us in
our callings—this, *this* is heavenly-mindedness. Such
is the counter-attraction to the "things on the earth,"
—the secularizing pursuits, the low-thoughted cares,
the carnal enjoyments,—which we so deeply need.
And this powerful, counteracting influence which we
possess is a realization of our resurrection with Christ,
and his enthronement in glory.

Individual and close intercourse with Jesus, in the
matter of confession of sin, and washing in the
atoning blood, strongly marks the state of spiritual-
mindedness. No Christian duty forms a surer test
of the spiritual tone of the believer than this. The
essence, the very life of spiritual-mindedness, is *holiness*; and the deepening of heart-holiness is the measure of our sanctity of life. Now, there can be no
progress in holiness apart from a habit of frequent
laying open of the heart in the acknowledgment of
sin to Christ. The conscience only retains its tenderness and purity by a constant and immediate confession; and the heart can only maintain its felt
peace with God as it is perpetually sprinkled with
the blood of Jesus. The soul thus kept beneath the
cross preserves its high tone of spirituality unim-
paired in the midst of all the baneful influences by
which it is surrounded. "To maintain a 'conscience

void of offence,' I am persuaded I ought to confess
sin more. I think I ought to confess sin the moment
I see it to be sin; whether in company, or in study,
or even preaching, the soul ought to cast a glance of
abhorrence at the sin. If I go on with duty, leaving
sin unconfessed, I go on with a burdened conscience,
and add sin to sin. I think I ought at certain times
of the day, to confess solemnly the sins of the previous hours, and seek their complete remission. I
feel when I have sinned an immediate reluctance
to go to Christ. I am ashamed to go. I feel as
if it would not do to go; as if it were making Christ
the minister of sin, to go straight from the swine-
trough to the best robe; and a thousand other excuses; but I am persuaded they are all lies direct
from hell. John argues the opposite way—'If any
man sin, we have an advocate with the Father;' and
a thousand other Scriptures are against it. I am
sure there is neither peace nor safety from deeper sin
but in going directly to the Lord Jesus Christ. This
is God's way of peace and holiness. It is folly to the
world and the beclouded heart, but it is *the way.*" *
Such were the holy sentiments and lofty aspirations
of an eminently spiritual mind; and if we follow
him as he followed the precepts of Christ, we must
transcribe, and make his experience our own. The
holy sensitiveness of the soul that shrinks from the
touch of sin, the acute susceptibility of the conscience
at the slightest shade of guilt, will of necessity draw

* Mc Cheyne.

the spiritual mind frequently to the blood of Jesus. And herein lies the secret of a heavenly walk. Acquaint yourself with it, my reader, as the most precious secret of your life. He who lives in the habit of a prompt and minute acknowledgment of sin, with his eye reposing calmly, believingly, upon the crucified Redeemer, soars in spirit where the eagle's pinion ranges not. He walks in secret places with God. " He shall dwell on high : his place of defence shall be the munitions of rocks." " There is a path which no fowl knoweth, and which the vulture's eye hath not seen"—"it is the new and living way," the royal highway wherein the saints alone walk with God. " No lion shall be there, nor any ravenous beast shall go up therein : it shall not be found there; but the redeemed shall walk there." Sprinkled with the blood of the Incarnate God, how holy, how awful the place ! Who can walk there, and not be spiritually-minded ?

The possession of the Holy Spirit in the fulness of his grace contributes essentially to the constitution of the spiritual mind. The great antagonist of carnality is the Spirit. " If we walk in the Spirit, we shall not fulfil the lusts of the flesh." " Be not overcome of wine, but be filled with the Spirit." As the Spirit of God, he is the Author of all that is spiritual. As the Spirit of holiness, he maintains and carries forward the work of sanctification in the soul. He it is who forms, and he it is who leads forward, the spiritual mind. The large possession of the Spirit ! nothing can exceed the blessing. Without the Spirit of God, what is man? He is the mark of every fiery assault, the prey of every prowling foe—a magazine of corruption, around which a thousand sparks—sparks of his own kindling—fall. But possessing the Spirit, even in its most limited measure, what is man? A living soul—a holy being—a temple of God—an heir of glory. But suppose him possessing the Spirit in the plenitude of His grace, not partially, but "filled with the Spirit,"—what must be the invincibility of his might in the resistance of sin! what the potency of his shield in disarming the power of temptation! and what the eminence of his attainments in spiritual-mindedness, as a child of God! While others are girding for the conflict, or are adjusting their armour, he is covering himself with glory on the battle-field. While others are training for the race, he has well-nigh reached the goal. Filled with the Spirit, he is filled with all the fruits of the Spirit. Faith is vigorous, hope is bright, love is fervent. He is mighty in the "Spirit of power, and of love, and of a sound mind." It was this possession of the Spirit in his fulness which gave to the Apostles, who until then were so timid and unbelieving, such irresistible boldness and power on the day of Pentecost. Some in their hearing exclaimed, "These men are full of new wine." But the secret was, "they were all filled with the Holy Ghost." And the hearts of the great mass to whom they preached the crucified Saviour, bowed before the power of their preaching, "as the

trees of the wood are moved with the wind." O seek
to be filled with the Spirit! then will your thirstings
for God be deeper—your breathings after holiness
intenser—your communion with your Heavenly Father
closer, and your faith in Jesus stronger. The inbeing
of the Spirit is the root of all holiness; but the
communication of the Spirit in the plenitude of His
gracious, sanctifying, Christ-transforming influence,
is the secret of an elevated tone of heavenly-mindedness.
Would you repel some strong assault, or vanquish
some powerful corruption, or throw off some clinging
infirmity, and wander by the verdant banks and quiet
waters of fellowship with the Father and with his Son
Christ Jesus? O ask, and you shall receive, the fulness
of the Spirit.

"To be spiritually-minded is life and peace." Such
are the fruits of a plant so divine and heavenly.
Spiritual-mindedness is "life." We fearlessly challenge every believer—What has been the effect in
your soul of a low state of grace? What has been
the effect of carnal indulgence—of allowed sin—of
needless intercourse with the world—of conformity to
its policy and its pleasures—of unruly temper—of a
volatile disposition, yea, of any species of carnality
whatever; has it not been *"death?"* When a process of spiritual relapse has been allowed to proceed
stealthily and unchecked; when the world, and sin,
and self have gained an ascendency, what has been the
consequence?—"death!" The habit of prayer may
not have been totally neglected, but there has been

no communion with God,—and so there has been death upon prayer. The Bible has not been entirely unread, but no light has beamed upon the sacred page —and so there has been death upon the Bible. The means of grace have not been utterly forsaken, but no grace has distilled from these channels—and so there has been death upon the means of grace. Thus a spiritual deathliness has crept over the soul, the effect and fruit of indulged and growing carnality. But " *life* " is the blessed effect of heavenly-mindedness. It is life springing from life, or rather the inner life in its outer actings. What spiritual mightiness, almost omnipotent, does he possess whose mind, and heart, and faculties are deeply immersed in the Spirit of Christ—closely allied to the divine and heavenly! As sin is weakness, so holiness is strength. As carnality impairs, so spirituality invigorates. The one deadens, the other vivifies. Close dealing with Essential Life increases the life of spirituality. Much intercourse with Jesus draws forth " life more abundantly." It is impossible to live a life of faith on the Son of God, constantly taking to his blood every sin, to his heart every care, to his sympathy every sorrow, to his grace every corruption, to his arm every burden, without being conscious of new life, of augmented power, of increased heavenliness. Inquire of the man of prayer, what is the effect in his soul of close, filial communion with God? Ask the reflective mind what is the effect upon his spirit of holy meditation? Ask the conscience much beneath the cross, what is

the result of the constant sprinkling of the atoning
blood? And, as with one voice, and with one utterance,
each believer will answer—"LIFE !" O, there is an
energizing influence in spirituality, a quickening of
the spiritual life in heavenly-mindedness, which he
only can understand, whose converse is much with
things heavenly, much with God. There is life in
prayer, life in the word, life in ordinances, life in the
enjoyment of vital religion, which transmits the thrill
of its deep pulsations through the whole soul. Nor
life alone in these. But when the storm of adversity
blows—when sore affliction comes—when the "noise
of the water-spout" is heard, and the tossing waves
and the foaming billows roll over the soul—when the
shadow of death is settling upon all creature-good—
then, even *then*, the spiritual mind panting after life
exclaims, "Though I walk in the midst of trouble,
Thou wilt *revive* me." "This is my comfort in my
affliction: for Thy word hath *quickened* me." And
what is all this but the pledge and the prelude of the
glorious consummation and crown of all—the life that
is to come, even life everlasting?

But not life alone; "peace" also is a fruit of
spiritual-mindedness. What peace of conscience does
that individual possess whose mind is stayed upon
spiritual things! It is as much the reward as it is
the effect of his cultivated heavenliness. The existence
of this precious blessing, however, supposes the exposure of the spiritual mind to much that has a
tendency to ruffle and disturb its equanimity and

repose. The Christian is far from being entirely exempt from those chafings and disquietudes which seem inseparable from human life. To the brooding anxieties arising from external things—life's vicissitudes, mutations, and disappointments—there are added, what are peculiar to the child of God, the internal things that distract—the cloudings of guilt, the agitations of doubt, the corrodings of fear, the mourning of penitence, the discipline of love. But through all this there flows a river the streams whereof make glad the city of God. Coursing its way along the windings of a soul,—often presenting to the eye the moral scenery of precipice and valley, undulating and wild, and all enshrouded in gloom,—this peace of God diffuses a calmness, serenity, and sunlight over the spirit, creating in the heart an emotion and a melody more like the repose of the upper sanctuary, and the chimings of the heavenly Sabbath, than the feelings and music of earth. It is the peace of the heavenly mind, the peace which Jesus procured, which God imparts, and which the Holy Spirit seals. A heavenly mind soars above a poor dying world, living not upon a creature's love, or smile—casting its daily need upon the heart of a kind Providence—careful for nothing, but with supplication and thanksgiving making known its requests unto God—indifferent to the turmoil, and vexations, and chequered scenes of worldly life, and living in simple faith and holy pleasing on Christ,—thus detached from earth, and moving heavenwards by the attractions of its placid coast, it

realizes a peace which passeth all understanding.
And if this be the present of the heavenly mind, what
will be the future of the *mind in heaven?* Heaven is
the abode of perfect peace. There are no cloudings
of guilt, no tossings of grief, no agitations of fear, no
corrodings of anxiety *there.* "There the wicked cease
from troubling, and the weary are at rest." It is the
peace of perfect purity—it is the repose of complete
satisfaction. It is not so much the entire absence of
all sorrow, as it is the actual presence of all holiness,
that constitutes the charm and the bliss of future
glory. The season of sorrow is frequently converted
into that of secret joy—Christ making our very griefs
to sing. But the occasion of sin is always that of
bitter grief; our backslidings often, like scorpions,
entwined around our hearts. Were there even—as
most assuredly there will not be—sadness in heaven,
there might still be the accompaniment of happiness;
but were there *sin* in heaven—the shadow of a shade
of guilt—it would becloud and embitter all. Thus,
then, as heaven is the abode of perfect peace, he who
on earth has his conversation most in heaven, approxi-
mates in his feelings the nearest to the heavenly state.
His "peace shall be as a river, and his righteousness
as the waves of the sea." O that our hearts were
more yielding to the sweet, and holy, and powerful
attractions of the heavenly world! Then would our
conversation be more in heaven.

In conclusion. How great and exalted the heavenly
calling of the Christian! Aim to walk worthy of it.

Debase it not by allying it with a carnal mind. Impair not your spiritual life by enchaining it to spiritual death. Let the friendships which you culti- vate, and the relationships of life which you form, be heavenly in their nature, and eternal in their duration. Seek to please God in all things. Rest not where you are, even though you may have attained beyond your fellows. Let your standard of heavenly-mindedness be not that of the saints, but of Christ. Study not a copy, but the Original. High aims will secure high attainments. He is the most heavenly, and the happiest, who the most closely resembles his Divine Master. Be much in your closet. There is no pro- gress in spiritual-mindedness apart from much prayer : prayer is its aliment, and its element. But leave not your religion there; let it accompany you into the world. While careful not to carry your business into your religion,—thus secularizing and degrading it,— be careful to carry your religion into your business— high integrity, holy principle, godly fear—thus impart- ing an elevation and sanctity to all its concerns. Be the man of God wherever you are. Let these solemn words be held in vivid remembrance—" I have created thee for my glory. I have formed thee for my praise. Ye are my witnesses, saith the Lord."

Heavenly-mindedness can only be maintained by the strictest vigilance. It is a delicate and fragile flower, susceptible of every variation of the spiritual atmosphere. Guard against that which checks its growth. Many are not aware how much great ex-

uberance of spirits, light conversation, foolish jesting,
witticisms at the expense of Scripture-sanctity, novel
reading, carnal music, unfit the heart for communion
with God, and lessen the tone of its spirituality.
Close intercourse with mere nominal religious professors is particularly to be avoided. Much more
injury to spiritual-mindedness accrues from intimate
friendship with such, than from those who assert no
pretensions to a religious character. With the one
we are apt to be less on our guard than the other.
Avoid the world's amusements: they will eat as a
canker into the very core of your spirituality. "Be
not conformed to this world," is a prohibition,—"Our
conversation is in heaven," is an exhortation which
should never be absent from the eye of a traveller to
the heavenly city. And why should not our conversation be in heaven? Are not its attractions many
and powerful? It is a holy place, and it is the place
of the holy. There are the city of the living God,
and the heavenly Jerusalem, and an innumerable
company of angels, and the general assembly and
church of the firstborn, which are written in heaven,
and God the Judge of all, and the spirits of just men
made perfect, and Jesus the Mediator of the new
covenant. How rich is heaven! And there we, too,
will shortly be. Why, then, should not our conversation be there? It will be recollected that when the
high priest entered within the veil, bearing in his
hands the blood of atonement and the smoking censer,
the eyes of the congregation, who stood without,

followed him to the entrance as the curtain parted,
and then veiled him from their gaze. And many a
thrilling heart and trembling hope followed him within
that holy place, its fervent sympathies clustering
around him while he presented the offerings, and
made intercession for the people. And many a longing eye intently and fondly watched for his *return*,
when, with uplifted hands, he would bless the waiting
congregation. Our great High Priest has passed
within the veil. As our Advocate he fills heaven's
high chancery. He loves us—remembers us—sym-
pathises with us—intercedes for us, and wears our
names on his breast-plate and his ephod. And soon
he will return in person to bless, with the first resur-
rection-glory, all those who " love his appearing."
Oh! shall not our hearts be more where our most
precious treasure is, and where our holiest and fondest
hopes centre, and where we ourselves shall shortly be?
" What manner of persons ought we to be in all holy
conversation and godliness," who are " looking for and
hastening unto the Lord's coming?" " The very
God of peace sanctify you wholly; and I pray God
your whole spirit, and soul, and body, be preserved
blameless unto the coming of the Lord Jesus." The
Lord grant that you may increasingly experience, that
" to be spiritually-minded is life and peace;" and that
in order to attain to this blessed state, we must live
upon the Lord Jesus—be filled with the Spirit—be
often at God's confessional—and, taking up our cross
daily, be pressing onward and upward, " denying all

ungodliness and worldly lusts, and living soberly, righteously, and godly in this present world; looking for that blessed hope, and the glorious appearing of the great God and our Saviour Jesus Christ; who gave himself for us, that he might redeem us from all iniquity, and purify unto himself a peculiar people, zealous of good works."

CHAPTER VII.

THE ENMITY OF THE CARNAL MIND.

"Because the carnal mind is enmity against God: for it is not
subject to the law of God, neither indeed can be."

ROMANS viii. 7.

HAVING spoken of carnal-mindedness, the Apostle
naturally proceeds to describe the carnal mind itself;
exhibiting its great distinctive feature—hostility to
God as manifested in subjection to the Divine government. To each of these particulars let us in the
present chapter direct our attention.

"The carnal mind is enmity against God." There
is something appalling to our moral feelings in the bare
announcement of the subject. The spectacle is an
awful one in the extreme, of the finite armed in dead
hostility to the Infinite—of a creature measuring his
power with God—opposing his will to God's will—his
way to God's way—his end to God's end. And yet
how disproportionate are our profoundest feelings of
horror and commiseration to the atrocious nature and
the tremendous consequences of the crime! Enmity
against God! the greatest and holiest, the best and
most powerful, of beings and of friends! And why

this enmity? Upon what, in the character of God, or in the nature of his government, is this sworn hostility grounded? Is it because he is essential love? perfectly holy? strictly righteous? infinitely wise and powerful? For which of these perfections does the sinner hate him? Is it because he gave his Son to die for man, laying him a bleeding sacrifice on the altar of justice for human transgression? Is it because the sun of his goodness shines upon every being, and that he opens his hand and supplies the need of every living thing? Is it because he exercises forbearance and long-suffering, and is slow to anger, and of great kindness? For which of these good works does the sinner hate him? And to what extent is this enmity displayed? It rests not short of the destruction of the Divine existence. Man is at war with the very being of God. Atheism is not so common a crime of our humanity as some suppose. Theism is the natural conviction of the human mind. The idea of a Supreme Being is coeval with man's existence. Where has there ever existed a people without a God? or a nation without a temple? Paganism, prostrate at the shrine of idolatry; and Christendom, bathing the standard of the cross in the blood of the martyrs; and Formalism, solemnly strutting in the crimson and purple of its gorgeous rites—each owns its belief in the existence of a God. But *what* God? Plainly not the God of the Bible; but a deity of its imagination. But in the existence of absolute atheism we are slow to avow our belief.

From the idea of a Deity it is impossible for the human mind to escape. "The fool hath said in his heart, No God;" that is, "I desire no God." He does not deny His existence; he does not say there is no God, but he desires no intercourse with Him. He may at times attempt to reason himself into a belief in the utter negation of a Deity; but in the still hour of night the truth flashes upon his mind with irresistible and overwhelming conviction—"There *is* a God! and I cannot overcome, I cannot escape him." Yes, the carnal mind is enmity with the being of God. Sin is destructive of all being. Man is a suicide—he has destroyed himself; a homicide—his influence destroys others; a deicide—he would, were it in his power, annihilate the very being of God. What a proof of this have we in the crucifixion of the Son of God! When God brought himself as near to man as Infinity could approach, he exclaimed, "This is the Heir; come, let us kill him!" and then proceeded to consummate the crime by nailing him to the tree!

But if further evidence were needed of man's decided and deadly hostility, we have it in the sentiments and feelings he cherishes towards the Lord Jesus Christ. "He that hateth me," says our Lord, "hateth my Father also." How completely this declaration sweeps away all the fancied reverence and admiration for God which floats before the imagination of the carnal mind in its profound slumber! The God of whom he has thus been dreaming is not

the God of revelation, but the god of his own creation. He is not the holy God whom the Bible
makes known—of whom Jesus is the living and
visible embodiment—but an ideal being clothed with
attributes, and administering a government harmoniz-
ing with the corrupt tastes and sinful propensities of
his carnal mind. Away with your religion of nature,
of sentiment, of poetry! All that you know of the
music of God, is the Æolian breathing of the wind;
all that you see of the glory of God, is the brilliance
of the star; all that you understand of the eternity of
God, is the expanse of the ocean; and of the omnipotence of God, is the fastness of the mountain and
the rock. A disciple, not of Christ, but of Spinoza,
your religion is sheer Pantheism, confounding with
His material works the Maker and Governor of the
universe. The god whom you profess to adore and
worship is not the God manifested in Christ, whose
justice and holiness, whose wisdom and truth, are
blended and harmonized with grace and love in the
cross of Calvary. Of what value is your fancied
admiration of God's character, whilst yet hating,
despising, and rejecting the Son, who is the "brightness of his glory, and the express image of his
person"? Your heart is a stranger to holiness, and
your mind to peace, whilst prostrate before a deity of
your own imagination—an ideal god. "Oh! give us
some steady object for our minds to rest upon!" was
a common exclamation in the prayers of the great
and good Chalmers, in the days of his unregeneracy,

when tossed amidst the breakers of Mirabaud's pan-
theistic philosophy.*   Of this want, you, my reader,
are perhaps deeply and painfully sensible.   There is
nothing in your creed; nothing in your vague,
shadowy, unreal conception of Deity, to fix your
thoughts, to soothe your spirit, to allay your fears,
to awaken your affections, and to inspire your hope.
Your altar is reared, and your incense is offered, but
it is to the " UNKNOWN GOD."

But what is the alleged ground of this hostility of
the carnal mind?   The non-subjection of the mind
to the government of God.   "It is not subject to
the law of God, neither indeed can be."   The secret
is now revealed.   God is the moral governor of the
universe.   Oh! this is the *casus belli* between him
and the sinner.   This constitutes the real secret of
his fell, inveterate hostility to the Divine Being.
The question at issue is—Who shall govern—God
or the sinner?   The non-subjection of the carnal
heart to God's law—its rebellion against the Divine
government—clearly indicates the side of this question which the carnal mind takes.   You may, my
reader, succeed in reasoning yourself into the belief
that you admire, adore, and love God as your Creator
and Benefactor, and only feel a repugnance, and
manifest an opposition, to him as a Lawgiver.   But
this is impossible in fact, however poetic or specious
it may be in theory.   In a purely human government we admit that the person and the office of the

* Memoir of Dr. Chalmers, vol. i. p. 46.

judge may be separable. For example, an individual may be a personal friend of the sovereign, and yet an avowed opponent of his government. Doubtless, during the Commonwealth there were many who loved Cromwell for his piety, and admired him for his manliness, who yet condemned many of the measures of his government as harsh and despotic. But the moral government of God does not admit of this refined distinction. His nature and his office, his person and his throne, are one and inseparable. No individual can possibly be a friend to the being of God, who is not equally friendly to the government of God. Now the moral law is offensive to the carnal mind. And why? Because of the holiness of its nature, and the strictness of its requirements. It not only takes cognizance of external actions, but it touches the very springs of action, the motives that lie concealed in the human heart, and regulate the life. It demands supreme affection and universal obedience. To this the carnal mind demurs. If Jehovah will relax the rigour of his law, and abate the stringency of its requirements, and soften the sternness of its demands,—if, in other words, God will lay aside his regal character, descend from his throne, forego his sovereignty, and lay aside his sceptre—then the war is at an end; the controversy ceases; the rebel lays down his weapons. It clearly appears, then, that the whole ground of dispute between these two extremes of being resolves itself into the question—" Who shall reign, God or the sinner?" But will God yield his right to the throne? Never! Can he relax one iota of the strictness of his law? Impossible! Heaven and earth shall pass away, but not one tittle of his law shall fail. If in any single case this could have been done, surely it would have been in that of his beloved Son. And yet, Jesus neither asked as a favour, nor accepted as a boon, the slightest abatement of the law he came to fulfil. He entered into no negotiation for the least compromise either of the stringency of the precept or the sternness of the penalty. It was the glory of the law that it demanded all from Christ, and it was the honour of Christ that he gave all the law demanded. Sinner! behold the true cause of your present hatred and hostility to God. You are not subject to the law of God, neither indeed can be, because your mind is unregenerate. Your heart is unholy, and you dispute God's right to govern you.

There are some solemn conclusions to which we may arrive from this subject.

The utter impossibility of the sinner's admission into heaven with the carnal mind unchanged is most clear. Suppose an opposite case. Imagine an unrenewed soul suddenly transported to heaven. In a moment it finds itself in the light, and holiness, and presence of God. What a scene of wonder, purity, and glory has burst upon its gaze! But, awful fact! horror of horrors! it is confronted face to face with its great enemy,—the God it hated, loathed, and denied!

Is it composed? Is it at home? Is it happy? Impossible! It enters the immediate presence of the Divine Being, its heart rankling with the virus of deadly hate, and its hand clutching the uplifted weapon. It carries its sworn malignity and its drawn sword to the very foot of the throne of the Eternal. "Take me hence," it exclaims; "this is not *my* heaven!" And then it departs "to its own place." But we are supposing an impossible case. For it is written of the heavenly city, "There shall in no wise enter into it anything that defileth, neither whatsoever worketh abomination, or maketh a lie; but they who are written in the Lamb's book of life." Listen to the declaration of the Great Teacher sent from God,—"Except a man be born again, he cannot see the kingdom of God." Ask you what this new birth means? We reply, you must become a new creature in Christ Jesus. You must ground your arms before the Eternal God of heaven and earth. You must give up the quarrel. You must relinquish the controversy. You must cease to fight against God. You must submit to the law and government of Jehovah. Your will must bow to God's will. Your heart must beat in unison with God's heart. Your mind must harmonize with God's mind. Implacable hatred must give place to adoring love—deep ungodliness to a nature breathing after holiness—stern opposition to willing obedience—the creature to the Creator—yourself to God. O blissful moment! when the controversy ceases, and God and your soul are at agreement through Christ Jesus. When, dropping the long-raised weapon, you grasp his outstretched hand, and rush into his expanded arms, fall a lowly, believing penitent upon his loving bosom, take hold of his strength, and are at peace with him. O happy moment! No more hatred, no more enmity, no more opposition now! It is as though all heaven had come down and entered your soul,—such joy, such peace, such love, such assurance, such hope do you experience! What music now floats from these words: "No condemnation in Christ Jesus." How blessed now to lean upon the breast which once you hated, and find it a pillow of love; to meet the glance which once you shunned, and find it the expression of forgiveness; to feel at home in the presence of him to whom once you said, "Depart from me, for I desire not the knowledge of thy ways."

What an evidence of the reign of grace in the soul, when the mind fully acquiesces in the moral government of God! "The Lord God Omnipotent reigneth," is the adoring anthem of every heart brought into subjection to the law of God. To the Christian how composing is the thought, that the government is upon Christ's shoulders, and that he sits upon the throne judging right. From hostility to the law of God, his heart is now brought to a joyful acquiescence in its precepts, and to a deep delight in its nature. "I delight in the law of God after the inward man." "O Lord!" he exclaims, "my holiness is in submission to thy authority. My happiness flows from doing and suffering thy will. I rejoice that the sceptre is in thy hands, and I desire that the thoughts of my mind, and the affections of my heart, may be brought into perfect obedience to thyself. Be my soul thy kingdom, be my heart thy throne, and 'let grace reign through righteousness unto eternal life.' "

CHAPTER VIII.

PLEASING GOD.

" So then they that are in the flesh cannot please God."
ROMANS viii. 8.

We have been contemplating, in the preceding ex-
positions of this chapter, some of the various phases
of the carnal mind. The Apostle now proceeds to a
necessary consequence of the hostility of a mind
governed by the flesh, and in rebellion against the
law of God. " So then they that are in the flesh
cannot please God." The doctrine thus set forth is,
the utter impossibility of the unregenerate pleasing
God. Having considered this primary truth, we shall
then place in contrast with it the especial points in
which the regenerate may be said to please God.

The utter impossibility of a carnal mind pleasing
God springs from the necessity of the case. As the
object of his displeasure, and as dwelling in a nature
not only diametrically opposite to his own, in which
lurks the latent virulence of a deep and implacable
hatred, but every faculty and power of which is armed
in the deadliest hostility to his government and being,

it is impossible that it can please him.   In whatever
point of light you contemplate the unregenerate—
taking the most intellectual and refined view,—the
utmost that can be said is, "He is in the flesh."
We do not forget that there are degrees of carnality,
even as there are degrees of spirituality; nevertheless,
the law of God takes into account no degrees, recog-
nizes no shades of difference, but regards all alike,
unregenerate.   The Bible solemnly and emphatically
affirms, that a carnal mind cannot please a holy and
righteous God.   How could it possibly be otherwise?
The apostle declares, "In me, that is in my flesh,
dwelleth no good thing."   What! *no* good thing?
Nothing spiritually good or morally lowly?   No,
nothing.   The purest ethics of the carnal mind are as
the ointment of the apothecary which the fly hath
spoiled; and the most zealous and costly duties and
sacrifices which it presents are but as 'splendid sins,'
so long as that mind is yet under the dominion of
the flesh.   But these are only general statements of
a most important truth; we pass to a few particulars.

There being no personal acceptance of those who
are in the flesh, consequently, whatever they do in
the way of religious service cannot be accepted of
God.   First, the *person*, and then the *gift*, is God's
order in the great method of our justification.   We
might refer to the narrative of Queen Esther's inter-
view with the King Ahasuerus, and to Jacob's meeting
with Esau, as illustrating this principle.   It is most
clear, that in both these instances,—had Esther urged

her suit in behalf of her nation without having awakened in the heart of the king a feeling of complacent regard towards her person—and had the offering of Jacob to his incensed brother preceded the presentation of himself,—in either case there must have been a decided and mortifying, if not fatal result. Apply these illustrations to the believer. What imparts divine acceptance to his service? Why do his prayers ascend before God like fragrant incense floating from a golden censer? Why does his meanest offering of love cast into the Lord's treasury outvalue the most splendid and affluent offerings of all others? Why is a sigh so full of meaning, and a tear so costly, and a desire so eloquent, and a heaven-lifted glance so expressive to God? Oh, it is because he is well pleased with his well-beloved Son, standing in whom the person of each believing sinner is fully accepted. We place this vital truth broadly before the unrenewed mind, and basing upon it the one important inquiry, we press its solemn consideration—How can you do that which is well-pleasing and acceptable to a holy God, while your *person* is to him an object of just, and holy, and utter abhorrence? While rejecting the Lord Jesus Christ, and refusing and despising the robe of his righteousness, with what complacency can God regard your meanless modes ot worship, your formal duties, and your heartless offerings? Will he not say, "When ye come to appear before me, who hath required this at your hand, to tread my courts? Bring no more vain oblations;

incense is an abomination unto me; the new moons
and Sabbaths, the calling of assemblies, I cannot
away with; it is iniquity, even the solemn meeting.
Your new moons and your appointed feasts my soul
hateth: they are a trouble unto me; I am weary to
bear them. And when ye spread forth your hands, I
will hide mine eyes from you: yea, when ye make
many prayers, I will not hear."* It was the robe of
the elder brother that made Jacob's offering of
venison savoury and acceptable to Isaac. It is the
righteousness of Christ, whose comeliness is upon us,
which makes our every act of service and homage of
love, an offering and a sacrifice to God of a sweet
smelling savour.

The absence of *faith* in the unregenerate must
render all the religious doings of the sinner equally
displeasing to God. "For without faith it is impossible to please him." The first life we live is sense;
the second is reason; the third, through the regenerating grace of the Spirit, is faith. And, until a man
reaches *this* life he moves in an orbit unillumined by
one ray from the sun of God's love. How can he
please God whose whole existence is a direct denial of
God? "He that believeth not hath made God a
liar!" God a *liar!* Astounding words! And yet
to this awful conclusion unbelief comes. Your unbelief is a practical denial of his existence. Your
unbelief is a practical denial of his sovereignty. You
live as if there were no God! And, in your non-

* Isaiah i. 12—15.

subjection to his law, you exclude him from the government of his own world. How can you, then, in your present course, do that which is pleasing to God? Oh, did you but truly, and in faith, grapple with that great foundation-truth of revealed religion, the being of God, believing that God is,—did you but really believe in the existence of a hell,—and did you but truly believe that God sent his beloved Son to save sinners from going down into that hell, you would not—nay, you could not—live the life of practical atheism and ungodliness you now are living—a life of sin and of unbelief, of impenitence and worldliness; without God, without Christ, without hope in the world! Impossible! Faith is a quickening, elevating, sanctifying principle. A living faith produces living works. A divine faith purifies the heart. A heaven-descending faith works by love, endures as seeing Him who is invisible, and has respect unto the recompense of reward. "That which is not faith is *sin.*" Apply this principle to all the religious duties of those who are still in the flesh, and by it test their real worth and acceptableness to God.

And what is the entire absence of *love* to God in the unregenerate but another confirmation of the same truth—God's displeasure against man, and man's utter inability to please him. The great constraining motive of the sacrifice with which God is pleased is *love.* Where this principle is not in operation there is wanting that which gives worth and acceptableness to the act, however valuable and

splendid that act may be. The divine moving-spring
is absent; and all the works of the soul, if they move
at all, are set in motion by a false action, and in a
wrong direction. " Love is the fulfilling of the law."
Without this heavenly affection there is no true obedience. A man may give " all his goods to feed the
poor, and his body to be burned," yet destitute of love
to God, his self-impoverishing charity, and his martyr
zeal, avail him nothing. His religion is still but as
" sounding brass, or a tinkling cymbal."

What an affecting picture have we presented here
of an individual living in deep, utter oblivion of God,
burying his one talent—perhaps, his ten—in the
earth,—himself a cumberer of the ground! What,
dear reader, has the past of your life been? Has it
all been displeasing to God? What! not one act,
not one service, not one sacrifice acceptable to, and
glorifying of, him? Astonished, if not appalled by
the charge, you perhaps reply, " Have I then done
nothing really pleasing to my Creator? I have given
my substance to extend the gospel, and my charity to
feed the poor, and my labour to promote the general
good; I have been punctual in the discharge of my
religious duties, and upright and generous in my
dealings with my fellows,—has all this not been
pleasing to God?" We ask, But have you given him
your *heart?* Have you fled out of your own righteousness, and taken refuge beneath the righteousness
of the incarnate God? Have not all these things of
which you boast, and upon which you place a strong

reliance, been but the working out a righteousness of
your own, in the spirit of the vain-glorying, self-
justifying Pharisee, who retired from the temple as
he entered it—a sinner under condemnation? Oh,
were your spirit to wing its way this night into the
presence of God, you would awake to the awful consciousness of having lived in this world without a
single act pleasing and acceptable to the holy, righteous Lord God. Oh, that the Eternal Spirit might
lay this solemn truth upon your heart, and lead you
to deep self-searching, to ascertain wherefore this life
—for every pulsation and for every act of which you
must one day give an account to God—has hitherto
been in opposition to the great end for which that
God created and placed you here!

But this gloomy picture has its opposite,—bright
and beautiful. Reversed, it presents to our notice
the character of those *with whom God is pleased*.
They are a *spiritual* people, and God, who is a Spirit,
must love and delight in that which harmonizes with
his own nature. Faith may be feeble, and grace may
be limited, and knowledge may be defective; yet, if
there be just that strength of faith that travels to,
and leans upon, the sacrifice of Jesus, and just that
measure of love that constrains to a sincere, though
imperfect, obedience, and just that extent of knowledge that knows Christ to be the Saviour of a poor
lost sinner, then, there is one who is pleasing to God.
They are also an *accepted* people, and therefore their
persons are pleasing to him. The delight of the

Father in the person of his Son reveals to us the great secret of his marvellous delight in us. "This is my beloved Son, *in whom I am well pleased.*" Blessed truth to those who see enough defilement and imperfection in their best doings to cover them with eternal confusion and shame! who, after the most spiritual performances, are constrained to repair in penitence and confession to Him who bears the iniquity of his people's holy things. Sweet truth to fall back upon in all the failures and flaws we are perpetually discerning in our works, in our motives, and our ends,—blots not appearing upon the surface, but visible to the microscopic eye of faith, which sees material for self-condemnation where others, in their fond and blind affection, approve and applaud. If God, my Father, is well pleased in his Son, then is it a truth, strictly inferential, that he is well pleased in me whom he beholds in his Son. But not their persons only, their offerings also are equally pleasing to God. "I will accept *you*," (the *person* first,) "with your sweet savour," (the offering next). Their preceptive walk likewise pleases him. Is the obedience of the child, springing from love, a pleasing and acceptable offering to a parent's heart? Ah! how imperfectly are we aware of the beauty and fragrance there are to God in a single act of filial, *holy* obedience, the fruit and offering of a Divine and deathless affection.

But it is a universal pleasing of God which the Scriptures of truth prescribe and enforce. "That ye might walk worthy of the Lord unto *all pleasing*, being fruitful in every good work, and increasing in the knowledge of God."* As a minister of the Lord Jesus, see how the apostle felt the weight of this great precept—" But as we were allowed of God to be put in trust with the gospel, even so we speak; not as pleasing men, but God, which trieth our hearts."† Human opinion weighed lightly with him. What men thought of him as a preacher was a matter of very little moment; the grand point, the all-absorbing thought and one aim of his life was, so to preach *as to please God*. Oh, for the Christianity and spirit of Paul! Lord! vouchsafe it in a double measure to all who preach thy great name. It is in this holy duty of aiming in all things to please God that we are sensible of such mighty power in prayer. " Whatsoever we ask, we *receive* of him, because we keep his commandments, *and do those things that are pleasing in his sight*."‡ Prayer is a precious, priceless privilege. A present and potent weapon. All our blessings flow through its medium, and all our achievements we owe to its instrumentality. Whatever, then, adds to the power of prayer, should be hailed by us with gratitude, and employed with vigour. Would we be more mighty and prevalent in prayer? then let us in all things desire so to walk as to please our heavenly Father. "Thou *meetest* him that rejoiceth and worketh righteousness, those that remember thee in thy ways."§

* Col. i. 10.   † 1 Thess. ii. 4.   ‡ 1 John iii. 22.
§ Isa. lxiv. 5.

But what are some of the footprints of this walk?
How may we trace it? *Unreserved obedience* is an
undoubted mark of well-pleasing. An obedience
that asks' no abatement of the precept, but that follows the Lord fully in its observance, not from an
enlightened judgment, but from a love-constrained
heart—walking, as did the primitive saints, in all the
commandments and ordinances of the Lord blame-
lessly—is indeed well pleasing to God. Oh, let there
be no reserves in our obedience! Let us withhold
from Christ no part of his purchased inheritance;
but surrender all at his feet, whose heart's blood was
the purchase-price of all. "Lord, however strait be
the path, and painful the cross, and self-denying the
precept, fain would I walk uprightly in all thy ways,
and fully follow thee in all thy commands, leaving
the consequences of my simple and implicit obedience to thy control. I can endure the obloquy of
the world, the alienation of friends, the coldness of
relatives, and can take the spoiling of my earthly
goods joyfully, if thou, my Lord, sustain me with
thy grace, and cheer me with thy presence, and
solace me with thy love."

Another footprint may be descried in the *walk of
faith* by which the Christian journeys to his heavenly
home. As unbelief is most dishonouring, so faith
is most honouring to the Lord Jesus. What a
revenue of praise accrues from it to his name! To
repair with our anxiety, the moment it occurs, to
his sufficiency; with our corruptions, the moment

they are discovered, to his grace; with our sorrow, the moment it is felt, to his sympathy; with our wound, the moment it is inflicted, to his love; with our guilt, the moment it is detected, to his blood,— oh! think you not that this walk of faith is most pleasing to the Lord? Let us beware of that which impairs the simplicity of this our walk, and causes us to stumble or start aside. We must be cautious, in the varied circumstances of our history, of applying first to a human arm for support, or to a human bosom for sympathy. With this, the Lord cannot be well pleased. But let us not hesitate to bear them at once to the one-appointed Source of all our supply: disclosing our wants to the full Saviour, our wanderings to our Heavenly Father, our griefs and burdens to our Elder Brother and Friend; and in thus walking by faith, we shall have the divine assurance in our souls, our rejoicing this—the testimony of our conscience that we please the Lord.

To believing *children* how touching and forcible is this precept—"Children, obey your parents in all things: *for this is wellpleasing unto the Lord.*" * Not less so to Christian *domestics*—"Servants, be obedient to them that are your masters according to the flesh, with fear and trembling, in singleness of your heart, *as unto Christ;* not with eyeservice, as menpleasers; but as the servants of Christ, doing the will of God from the heart; with good will doing service, *as to the Lord,* and not to men." † Yea, to

* Col. iii. 20.   † Eph. vi. 5—7.

all who bear the Saviour's name how solemn the exhortation—" Whether therefore ye eat or drink, or whatever ye do, do all to the glory of God." Thus universal and binding is this sublime principle of action, which the gospel furnishes to all the followers of Christ. Oh, let us seek closely to resemble the two illustrious examples set before us in the Word, of this high and holy walk. The minor one—because purely human—of Enoch, who, " before his translation had this testimony, that he *pleased God.*" The higher one—because the human was blended with the Divine—of Jesus, who could say, " I do always those things which *please Him.*" Breathing from our heart on your behalf, beloved reader, the sublime and touching prayer of the Apostle, we conclude this chapter : " The God of peace, that brought again from the dead our Lord Jesus, that great Shepherd of the sheep, through the blood of the everlasting covenant, make you perfect in every good work to do his will, *working in you that which is wellpleasing in his sight*, through Jesus Christ ; to whom be glory for ever and ever. Amen."

CHAPTER IX.

THE INDWELLING OF THE SPIRIT IN THE REGENERATE.

"But ye are not in the flesh, but in the Spirit, if so be that the Spirit of God dwell in you. Now if any man have not the Spirit of Christ, he is none of his."—ROMANS viii. 9.

WE have now arrived at those truths contained in this sublime chapter which have a more direct bearing on the experience of the children of God. Hitherto our topics have led us to address ourselves more especially to the unregenerate. Oh, that the solemn and searching delineations of unrenewed mind, of unsanctified affection, and of supreme devotion to self, gathered from the opening of the chapter, and pressed upon the reader's attention, may, by the power of the Holy Ghost, be received to the saving of the soul. Dismissing, then, the awful condition of the unconverted, the Apostle proceeds to address himself to the Christian Romans, and at once plunges into the great mysteries and privileges, glories and hopes, of the believer's inner life. Two topics of thought invite our attention in this verse—The indwelling of the

Spirit of God in the regenerate; and the great authenticating evidence of the fact—the possession of the Spirit of Christ. Let us discuss them in their order.

Scoffed at by the proud boaster of human reason, rejected by the cold formalist, and hated by the avowed enemy of practical godliness, as this doctrine is, it is yet a vital truth, and of marvellous interest to the child of God. It is, in fact, his life. We admit its profoundness, mysteriousness, and inexplicability; yet, apart from its individual, heartfelt experience, all religion, so called, is a counterfeit and a delusion.

The doctrine of the personal inbeing of the Spirit has been reduced, in the creed of some, to a mere poetical conception. Assimilation to the character and disposition of the Spirit in that which is amiable, sympathizing, and generous, has been made to take the place of an actual and personal residence of the Holy Ghost. And thus the indwelling of the Spirit of God in the soul of the regenerate—one of the fundamental verities of our faith—is narrowed down to the skeleton idea of a mere resemblance to spiritual grace and excellence. But in opposition to this dwarfish conception of a gigantic truth, how bold and explicit are the delineations and assertions of the Holy Scriptures. "Know ye not that ye are the temple of God, *and that the Spirit of God dwelleth in you?*"* "And because ye are sons, God hath sent

* 1 Cor. iii. 16.

forth *the Spirit of his Son into your hearts.*" * Observe where the Spirit is said to dwell,—not in the understanding, the fatal error of many—but in the heart. Most certainly he enlightens the understanding with the truth, but he does not rest there. He makes his way to, and takes up his abode in, the renewed and sanctified *heart*. There he sheds abroad the love of God. There he inspires the cry of "Abba, Father." And be that cry never so faint, it yet is the breathing of the indwelling Spirit, and meets a response in the heart of God. How affecting are Paul's words to Timothy: "That good thing which was committed unto thee keep *by the Holy Ghost which dwelleth in us.*" † Timothy had no spiritual strength of his own. The Apostle therefore reminds him of a truth which, in his conscious weakness, was well calculated to cheer his heart, and encourage him to cultivate and use for Christ's glory the spiritual gift bestowed upon him, namely, the power of the indwelling Spirit. That self-same Spirit dwells in all true believers. Let it constrain us to stir up our spiritual gifts and graces—so prone to slumber and become inert,—and employ them more devotedly for the Lord.

But what is the great evidence of the inbeing of the Spirit? Our possession of the Spirit of Christ. "If any man have not the Spirit of Christ he is none of his." Let us briefly direct our attention to this truth.

* Gal. iv. 6.   † 2 Tim. i. 14.

It will be observed that the title is changed. In the former clause of the verse he is styled the " Spirit of God." In the latter clause, he is denominated the " Spirit of Christ." Why the Spirit of Christ? Because he proceeds from Christ, equally as of the Father. " Upon whom thou shalt see the Spirit descending, and remaining on him, the same is he which baptizeth with the Holy Ghost,"*—clearly recognizing a power on the part of Christ to send the Spirit. Our Lord, when alluding to the Holy Ghost, emphatically says, " Whom I will send unto you." What declaration could more clearly set forth the emanation of the Spirit from Christ, than this, thus justifying the title ascribed to him by the Apostle, as the " Spirit of Christ?" We are here supplied with a strong argument in favour of the Deity of the Spirit predicated upon the unity of the Father and the Son in the one Divine Spirit: the Holy Ghost, proceeding from, and wearing the title of both, must conclusively establish an essential unity of mind.

The reasonableness of such an evidence, authenticating the fact of the indwelling of the Spirit, is too obvious to question. An individual claiming to be Christ's, yet not possessing the Spirit of Christ, lacks the only irrefragable proof which establishes the validity of his claim, and thus his profession is falsified. But what is it to possess the Spirit of Christ?

The Spirit of Christ is the great convincer of sin. " He shall convince the world of sin." Have you

* John i. 33.

thus received him? Has he discovered to you the moral leprosy of your nature, the exceeding sinfulness of sin? Do you know aught of the conflict of which the Apostle speaks in the preceding chapter of this Epistle—the law of the mind in battle with the law of the members? And has this discovery led you to self-condemnation, to self-renunciation, to lay your mouth in the dust before God? If this be so, then the Spirit of Christ is a Spirit of conviction in you, and by this you may know that you are Christ's.

The Spirit of Christ leads to Christ. He is to the sinner what John was to the Messiah—he goes before as the Forerunner of the Lord's salvation. He prepares the way, and heralds the coming of Jesus into the soul. This was one specific object for which he was sent, and which entered essentially into his mission—to lead men to Christ. Has he led you to Christ? Can you say, " Christ is made unto me wisdom, and righteousness, and sanctification, and redemption?" What think you of Christ? Is his blood precious? Does his righteousness give you peace? Does his grace subdue your sins? Do you in sorrow travel to his sympathy, in weakness take hold of his strength, in perplexity seek his counsel, in all your steps acknowledge and wait for him? Is Christ thus all and in all to you? Then you have the Spirit of Christ. This we venture to assert for your encouragement.—You may resort to Christ, and there may be no sensible apprehension, no realizing touch, no manifested presence; yet, if your heart

goes out after Jesus, if your spirit travels alone to
him—praying for his sympathy, panting for his grace,
thirsting for his love, and you are led to say, "Lord,
the desire of my heart is to thy name, and to the
remembrance of thee. I seem not to see thee, to
touch thee, to apprehend thee; yet I come, and I
find a heaven in coming; and for ten thousand worlds
I dare not, I could not stay away"—then, dear reader,
you have the Spirit of Christ, and are Christ's.

Not only does the Spirit lead to Christ, but he also
conforms those thus led to the image of Christ. He
guides us to Christ, not for consolation and instruction only, but also for assimilation. If we are humble,
we have the Spirit of Christ—for he was humble.
If we are meek, we have the Spirit of Christ—for he
was meek. If we believe, we have the Spirit of
Christ—for he lived a life of faith. If we love God,
we have the Spirit of Christ—for he was the incarnation of love. If we are holy, we have the Spirit of
Christ—for he was without sin. If we are obedient,
meek, and self-denying in suffering, silent in provoca-
tion, submissive in chastisement, patient in tribulation,
and rejoicing in hope, then have we the Spirit of
Christ, for he was all this. Thus, the possession of
this immense, this indispensable blessing, comprises
two grand things—first, to become the subject of an
actual and permanent inbeing of the Spirit; and,
second, to be assimilated in character and disposition
to the Saviour. And while it is most certain that, if

the first-mentioned blessing is attained, the second follows, yet it is to the second we are to look as the fruit and evidence of the first. The question, "Am I Christ's?" hinges upon the question, "Have I the Spirit of Christ?"

The subject lays the basis for the most solemn exhortation and appeal. As a temple of the Holy Spirit, yield yourself to his Divine and gracious power. Bend your ear to his softest whisper—your will to his gentlest sway—your heart to his holy and benign influence. In not hearkening to his voice, and in not yielding to his promptings, we have been great losers. Often has he incited to communion with God, and because the time was not seasonable, or the place not convenient, you stifled his persuasive voice, resisted his proffered aid, and thus slighted and grieved, he has retired. And lo! when you have risen to pray, God has covered himself as with a cloud that your prayer could not pass through. Oh, seek to have an ear attuned to his softest accents, and a heart constrained to an instant compliance with his mildest dictates. The greatest blessing we possess is the possession of the Spirit.

And Oh, to be Christ's—to be his gift, his purchase, his called saint, his lowly disciple—what an inestimable privilege! But how may we be quite sure that this privilege is ours? If we have the Spirit of Christ, we are in very deed Christians. It is the superscription of the King, the mark of the

Shepherd, the Lord's impress of himself upon the heart. And how sanctifying this privilege! "They that are Christ's have crucified the flesh with its affections and lusts." "Let those that have named the name of Christ depart from all iniquity." And if we are Christ's now, we shall be Christ's to all eternity. It is a union that cannot be dissolved. Every believer in Jesus is "sealed with that Holy Spirit of promise which is the earnest of our inheritance." And as we have the earnest of the inheritance, we shall as assuredly possess the inheritance itself.

Lastly, the Spirit of Christ is an active, benevolent Spirit. It bore the Saviour, when he was in the flesh, from country to country, from city to city, from house to house, preaching his own gospel to lost man. " He went about doing good." If we have the Spirit of Christ we shall be prompted to a like Christian love and activity on behalf of those who possess not the gospel, or who, possessing it, slight and reject the mercy. The Spirit of Christ is essentially a *missionary* Spirit. It commenced its labour of love at Jerusalem, and from that its centre, worked its way with augmenting sympathy and widening sphere until it embraced the world as the field of its labour. Ah! that we manifest so little of this Spirit, ought to lead us to deep searchings of heart, and stir us up to earnest prayer: "Lord, make me more earnest for the salvation of souls, for the advancement of thy kingdom. Grant me this evidence of being thine—

the possession of thy Spirit, constraining me to a more simple and unreserved consecration of my talents, my substance, my rank, my influence, my time, myself, to the establishment of thy truth, the advancement of thy cause, and thus to the wider diffusion of thy glory in the earth."

CHAPTER X.

THE BODY DEAD, BUT THE SPIRIT LIFE.

"And if Christ be in you, the body is dead because of sin; but
the Spirit is life because of righteousness."

ROMANS viii. 10.

WE are, in the first clause of this passage, conducted to another and more advanced stage in the
spiritual life—the indwelling of Christ, and the great
blessing which follows. There are some experimental
truths in the Christian faith which, from their overpowering magnitude and sanctity, the timid mind is
slow to recognize, and the heart to believe. Of
such is the doctrine before us. And yet this truth—
the inbeing of Christ—is interwoven with the very
texture of the Bible. With what distinctness and emphasis it is declared—" Examine yourselves, whether
ye be in the faith; prove your own selves. Know ye
not your own selves, how that *Jesus Christ is in you,*
except ye be reprobates?"* "He that eateth my
flesh, and drinketh my blood, dwelleth in me, *and I
in him.*"† "I in them."‡ What single truth can
be more clearly affirmed? That it has been but

* 2 Cor. xiii. 5.   † John vi. 56.   ‡ John xvii. 23.

dimly perceived, and in some cases awfully perverted, is but to assert that to which every truth is exposed. Its greatest abuse has been that which affirmed that the indwelling of Christ is an incorporation, and not a union of Christ and the believer only. So that some, predicating their heresy of this doctrine, have affirmed, "I am Christ!" "I am the Holy Ghost!" and thus many have been deluded and drawn away. But the inbeing of Christ in the believer is no more an incorporate union than the land and the sea, or the light and the air, or the soul and the body are an incorporation, or are essentially the same, because they have a union of contact one with the other. And yet the truth for which we plead is a close, personal union. Christ is in the believer, just as the believer is in Christ. We cannot be said to be in the grace of Christ, but we are in Christ himself as the Head of his mystical body. So Christ is in us, not figuratively by his grace, but really by his Spirit. Now, that Christ should thus spiritually dwell in his saints is no wonder, since he received them as a gift, purchased them by his blood, won them by his grace, called them by his Spirit, and is now in heaven preparing for them an eternal mansion. That he should thus dwell in the hearts of all the regenerate, taking a personal, full, and irrevocable possession of them for himself, is perfectly congruous with all that he has done and still is doing for them.

We now approach a solemn fact asserted in this passage: "The body is dead because of sin." What

body is referred to here? Certainly not, as some
have supposed, the body of sin. Who can with truth
affirm of it that it is dead? The individual who
claims as his attainment a state of sinless perfection,
an entire victory over the evil propensities and actings of his fallen nature, has yet to learn the alphabet
of experimental Christianity. Pride is the baneful
root, and a fall is often the fatal consequence of such
an error. Oh no! the body of sin yet lives, and
dies not but with death itself. We part not with
innate and indwelling sin but with the parting breath
of life, and then we part with it for ever. But it is
the natural body to which the Apostle refers. And
what an affecting fact is this! Redeemed by the
sacrifice, and inhabited by the Spirit of Christ,
though it be, yet this material fabric, this body of
our humiliation, tendeth to disease, decay, and death;
and, sooner or later, wrapped in its shroud, must
make its home in the grave, and mingle once more
with its kindred dust. "The body is dead because of
sin." Our redemption by Christ exempts us not from
the conflict and the victory of the last enemy. We
must confront the grim foe, must succumb to his
dread power, and wear his pale conquests upon our
brow. We must die—are dying men—because of sin.
"Death hath passed upon all men, for that all have
sinned." And this law remains unrepealed, though
Christ has delivered us from the curse. From this
humiliating necessity of our nature, even the non-con-
demned find no avenue of escape; from this terrible

conflict, no retreat. One event happens to the wicked and the righteous—they both leave the world by the same dismal process of dissolution. But the character of death is essentially changed; and herein lies the great difference. In the one case, death is armed with all its terrors; in the other, it is invested with all its charms—for death has an indescribable charm to the believer in Jesus. Christ did not die to exempt us from the process of death, but he died to exempt us from the sting of death. If, because of original and indwelling sin in the regenerate, they must taste of death; yet, because of pardoned sin in the regenerate, the "bitterness of death is past." If, because there exists a virus in the body, the body must dissolve; yet, because there exists an infallible antidote, the redeemed soul does not see death as it passes through the gloomy portal, and melts away into its own light, life, and immortality. How changed the character of death! If the body of the redeemed is under the sentence, and has within it the seeds of death, and must be destroyed, yet that death is to him the epoch of glory. It is then that the life within germinates and expands; it is then that he really begins to live. His death is the birthday of his immortality. Thus, in the inventory of the covenant, *death* ranks amongst the chief of its blessings, and becomes a covenant mercy. "Death is gain." "What!" exclaims the astonished believer, "death a blessing—a covenant blessing! I have been wont to contemplate it as my direst curse, to

dread it as my greatest foe." Yes; if death is the
sad necessity, it is also the precious privilege of our
being. In the case of those who are in Christ Jesus,
it is not the execution of a judicial sentence, but the
realization of a covenant mercy. And as the Christian
marks the symptoms of his approaching and inevi-
table dissolution—watching the slow but unmistake-
able advances of the fell destroyer—he can exclaim,
as he realizes that there is now no condemnation to
them that are in Christ Jesus—

> " Come, Death, shake hands ;
>   I'll kiss thy bands,—
>   'Tis happiness for me to die.
>   What ! dost thou think
>   That I will shrink ?—
>   I go to immortality."

" Because of sin." Ah! it is this truth whose
dark shadow flits across the brightness of the
Christian's condition. To what are all our ailments,
calamities, and sorrows traceable, but to sin? And
why do we die? " Because of sin." The immediate
and proximate causes of death are but secondary
agents. Had we not transgressed, we then had not
died. Deathlessness would have been our natural
and inalienable birthright. And were we more
spiritually-minded than we are, while we looked
onward with steady faith to a signal and glorious
triumph over the King of Terrors, we should blend
with the bright anticipation of the coming victory
the humbling conviction that we have sinned, and
that therefore the body is dead.

"But the Spirit is life because of righteousness." What are we to understand by the term spirit? Our reply will at once go to exclude the idea of the Holy Spirit. Of the Third Person of the blessed Trinity it cannot be of whom the Apostle speaks. The only remaining interpretation, then, is that which restricts its meaning to the spiritual and immortal part of the believer—the regenerated spirit of man, and not the regenerating Spirit of God. If, as we have shown, the first part of the antithesis must be understood of the material frame, the second part must be understood of the spiritual nature, body and soul being placed in direct contrast. The cheering declaration, then, of the Apostle is, that the spiritual and immortal part of our nature is recovered from the curse, renewed and quickened with a divine and heavenly life. If the body is dead because of sin, the spirit is life because of righteousness. The spirit is life—instinct with a new and deathless principle—because Christ is the righteousness of his people. On the broad basis of God's method of justification our spirit lives. In every point of view, Christ is identified with our spiritual life. We live a life of justification by Christ—a life of holiness from Christ—a life of faith in Christ—and a life of immortality with Christ. Thus, in all its phases, "Christ is our life." O glorious truth! Welcome death — the spirit lives! Welcome the grave—the spirit is beyond it! Death! thou canst but touch the material fabric—the inner life towers above thy reach, hid with Christ in God. Grave! thou canst but imprison the body—the soul is at home with Jesus. I live, not because of any righteousness which I have wrought, but because Christ is my righteousness. I live on account of the Righteous One—I live in the Righteous One—and I shall live for ever with the Righteous One. Thus is the spirit life because of righteousness. Oh, what a glorious immortality unveils to the eye of faith. If through the gloomy portals of death the spirit of the believer must pass, in its transit to eternity, life attends it, and life awaits it, and life crowns it. Animated with a deathless existence, clothed with the robe of a newborn immortality, it burst forth from its enthralment, and, smiling back upon death, speeds its way to glory, honour, and endless life. To this life let us look forward. From a life now experienced, let us live for a life so soon to be enjoyed. The body must die. But what of that? the spirit is life. And the life-inspired spirit will come back again, re-enter and re-animate the slumbering dust—and now, re-modelled and spiritualized—it will be with Christ and all the saints in the new heaven and the new earth, wherein will dwell righteousness.

CHAPTER XI.

THE RESURRECTION OF CHRIST.

"But if the Spirit of him that raised up Jesus from the dead
dwell in you, he that raised up Christ from the dead shall
also quicken your mortal bodies by his Spirit that dwelleth
in you."—ROMANS viii. 11.

HAVING affirmed of the redeemed body that it was
dead because of sin, the Apostle, as if anxious to
rescue the saints from the humiliation of so affecting
a truth, hastens to unveil the light which plays so
brightly and cheeringly around each believer's tomb.
He shows that light to spring from the fact of the
resurrection of the Saviour. This doctrine is the
grand luminary of the Christian system—it touches
and gilds with its brilliance each cardinal doctrine of
our faith. If Christ be not risen from the dead, then
is that faith vain and lifeless; but if he be risen, then
each truth becomes instinct with life; and hope, like
the day-spring from on high, rises with light and
glory upon the soul.

The credibility of this great fact is perhaps the
first point to which the mind naturally directs its
inquiry. But in the present instance the truth of

the doctrine must be assumed rather than established. We are not writing for the sceptic, but for the believer. Not so much to convince as to confirm the mind. And yet, were we arguing the question with a disputant, we might pursue a simple line of reasoning, somewhat like this,—

That the body of our Lord left the tomb is a fact which even those who have attempted to invalidate the doctrine readily concede. The great question in dispute, then, is—Who removed it? Did the enemies of Christ? What would they have gained by that step? Would they not on the contrary have lost much? Would it not have weakened their declaration that he was an impostor, and have strengthened that of his apostles, that he was risen? Why did not the priests and rulers, who bribed the Roman soldiers to affirm that his disciples had first surreptitiously possessed themselves of the body, and then secreted it, prove their assertion to the satisfaction of all Jerusalem, and thus at once strike the death-blow at the infant religion, and overwhelm the apostles with infamy and scorn? With the power of search which they possessed, surely, this were a natural and an easy process. To have produced the still lifeless body of our Lord would have substantiated their assertion, and thus have set at rest a question, upon which interests of such moment hung, at once and for ever. But what were the circumstances of our Lord's interment? They were all such as to strengthen the fact of his resurrection.

He was buried in a tomb hewn out of a rock. To have excavated that rock would have been a work of time, of immense difficulty, if not of utter impossibility. The exit of our Lord therefore from the tomb could only have been by the door through which he passed within it. And, as if to encircle the grave of the Saviour with sentinels of unimpeachable veracity, the Holy Ghost informs us, that in the " place where he was crucified, there was a garden, and in the garden a *new* sepulchre, *wherein was never man laid."* Thus, then, if that sepulchre were emptied, none other than the body of Jesus had broken from its lone captivity. The substitution of another for the corpse of the Saviour, was beyond the range of possibility. And who are the *witnesses?* A company of poor, unlearned, and timid fishermen— as unskilled in the art of falsehood and collusion, as they were in the lettered sciences of their age. They had nothing earthly to gain in testifying to the fact, but everything to lose. Instead of human applause, and honour, and wealth, they were rewarded with every species of obloquy, deprivation, and suffering. And yet, oppressed by poverty and persecution, and with the gloomy machinery of torture—the dungeon, the rack, and the cross—staring them in the face, they travelled everywhere, testifying to the sceptic philosophers of Athens, as to the unlettered peasants of Rome, that Christ was risen from the dead. Nor were they men likely to be imposed upon. They were at first strangely incredulous of the fact itself.

How slow of heart were they to welcome the testimony that their Lord was indeed alive. Retired from the sepulchre, where in love and sadness they had laid him, they met the holy women, who at the dawn of day had borne their aroma to the tomb, and returning, who proclaimed to the "eleven and to all the rest," that he was alive. Yet we are told, "their words seemed to them as idle tales." And when one of the witnesses to the credibility of the fact testified to Thomas, "We have seen the Lord," how was the testimony received? "Except I shall see in his hands the print of the nails," were the words of that disbelieving disciple, "and put my finger into the print of the nails, and thrust my hand into his side, I will not believe." Thus reluctant to receive the fact of his resurrection, is it possible that they could have been easily imposed upon by a fiction? We may, then, safely leave the credibility of this cardinal doctrine of our faith to its own evidence, and pass on to other and more experimental views of the glorious truth.

We may refer for a moment to the *necessity* that Jesus should rise again from the dead; and this will supply a collateral argument in favour of the truth of the doctrine. It was necessary that he should make good his own prediction, "Destroy this temple, and in three days I will raise it up." That some of his enemies rightly understood him to refer to the temple of his body is evident from their subsequent allusion to these words, "We remember

that that deceiver said, while he was yet alive,
After three days I will rise again." Our Lord thus
fulfilled his own undeviating prediction. But the
perfection of his mediatorial work also pleaded for
its necessity. "He was delivered for our offences,
and *raised again for our justification.*" The Father's
glory was clearly interwoven with the fact—his
honour, faithfulness, and power. Thus it is said,
"Therefore are we buried with him by baptism unto
death : that like as Christ was raised up from the
dead *by the glory of the Father,* even so we also
should walk in newness of life."

But let us trace the effect of this truth in the
believing soul, and this will supply us with no mean
evidence in favour of its credibility. For if the
power of the fact is experienced, the fact itself must
be certain. It is one thing to yield the assent of
an informed understanding to a truth, and it is
another to feel the influence of that truth in the
heart. But what is it to sympathize with Christ's
resurrection? It is to be a partaker of its quickening energy, to be sensible of its life-giving, life-
elevating power. Oh, there is no single truth which
embodies and conveys so much blessing to the
believer as his Lord's resurrection. Trace its sanctifying tendency : "Blessed be the God and Father
of our Lord Jesus Christ, which according to his
abundant mercy hath begotten us again unto a
lively hope by the resurrection of Jesus Christ from
the dead." To be sensible of this amazing power

in the soul is to be born again—to be raised from the grave of corruption—to live on earth a heavenly, a resurrection-life—to have the heart daily ascending in the sweet incense of love, and prayer, and praise, where its risen Treasure is. It possesses, too, a most *comforting* power. What but this sustained the disciples in the early struggles of Christianity, amidst the storms of persecution which else had swept them from the earth? They *felt* that their Master was alive. They needed no external proof of the fact. They possessed in their souls God's witness. The truth authenticated itself. The three days of his entombment were to them days of sadness, desertion, and gloom. Their sun had set in darkness and in blood, and with it every ray of hope had vanished. All they loved, or cared to live for, had descended to the grave. They had now no arm to strengthen them in their weakness—no bosom to sympathise with them in sorrow—no eye to which they could unveil each hidden thought and struggling emotion. But the resurrection of their Lord was the resurrection of all their buried joys. They now travelled to him as to a living Saviour, conscious of a power new-born within them, the power of the Lord's resurrection. "Then were the disciples glad when they saw the Lord." But is this truth less vivifying and precious to us? Has it lost aught of its vitality to quicken, or its power to soothe? Oh, no! truth is eternal and immutable. Years impair not its strength, circumstances change not its character.

The *same* truths which distilled as dew from the lips of Moses; which awoke the seraphic lyre of David; which winged the heaven-soaring spirit of Isaiah; which inspired the manly eloquence of Paul; which floated in visions of sublimity before the eye of John; and which in all ages have fed, animated, and sanctified the people of God—guiding their counsels, soothing their sorrows, and animating their hopes—still are vital and potent in the chequered experiences of the saints, hastening to swell the cloud of witnesses to their divinity and their might. Of such is the doctrine of Christ's resurrection. Oh, what consolation flows to the church of God from the truth of a living Saviour—a Saviour alive to know and to heal our sorrows—to inspire and sanctify our joys—to sympathise with and supply our need! Alive to every cloud that shades the mind, to every cross that chafes the spirit, to every grief that saddens the heart, to every evil that threatens our safety, or perils our happiness! What power, too, do the promises of the gospel derive from this truth! When Jesus speaks by these promises, we feel that there is life and spirit in his word, for it is the spoken word of a living Saviour. And when he invites us to himself for rest, and bids us look to his cross for peace, and asks us to deposit our burdens at his feet, and drink the words that flow from his lips, we feel a living influence stealing over the soul, inspiriting and soothing as that of which the trembling Evangelist was conscious, when the glorified Saviour gently laid his right hand upon him, and said, " Fear not; I am the first and the last: I am he that liveth, and was dead; and, behold, I am alive for evermore, Amen; and have the keys of hell and of death." Is Jesus alive? Then let what else die, our life, with all its supports, and consolations, and hopes, is secure in him. "Because I live, ye shall live also." A living spring is he. Seasons vary, circumstances change, feelings fluctuate, friendships cool, friends die, but Christ is ever the same. He is that "Tree of Life," whose boughs overhang either side of the river, and which yieldeth its fruit every month. Travel to it when we may, we find it fruitful. It may be winter with us, it is always summer with the Tree. Cold and dreary may be the region whence we have come, all chilled and desolate, to the spot where it stands: in an instant it is as though we had emerged into a southern clime—its balmy air, its spicy breezes, and its warm sunlight, encircling us in their soft robes. Oh, the blessedness of dealing with a risen, a living Redeemer! We take our wants to him—they are instantly supplied. We take our sins to him—they are immediately pardoned. We take our griefs to him—they are in a moment assuaged. " Every month," ay, and each moment of every month, finds this Tree of Life proffering its ample foliage for our shade, and yielding its rich fruit for our refreshment. Such are some of the blessings which flow from the resurrection of Christ. The identity of this great fact with the resurrection of the saints we reserve for the next chapter; closing the present with the fervent prayer that the Eternal Spirit may give us a heartfelt possession of its power, enabling us to exclaim, with the unwavering faith and undimmed hope of the holy patriarch—"I KNOW THAT MY REDEEMER LIVETH."

CHAPTER XII.

THE RESURRECTION OF THE CHRISTIAN.

" He that raised up Christ from the dead shall also quicken your
mortal bodies, by his Spirit that dwelleth in you."

ROMANS viii. 11.

IDENTICAL with, and consequent upon, the resurrection of the Saviour, is the resurrection—not less
divine, and scarcely less glorious — of the saints.
Seeing that our Lord entered the grave as a public
person, sustaining a representative character, when,
therefore, he broke from its thraldom, he rose, the
" first-fruits of them that slept." The Head of the
Church alive, the resurrection-life of the Church
became a fact, at once certain and glorious. Now,
if the gospel be a myth—how charming the fiction!
If untrue—how blissful the lie! With what sunlight joyousness does it gladden all the present,
and with what effulgent hope does it gild all the
future! Robbing us of this, what does Infidelity
proffer as its substitute? It proposes to soften our
ills, and to soothe our sorrows, by annihilating our
faith, and extinguishing our hope! But we believe,

and are sure that Christ was no impostor, that Christianity is no fiction, that the Gospel is no lie; and, confirmed in our faith in the resurrection of the Saviour, "why should it be thought a thing incredible that God should raise the dead?" Having contemplated the "first-fruits," now waving before the golden altar in heaven, let us take a perspective view of the coming harvest—the quickening of our mortal bodies by Christ's Spirit that dwelleth in us.

"Your mortal bodies" — words which at once define our present existence as one of suffering, and humiliation. And such verily it is. In asserting this fact, let it not be supposed that we deny that there is much dignity and grandeur connected with our material frame. We are fearfully and wonderfully made; a piece of mechanism displaying in each part and combination of the whole, the infinite wisdom, and elaborate skill, and boundless benevolence of the Divine Framer. And yet, from the most pleasing survey of this wondrous creature, man, we are compelled to revert to the sad truth, that our present existence is one of deep humiliation and certain decay. The language of Scripture in depicting this condition—a condition well calculated to lay human pride in the dust — is strong and emphatic. The Apostle characterises our material frame as "this vile body," literally, "the body of our humiliation." And in his sublime and triumphant argument on the resurrection, he employs terms equally as descriptive of our present state: "When *this corruption* shall put on incorruption, and *this mortal* shall put on immortality." Thus is our physical structure, which we adorn with so much care, and which others so extravagantly admire, described as a "vile body," as "corruption," as "mortal." Ah! has the fact with many, perhaps, my reader, with you, become so common-place as to have changed its character, from one of the most affecting and humbling, to one the existence and contemplation of which awakens in the mind no deep and serious reflection? Have you grown so familiar with disease, and become so conversant with death—the inanimate clay, the shroud, the coffin, the hearse, the grave, —those sad emblems of our mortality—as to feel sensible of no solemn emotions when the Holy Ghost brings the fact before the mind? Is it with you a light matter to die? Ah! death is no trifle; and he will find it so who knows not Him who is the "Resurrection and the Life." But, display the stoic and act the philosopher as you may, give place to mirth, and hilarity, and thoughtlessness as you will, —in all your vivacity, your pomp and power, you are mortal, and must die. "Dust thou art, and unto dust shalt thou return." You shall "say to corruption, Thou art my father; and to the worm, Thou art my mother and my sister." To this humiliating end all are tending. And although some of our race move to the tomb in greater state and luxury than others, yet, "The grave is my house," is the affecting exclamation of all. There the rich and the poor meet together — Dives and Lazarus side by side. "There the wicked cease from troubling, and the weary are at rest." And yet how few feel the solemnity, and admit the force of this truth. How few pause to consider that this body which they now pamper with such studied luxuriance, and adorn with such refinement of taste, will ere long need no clothing but the winding sheet, no house but the coffin, and no home but the grave! And that so changed will be the countenance, once lined with beauty and radiant with thought,—and so decayed the body, once so graceful and athletic,—that those who regarded it with the fondest love, and who worshipped it with the deepest devotion, will be the first to exclaim, " Bury my dead out of my sight." Oh, how dire the humiliation of our present existence ! " The body is dead because of sin."

But there glows around the grave of the believer in Jesus the halo of a blessed hope. " He that raised up Christ from the dead shall also quicken your mortal bodies." But for this animating and sustaining hope how starless and cheerless were his present existence. Strange as it may sound, that existence derives a character of peculiar sadness from the very circumstance of his Christianity. He is one to whom the Spirit has made known the inward plague. He is one whose frequent cry is, " O, wretched man that I am ! who shall deliver me from the body of this death ? " He is one who conflicts with principalities and powers.

He is one who is often placed in the fiery furnace of
affliction. There is a secret in the history of every
believer known only to God and his own soul. Oh,
then, what a rayless, desolate path through this vale
of tears were his, but for the hope of the resurrection
—that hope which, like the stars of evening, shines
the sweetest and the brightest when life seems the
gloomiest and the darkest. No pomp or circumstance may attend him to the tomb, no marble
monument may rear its chiselled form to record his
virtues, to perpetuate his name, or mark the spot
where his ashes repose. Those ashes the ocean's cave
may contain; his only tombstone the crested billows;
his only requiem, chanted to the wild sea-bird, the
solemn music of the waves as they dash and die upon
the shore: but he sleeps in Jesus, and slumbering
thus, his flesh rests in hope of a glorious resurrection
and a blissful immortality. Oh, what a new and
impressive character does Christianity give to the
entire scene of the believer's departure out of this
world to go unto the Father! To the eye of sense
the outer door of the tomb appears hideous and
forbidding. The deadly nightshade, and the overshadowing ivy, entwine darkly and thickly over its
dismal arch; while the trail of the worm and the
time-gathered mould upon its bars, deepen the air of
its repulsiveness. But viewed by faith, how changed
that tomb! As seen by its piercing eye, it is all
radiant around, and all refulgent within. The Lamb
of God has been there, touching and gilding all with

life and glory. There rears the tree of life—there clusters the living vine—there flow the heavenly waters—there float the celestial breezes—there are redolent all the sweets of the upper paradise. And when the inner door opens upon heaven, what a scene of grandeur bursts upon the spirit's view! Glory, streaming from above, bathes it in its liquid beams, and lights its pathway to the skies. This is the tomb of a believer in Jesus. No; it is no longer a *tomb*— it is a triumphal arch, all radiant and garlanded, through which the spiritual conqueror, laden with the spoils of his last victory, passes, amidst the acclaim of angels and the welcomings of sister spirits, to his crown and his rest.

But what will be the *order* of the believer's resurrection? Will it be anterior to, or contemporaneous with, the general resurrection of the dead? This is a question of the tenderest, holiest, interest. We believe that in this, as in each former part of his history, God will maintain the same difference he has ever put between the righteous and the wicked. The resurrection of the just is distinctly placed in Scripture in the foreground of the great and solemn scene. It is evidently made to take the precedence by a thousand years of the resurrection of the unjust. "The dead in Christ shall *rise first*."* "Blessed and holy is he that hath part in the *first resurrection*."† Speaking of the ungodly, the Psalmist thus refers to the difference between them and the just at the resur-

* 1 Thess. iv. 16.   † Rev. xx. 6.

rection: "Like sheep they are laid in the grave: death shall feed on them; *and the upright shall have dominion over them in the morning.*"* Oh, what a scene of joy will that be when, emerging from the gloom and impurity of the grave, the dead in Christ shall find themselves bathing in the golden beams, and inhaling the heavenly odour, of the morning of the "first resurrection." No demon of darkness shall shade its glory with his raven wing. No wail of despair shall blend with its entrancing music; it will be as when this magnificent creation first burst into being, and all the morning stars sang together for joy. And as the Saviour cleaves the air, descending in the clouds of heaven, and nearing the earth he had touched and consecrated with his blood, a shout will be heard, so melodious, that all the heavenly minstrelsy will suspend their harpings to listen in breathless silence to its strains—"Lo, this is our God: we have waited for him, and he will save us: this is the LORD; we have waited for him; we will be glad and rejoice in his salvation."

"By his Spirit that dwelleth in us." Such is the agency by which the resurrection of the saints will be effected. The indwelling of the Holy Ghost secures the reanimation of our slumbering dust, and supplies the power by which it will be accomplished. The resurrection of the redeemed body will be the resurrection of an entombed, not a lost—the re-construction of a dilapidated, not a destroyed temple of

* Psa. xlix. 14.

the Holy Ghost. The same Spirit dwelling in us now, will dwell in us then. Quickening with his Divine energy our mortal body, he will re-model, re-animate, and re-enter his former abode, replenishing it with his glory through eternity. In this marvellous work of resuscitation each Person of the ever blessed Trinity will be engaged. The Father will welcome home, as from a long exile, his adopted family; the Son will openly espouse his ransomed bride; and the Spirit will rebuild and re-occupy his sacred temple. Then will the Prophet's prediction receive its fullest and sweetest accomplishment—"The Lord God in the midst of thee is mighty; he will save, he will rejoice over thee with joy; he will rest in his love, he will joy over thee with singing."

CHAPTER XIII.

THE BELIEVER'S OBLIGATION TO MORTIFY SIN.

"Therefore, brethren, we are debtors, not to the flesh, to live
after the flesh. For if ye live after the flesh, ye shall die:
but if ye through the Spirit do mortify the deeds of the
body, ye shall live."—Romans viii. 12, 13.

AFTER the lucid statement which the Apostle had
in earlier verses made of the doctrine of justification,
it was but natural and proper that he should proceed
to illustrate the close affinity to its cognate truth—
sanctification. So far from the doctrine of completeness in Christ engendering a spirit of laxity in the
believer, it is his aim to show that it was the parent
of all true holiness; that instead of weakening the
motive of sanctification, it rather strengthens it,
binding the justified by the most solemn obligation to
an entire mortification of all sin. "Therefore,"—is
the conclusion to which his reasoning brings him,—
"_Therefore_, brethren, we are debtors, not to the
flesh, to live after the flesh." There are three distinct, yet consecutive points of truth in this passage—
The solemn obligation of the children of God—The

duty to which that obligation binds them—and The Divine agency by which that duty is discharged.

"We are debtors." That around a subject so momentous as this no obscurity might gather, tending to misguide the judgment, the Apostle most distinctly and emphatically affirms that the flesh has no valid claim whatever upon the believer; and that, consequently, he is under no obligation to yield compliance with its feigned exactions. We are debtors; but the flesh is not our creditor. What are its demands, that it is incumbent upon us to comply? Do we owe anything to sin, the parent of all our woe? Nothing. To Satan—who plotted our temptation and accomplished our downfall? Nothing. To the world—ensnaring, deceitful, and ruinous? Nothing. No; to these, the auxiliaries and allies of the flesh, we owe nothing but the deepest hatred, and the most determined opposition.

And yet the saints of God are "debtors." To whom? What debtors are they to the *Father,* for his electing love, for the covenant of grace, for his unspeakable gift, for having blessed us with all spiritual blessings in Christ Jesus! We but imperfectly estimate the debt of love, gratitude, and service which we owe to him whose mind the Eternal Son came to reveal, whose will he came to do, and whose heart he came to unveil. It was the Father who sent the Son. With him originated the wondrous expedient of our redemption. He it was who laid all our sins on Jesus. It was his sword of justice that smote the Shepherd, while his hand of love and protection was laid upon the little ones.* We have too much supposed that the atonement of Jesus was intended to inspire the mercy, rather than to propitiate the justice of God; to awaken in his heart a love that did not previously exist. Thus we have overlooked the source from whence originated our salvation, and have lost sight of the truth, that the mediation of Jesus was not the cause, but rather the effect of God's love to man. "Herein is love, not that we loved God, but that he loved us, and gave his Son to be a propitiation for our sins." Oh for the Spirit to understand, and for grace to feel, and for love to exemplify, our deep obligation to God for the everlasting love that gave his Son!

Equal debtors are we to the *Son*. He was the active agent in our redemption. He it was who undertook and accomplished all that our salvation required. He left no path untrodden, no portion of the curse unborne, no sin unatoned, no part of the law uncancelled—nothing for us in the matter of our salvation to do, but simply to believe, and be saved. Oh, to raise the eye to him—strong in faith, beaming with love, moist with contrition—and exclaim, "Thou hast borne my sin, endured my curse, extinguished my hell, secured my heaven. Thy spirit was wounded for me; thy heart bled for me; thy body was bruised for me; for me thy soul was stricken—for me, a sinner, the chief of sinners. I

* Zech. xiii. 7.

am thy debtor—a debtor to thy dying love, to thy eternal, discriminating mercy. Surely, an eternity of love, of service, and of praise, can never repay thee what I owe thee, thou blessed Jesus." Oh, how deep the obligation we are under to Christ!

And not less indebted are we to the *Holy Spirit*. What do we not owe him of love and obedience, who awoke the first thrill of life in our soul; who showed to us our guilt, and sealed to us our pardon? What do we not owe him for leading us to Christ; for dwelling in our hearts; for his healing, sanctifying, comforting, and restoring grace; for his influence which no ingratitude has quenched; for his patience which no backsliding has exhausted; for his love which no sin has annihilated? Yes, we are the Spirit's lasting debtors. We owe him the intellect he has renewed, the heart he has sanctified, the body he inhabits,—every breath of life he has inspired, and every pulse of love he has awakened. Thus are all real believers debtors to the Triune God. Debtors to the Father's everlasting love, to the Son's redeeming grace, and to the Spirit's quickening mercy. To the flesh we owe nothing but uncompromising hatred; to JEHOVAH we owe undivided and supreme affection.

Holiness, or the mortification of sin, is the obligation to which this indebtedness binds us. In a previous chapter of this work we explained the import of the phrase, "living after the flesh." We now consider its opposite condition, "mortifying the deeds of the body." It is marvellous how strangely the subject of mortification of sin in the godly has been mystified and misunderstood. Some have resolved it into a mere maceration or mortification of the body. Others have restricted it to the mere excision of outward sins. While yet others have represented it as consisting in the destruction of sin altogether in the believer. But none of these views convey any correct idea of the mortification spoken of in the passage under consideration. What, then, is it to "mortify the deeds of the body?" True mortification has its foundation in the life of God in the soul. A spiritual, yea, a most spiritual work, it can only spring from a most spiritual principle. It is not a plant indigenous to our fallen nature. It cannot be in the principle of sin to mortify itself. Nature possesses neither the inclination, nor the power, by which so holy an achievement can be accomplished. A dead faith, a blind zeal, a superstitious devotion, may prompt severe austerities; but to lay the axe close to the root of indwelling evil, to marshal the forces against the principle of sin in the heart—thus besieging and carrying the very citadel itself; to keep the body under, and bring it into subjection, by a daily and a deadly conflict with its innate and desperately depraved propensities, — is a work transcending the utmost reach of the most severe external austerities. It consists, too, in an annulling of the covenant with sin : " Have no fellowship with the unfruitful works of darkness"—enter into no truce, make no agreement, form no union—" but rather reprove them."

" Ephraim shall say, What have I to do any more
with idols?" The resources of sin must be cut off:
"Put ye on the Lord Jesus Christ, and make no
provision for the flesh, to fulfil the lusts thereof."
Whatever tends to, and terminates in, the sinful
gratification of the flesh, is to be relinquished, as
frustrating the great aim of the Christian in the
mortification of the deeds of the body. Mortification
is aptly set forth as a crucifixion: "They that are
Christ's have crucified the flesh." Death by the cross
is certain, yet lingering. Our blessed Lord was suspended upon the tree from nine in the morning until
three in the afternoon. It was a slow, lingering
torture, yet terminating in his giving up the ghost.
Similar to this is the death of sin in the believer. It
is progressive and protracted, yet certain in the issue.
Nail after nail must pierce our corruptions, until the
entire body of sin, each member thus transfixed, is
crucified and slain. Let us now contemplate the
two-fold agency by which the work of mortification is
accomplished.

"If ye through the Spirit do mortify the deeds of
the body, ye shall live." "If ye." The believer is
not a cipher in this work. It is a matter in which
he must necessarily possess a deep and personal
interest. How many and precious are the considerations that bind him to the duty! His usefulness, his
happiness, his sunny hope of heaven, are included in
it. The work of the Spirit is not, and never was
designed to be, a substitute for the personal work of

the believer. His influence, indispensable and sovereign though it is, does not release from human and individual responsibility. " Work out your own salvation "—" Keep yourselves in the love of God " —" Building up yourselves," are exhortations which emphatically and distinctly recognize the obligation of personal effort and human responsibility. The reasoning which bids me defer the work of battling with my heart's corruptions, of mortifying the deeds of the body, until the Spirit performs his part, argues an unhealthy Christianity, and betrays a kind of truce with sin, which must on no account for a moment be entertained. As under the law, the father was compelled to hurl the first missile at the profane child, so under the gospel — a milder and more benignant economy though it be—the believer is to cast the first stone at his corruptions; he is to take the initiative in the great work of mortifying and slaying the cherished sin. " If ye do mortify." Let us, then, be cautious of merging human responsibility in Divine influence; of exalting the one at the expense of the other; of cloaking the spirit of slothfulness and indolence beneath an apparently jealous regard for the honour of the Holy Ghost. How narrow is the way of truth! How many diverging paths there are, at each turning of which Satan stands, clothed as an angel of light, quoting Scripture with all the aptness and eloquence of an apostle! But God will never release us from the obligation of " striving against sin." " I keep under my body and bring it into subjection," was Paul's noble declaration. Is no *self-effort* to be made to escape the gulf of habitual intoxication, by dashing the ensnaring beverage from the lips? Is no *self-effort* to be made to break away from the thraldom of a companionship, the influence of which is fast hurrying us to ruin and despair? Is no *self-effort* to be made to dethrone an unlawful habit, to resist a powerful temptation, to dissolve the spell that binds us to a dangerous enchantment, to unwind the chain that makes us the vassal and the slave of a wrong and imperious inclination? Oh, surely, God deals not with us as we deal with a piece of mechanism—but as reasonable, moral, and accountable beings. "I drew you with the bands of a *man*." Mortification, therefore, is a work to which the believer must address himself, and that with prayerful and resolute earnestness.

And yet we must acknowledge that it infinitely transcends the mightiest puttings forth of creative power. "If ye *through the Spirit* do mortify." This he does by making us more sensible of the existence of indwelling sin,—by deepening our aspirations after holiness,— by shedding abroad the love of God in the heart. But above all, the Spirit mortifies sin in the believer by unfoldings of the Lord Jesus. Leading us to the cross, he would show us that as Christ died for sin, so we must die to sin—and by the selfsame instrument too. One real, believing sight of the cross of Jesus!—oh, what a crucifying power has it! Paul, standing beneath its awful shadow, and gazing upon its Divine victim, exclaimed, "God forbid that I should glory save in the cross of our Lord Jesus Christ, by which the world is crucified unto me, and I unto the world." Get near the Saviour's cross, if you would accomplish anything in this great and necessary work of mortification. The Spirit effects it, but through the instrumentality of the Atonement. There must be a *personal contact* with Jesus. This only is it that draws forth his grace. When the poor woman, in the Gospel, touched the Saviour, we are told that multitudes thronged him. And yet, in all that crowd that pressed upon his steps, one only extracted the healing virtue. Thus do multitudes follow Christ externally; they attend his courts, and approach his ordinances, and speak well of his name, who know nothing by faith of personal transaction with the Lord. They crowd his path, and strew their branches in his way, and chant their Hosannahs; but of how few can Christ say, " Somebody hath *touched me !*" Oh, let us have more personal dealing with the Lord Jesus. He delights in this. It pleases, it glorifies him. He bids us come and disclose every personal feeling, and make known every want, and unveil every grief, and confide to his bosom each secret of our own. He loves us to bathe in his blood—to enfold ourselves in his righteousness—to draw from his grace—and to cast ourselves upon his boundless sympathy. The crowd cannot veil us from his eye. He sees the poor and contrite; he descries the trembling and the lowly; he meets the uplifted glance; he feels the thrill of the trembling, hesitating, yet believing touch. "Somebody hath touched me." Who? Is it *you*, my reader?

Thus does the Spirit mortify sin in the believer. "But how may I know," is the anxious inquiry of many, "that sin is being mortified in me?" We reply—By a weakening of its power. When Christ subdues our iniquities, he does not eradicate them, but weakens the strength of their root. The principle of sin remains, but it is impaired. See it in the case of Peter. Before he fell, his easily besetting sin was self-confidence: "Though all should deny thee, yet will I not." Behold him after his recovery—taking the low place at the feet of Jesus, and at the feet of the disciples too, meekly saying, "Lord, thou knowest all things; thou knowest that I love thee." No more self-vaunting, no more self-confidence: his sin was mortified through the Spirit, and he became as another man. Thus often the very outbreak of our sins may become the occasion of their deeper discovery, and their more thorough subjection. Nor let us overlook the power of the truth by the instrumentality of which the Spirit mortifies sin in us: "Sanctify them through thy truth." The truth as it is in Jesus, revealed more clearly to the mind, and impressed more deeply on the heart, transforms the soul into its own Divine and holy nature. Our spiritual and experimental acquaintance, there-

fore, with the truth—with Him who is Essential
Truth—will be the measure of the Spirit's mortification of sin in our hearts. Is the Lord Jesus
becoming increasingly precious to your soul? Are
you growing in poverty of spirit, in a deeper sense
of your vileness, and weakness, and unworthiness?
Is pride more abased, and self more crucified, and
God's glory more simply sought? Does the heart
more quickly shrink from sin, and is the conscience
more sensitive to the touch of guilt, and do confession and cleansing become a more frequent habit?
Are you growing in more love to all the saints—
to those who, though they adopt not your entire
creed, yet love and serve your Lord and Master?
If so, then you may be assured the Spirit is mortifying sin in you. But oh, look from everything to
Christ. Look not within for sanctification; look for
it from Christ. He is as much our " sanctification,"
as he is our " righteousness." Your evidences, your
comfort, your hope, do not spring from your fruitfulness, your mortification, or anything within you;
but solely and entirely from the Lord Jesus Christ.
" Looking unto Jesus " by faith, is like removing
the covering and opening the windows of a conserva-
tory, to admit the sun, beneath whose light and
warmth the flowers and fruits expand and mature.
Withdraw the veil that conceals the Sun of Righteousness, and let him shine in upon your soul, and
the mortification of all sin will follow, and the fruits
of all holiness will abound.

CHAPTER XIV.

THE GUIDANCE OF THE SPIRIT.

"For as many as are led by the Spirit of God, they are the sons of God."—ROMANS viii. 14.

WE are here presented with another and a beautiful view of the Spirit as the Leader of his people. Man is a traveller to the eternal world. Left to self-guidance, as a fallen creature, he possesses vast and uncontrollable powers of self-destruction. What is he without a guide in the wilderness? what is he without a pilot on the ocean? Some recognize no other spirit—invoke no other spirit—and are guided by no other spirit, than the spirit of the world. And what is the spirit of the world but the all-pervading and controlling power of the spirit of darkness, who is emphatically denominated the "god of this world?" Others are more manifestly guided by their own spirit, their unsanctified, unsubdued spirit, and thus, "like a city that is broken and without walls," they are exposed to the perpetual invasion of every prowling evil. How evident is it, then, that threading his way to eternity along a path of difficulty and peril, man needs a Divine guide !

Such is the Guide. of the saints. They are "led by the Spirit." It is the office of JEHOVAH the Spirit in the covenant of redemption, after he has called a people out of the world, to place himself at their head, and undertake their future guidance. He knows the path to heaven. With all its intricacies and dangers he is acquainted;—with the sunken rock, and the treacherous quicksand, and the concealed pit, and the subtle snare, he is familiar. He knows, too, the individual and ordained path of each celestial traveller. All that God has appointed in the everlasting covenant—all the windings, and intricacy, and straitness of the way he knows. All the future of our history is infinitely more vivid and transparent to his mind than is the past, already trodden, to our eye. It is utterly impossible, then, that he should mislead. And what is equally as essential to him as a guide, he knows his own work in the soul. All its light and shade, its depressions and its revivings, its assaults and victories, are vivid to his eye. Dwelling in that heart — his sacred temple—his chosen abode—he reads his own writing inscribed there; understands the meaning of every groan, interprets the language of every sigh, and marks the struggling of every holy desire; he knows where wisely to supply a check, or gently to administer a rebuke, or tenderly to whisper a promise, or sympathetically to soothe a sorrow, or effectually to aid an incipient resolve, or strengthen a wavering purpose, or confirm a fluctuating hope. But, in less general terms—what is it to be led by the Spirit?

The existence of spiritual life in those he leads is an essential point assumed. He does not undertake to lead a spiritual corpse, a soul dead in sins. Many are moved by the Spirit, who are not led by the Spirit. Was not Saul, the king of Israel, a solemn instance of this? And when it is said, "the Spirit of God departed from him," we see how, in an ordinary way, the Spirit may strive with a man's natural conscience, and powerfully work upon his feelings through the word, and even employ him as an agent in the accomplishment of his will, and yet never lead him one step effectually and savingly to Christ, and to heaven. There is, as in Ezekiel's vision of the bones, "a voice, and behold a shaking, and the bones come together, bone to his bone, *but there is no breath in them.*" But there is spiritual life in those whom the Spirit leads. They thus become in a sense voluntary in the movement. They are not forced; it is not by compulsion they follow; they are led—persuasively, gently, willingly led. The leading of the Spirit, then, is his acting upon his own life in the soul.

It supposes, too, entire inability to lead themselves in those who are led by the Spirit: "I will lead the blind by a way they know not." And such are we. Unable to discern a single step before us, and incapable of taking that step even when discerned, we need the guidance of the Holy Ghost. What can we see of truth—what of providence—what of God's mind and will, of ourselves? Absolutely nothing. Oh, what unfoldings of ignorance, what exhibitions of weakness, have marked some of the wisest and mightiest of God's saints, when left to self-teaching and to self-guidance! Thus there is a strong and absolute necessity that wisdom, and strength, and grace, infinitely transcending our own, should go before us in our homeward journey.

The first step the Spirit takes in this great work is, *to lead us from ourselves*—from all reliance on our own righteousness, and from all dependence upon our native strength. But let us not suppose that this divorce from the principle of self entirely takes place when we are "married to another, even to Christ." It is the work of a life. Alas! Christ has at best but a portion of our affections. Our heart is divided. It is true there are moments—bright and blissful— when we sincerely and ardently desire the full, un-reserved surrender. But the ensnaring power of some rival object soon discovers to us how partial and imperfect that surrender has been. This severing from ourselves—from all our idols—is a perpetual, unceasing work of the Spirit. And who but this Divine Spirit could so lead us away from self, in all its forms, as to constrain us to trample all our own glory in the dust, and acknowledge with Paul that we are "less than the least of all saints?" But more than this. He leads from an opposite extreme of self —from a despairing view of our personal sinfulness. How often, when the eye has been intently bent within, gazing as it were upon the gloom and confusion of a moral chaos, the Spirit has gently and graciously led us from ourselves to an object, the sight of which has at once raised us from the region of despair! How many walk in painful and humiliating bondage from not having thus been sufficiently led out of themselves! Always contemplating their imperfect repentance, or their weak faith, or their little fruitfulness, they seem ever to be moving in a circle, and to know nothing of what it is to walk in a large place. Thus from sinful self, as from righteous self, the Spirit of God leads us. To what does he lead?

He leads us to Christ. To whom else would we, in our deep necessity, wish to be led? Now that we know something experimentally of Jesus, to whom would we go but to him? Having severed us in some degree from ourselves, he would bring us into a closer realization of our union with the Saviour. " He shall glorify me, for he shall take of mine and show it unto you." And this promise is fulfilled when, in all our need, he leads us to Christ. Are we guilty?—the Spirit leads us to the blood of Jesus. Are we weary?—the Spirit leads us to abide in Jesus. Are we sorrowful?—the Spirit leads us to the sympathy of Jesus. Are we tempted?—the Spirit leads us to the protection of Jesus. Are we sad and desolate?—the Spirit leads us to the tender love of Jesus. Are we poor, empty, and helpless?—the Spirit leads us to the fulness of Jesus. And still it is to the Saviour he conducts us. The Holy Spirit is our Comforter, but the holy Jesus is our comfort. And to Jesus—to his person, to his offices, and to his work, in life and in death, the Divine Guide ever leads us.

He leads us to truth. The promise of the Saviour is, " He shall guide you into all truth." When professing Christians have been led into error, nothing is more certain than that they have not been led by the Spirit. Though many claim him as their Teacher, he disowns them as his disciples. As the " Spirit of truth" he can reveal nothing but truth; can teach nothing but truth; can lead to nothing but truth. All who have received the truth—who are walking in the truth—and who are growing in the truth—are brought under the guidance of the Spirit of truth. Tossed from opinion to opinion, agitated and perplexed by the conflicting views of men and the antagonist creeds of churches, are you anxiously inquiring, " What is truth?"—Commit yourself to the guidance of the Spirit. Cast yourself in faith upon the promise, and plead it at the feet of your Divine Teacher—"*He shall guide you into all truth.*" He can harmonize apparent contradictions, he can reconcile alleged discrepancies, he can clear away overshadowing mists, and place each essential doctrine, and each enjoined precept, and each divine institution before your mind, clear, transparent, and effulgent as a noontide sunbeam. Oh, betake yourself, in your anxious, perilous search for the truth, to the simple guidance of the Spirit, and what the Greek philosopher, in transport at his discovery, shouted, you, with infinitely greater joy of heart and emphasis of meaning, shall echo, "I have found it! I have found it!"

He leads to all holiness. As the "Spirit of holiness," it is his aim to deepen the impress of the restored image of God in the soul, to increase our happiness by making us more holy, and to advance our holiness by making us more like God. Thus he leads to nothing but what is sanctifying. All the unfoldings he makes of Christ, all the views he unveils of God, all the deeper insight to truth which he imparts, all the rebukes he faithfully yet gently whispers, all the chambers of imagery in our hearts which he opens, and all the joy which he inspires, have this for their single object—the perfection of us in holiness. Christ is the source, the truth is the instrument, and the Spirit is the agent of our sanctification.

He leads to all comfort. Hence he is emphatically denominated, "the Comforter." There is no sorrow of the believing heart of which he is ignorant, to which he is indifferent, or which his sympathy does not embrace, and his power cannot alleviate. The church in which he dwells, and whose journeyings he guides, is a tried church. Chosen in the furnace of affliction, allied to a suffering Head, its course on earth is traced by tears, and often by blood. Deeply it needs a Comforter. And who can compute the individual sorrows which may crowd the path of a single traveller to his sorrowless home? What a world of trial, and how varied, may be comprised within the history of a single saint! But if sorrows abound, consolation much more abounds, since the Comforter of the Church is the Holy Ghost. What a mighty provision, how infinite the largess, the God of all consolation has made in the covenant of grace for the sorrows of his people, in the appointment of the Third Person of the blessed Trinity to this office! What an importance it attaches to, and with what dignity it invests, and with what sanctity it hallows our every sorrow! If our heavenly Father sees proper in his unerring wisdom and goodness to send affliction, who would not welcome the message as a sacred and precious thing, thus to be soothed and sanctified? Yes, the Spirit leads the sorrowful to all comfort. He comforts by applying the promises—by leading to Christ—by bending the will in deep submission to God—and by unveiling to faith's far-seeing eye the glories of a sorrowless, tearless, sinless world. And oh, who can portray his exquisite character as a Comforter? With what promptness and tenderness he applies himself to the soothing of each grief—how patiently he instructs the ignorant—how gently he leads the burdened — how skilfully he heals the wounded—how timely he meets the necessitous—how soothingly he speaks to the mourner! When our heart is overwhelmed within us, through the depth and foam of the angry waters, he leads us to the Rock that is higher than we.

He leads to glory. There he matures the kingdom, and perfects the building, and completes the temple he commenced and occupied on earth. No power shall oppose, no difficulty shall obstruct, no contingency shall thwart the consummation of this his glorious purpose and design. Every soul graced by his presence, every heart touched by his love, every body sanctified as his temple, he will lead to heaven. Of that heaven he is the pledge and the earnest. While Jesus is in heaven, preparing a place for his people, the Spirit is on earth, preparing his people for that place. The one is maturing glory for the Church, the other is maturing the Church for glory.

" They are the sons of God." Such are they who are led by the Spirit. All who are conscious of this Divine guidance have an indubitable evidence of their Divine sonship. It is a dignified and holy relationship. It implies an assimilation of nature with God. The Apostle speaks of some whom he denominates the " children of the devil," because of their Satanic nature. The regenerate are denominated the " sons of God," because they are " partakers of the Divine nature." Thus does one of the beatitudes express it —" Blessed are the peacemakers, for they shall be called the children (Greek, sons) of God," because their nature assimilates with him who is the " God of peace." Again : " Love your enemies, bless them that curse you, pray for them that despitefully use you and persecute you, that ye may be the children (sons) of God ;"—like Him who maketh his sun to shine upon the evil and the good. Now, are we sensible that in any measure we are under the guidance of the Spirit? Has he led us from ourselves to Christ— through Christ to God? Hear we his " still small voice?" feel we his gentle constraints, his gracious drawings, his soothing love? Then are we the sons of God. " For as many as are led by the Spirit, they are the sons of God."

In conclusion, receive, my beloved reader, a word of tender caution. Beware of being guided by any other than by the Spirit of God. The temptation is strong, and the tendency to yield to it equally so, of being biassed in forming our theological views, and in modelling our Christian practice, by the profound research, the distinguished talents, the exalted piety, and admired example of men. But this must not be. It is inconsistent with the honour that belongs, and with the love that we owe to the Spirit. A human must necessarily be a fallible guide; against the influence of whose doctrinal error, and practical mistakes, no extent of learning, or depth of spirituality, or eminence of position on their part, can ensure us. We are only safe, as we constantly and strictly follow our Divine and heavenly guide. Blessed and Eternal Spirit! to thy teaching would I bow my mind. To thy love would I yield my heart. To thy consolation would I carry my sorrows. To thy government would I resign my entire soul. "Thou shalt guide me by thy counsel, and afterwards receive me to glory."

CHAPTER XV.

THE SPIRIT OF ADOPTION.

" For ye have not received the spirit of bondage again to fear ;
but ye have received the Spirit of adoption, whereby we cry,
Abba, Father."—ROMANS viii. 15.

IT is most distinctly affirmed in this passage, that
the children of God are emancipated from the spirit
of bondage—the present and mournful condition of
all the unregenerate.   The question here arises, what
is the spirit of bondage of which the Apostle speaks?
It exhibits itself in various forms, yet, essentially,
it is the same spirit.   The world, for example, holds
in cruel bondage all its devotees.   It enslaves the
intellect by its opinions, the heart by its pleasures,
the imagination by its promises, the soul by its
religion—leading it a willing captive, a victim garlanded for the sacrifice.   They are described as
" walking according to the course of this world,
according to the prince of the power of the air,
the spirit that now worketh in the children of disobedience."

But it is the moral law—the spirit of bondage

which gendereth fear—to which the passage particularly refers. Its commands are exceedingly broad, and the obedience upon which it insists unqualifiedly perfect; and yet, with all the breadth of the precept, and the rigidness of the requirement, it proffers no helping hand. It shows a man his sin, but not his pardon. It teaches him his weakness, but tells him not where his great strength lieth. It thunders in his ear his misery and condemnation, but whispers not a word of mercy and of hope. Emancipated, as the justified believer really is, from the condemning power of this law, yet, alas! how much of its bondage spirit does he still retain! How few of the sons of God realize the possession and largeness of their birthright! How few rise to the dignity and the privilege of their adoption! How few see their completeness in Christ Jesus, and read the sentence of their pardon written in the heart's blood of Immanuel! How few walk in a large place, and by the sunny joyousness and lofty aspirations of their spirit, evidence that they have " not received the spirit of bondage again to fear!"

"But ye have received the Spirit of adoption." The Spirit of adoption is the same as the Spirit of God. There are two essential features which identify him as such. The first is, he imparts the nature of the Father to all the children of the family. In this there is a wide difference between a human and a Divine adoption. Man can only confer his name and his inheritance upon the child he adopts. But in the adoption of God, to the name and inheritance of God is added the Divine nature imparted in regeneration; so that, in the words of our Lord, we become manifestly the "children of our Father who is in heaven." The second feature is,—having begotten the nature of the Father, he then breathes the spirit of the child into the heart. He inspires a *filial love*. The love which glows in the believer's heart is the affection of a child to its parent. It is not a servile bondage, but a filial and free spirit. Oh, sweet and holy emotion! How tender and confiding, how clinging and childlike is it! Such ought to be our love to God. He *is* our Father, — we *are* his children. Why should not our love to him be marked by more of the exquisite tenderness, and the unquestioning confidence, and the calm repose of a child reclining upon a parent's breast? A childlike *fear of God* is another inspiration of the Spirit of adoption. Love and fear are twin graces in the Christian character. The Spirit of God is the Author of both; and both dwell together and co-operate in the same renewed heart. It is not the dread of the servant, but the holy trembling of the child, of which we speak. It is a filial, loving, reverential fear. A childlike *trust in God* also springs from the Spirit of adoption. The trust of a child is implicit, affectionate, and unquestioning. Upon whose counsel may he so safely rely, in whose affection may he so fully confide, upon whose fidelity may he so confidently trust, as a parent's? God is your Father, O child of a divine adoption, of a heavenly birth!—let your trust in him be the result of the relationship you sustain. It admits you to the closest intimacy, and invites you to the most perfect confidence. You have not a want, nor an anxiety, nor a grief which is not all his own. His adoption of your person—an act of his spontaneous and most free grace—pledged him to transfer all your individual interests to himself. To these we must add a filial *obedience:* "If ye love me, keep my commandments." Obedience, whether to the Saviour's precept, or to the Father's law, is the test of love; and love is the spring of obedience. "All that the Lord God hath spoken to us will we do," is the language of that heart where the Spirit of adoption dwells. Such are some of the features of adoption.

"Whereby we cry, Abba, Father." The Apostle employs in the original two different languages. It may not be improper to infer, that in using both the Syriac and the Greek form—the one being familiar to the Jew, and the other to the Gentile—he would denote that both the Christian Jew and the believing Gentile were children of one family, and were alike privileged to approach God as a Father. Christ, our peace, hath broken down the middle wall of partition that was between them; and now, at the same mercy-seat, the Christian Jew and the believing Gentile, both one in Christ Jesus, meet, as rays of light converge and blend in one common centre—at the feet of their reconciled Father. The expressions, too, set forth the peculiarity and intensity of the affection. Literally, " Abba, Father," signifies " My Father." No bond-servant was permitted thus to address the master of the family; it was a privilege peculiar and sacred to the child. And when our blessed Lord would teach his disciples to pray, he led them to the mercy-seat, and sealed these precious words upon their lips — " Our *Father,* which art in heaven." And after his resurrection, with increased emphasis and intensity did he give utterance to the same truth. Previously to his death his words were, " I go to the Father." But when he came back from the grave, every truth he had before enunciated seemed quickened as with new life. How tender and touching were his words—" I ascend unto my Father, and to *your* Father; to my God, and to *your* God." No longer a bond-slave, but a son, oh, claim the dignity and privilege of your birthright ! Approach God as *your* Father. " Abba, Father !" How tender the relation ! how intense the affection ! what power it imparts to prayer ! What may you not ask, and what can God refuse, with " Abba, Father " breathing in lowliness and love from your lips? Remember, it is an inalienable, unchangeable relation. Never, in any instance, or under any circumstance the most aggravated, does God forget it. He is as much our Father when he chastises, as when he approves; as much so when he frowns, as when he smiles; as much so when he brims the cup of adversity, as when he bids us drink the cup of salvation. Behold the touching display of it in his gracious restorings: "But when he was yet a great way off, *his father* saw him, and had compassion, and ran, and fell on his neck and kissed him." In all his wanderings, that father's love had never lost sight of his wayward child. It tracked him along all his windings, followed him to the very swine-trough, hovered around him even then, and waited and welcomed his return. We may doubt, and debase, and deny our Divine relationship, yet God will never disown us as his children, nor disinherit us as his heirs. We may cease to act as a child, he will never cease to love as a Father. To him, then, as to a Father at all times repair. "Have faith in God." Confide in his heart to love you; in his counsel to guide you; and in his power to sustain you. Cast from you the fetters that enthral, and pray to be upheld by his *free* Spirit. "Where the Spirit of the Lord is, there is liberty."

CHAPTER XVI.

THE SPIRIT TESTIFYING TO THE BELIEVER'S
ADOPTION.

"The Spirit itself beareth witness with our spirit, that we are the
children of God."—ROMANS viii. 16.

HAVING affirmed the Divine relationship of the believer, the Apostle now proceeds to adduce the divine
evidence of a truth so great. He assumes that the
actual existence of the believer's sonship, may, to his
own soul, at times be a matter of painful uncertainty.
This leads him to unfold the agency of the Spirit in
authenticating the fact, thus at once neutralizing in
the mind all doubt, and allaying all fear. "The
Spirit itself bearing witness with our spirit, that we
are the children of God."

With regard to the first point; it is not strange
that the fact of his adoption should meet with much
misgiving in the Christian's mind, seeing that it is a
truth so spiritual, flows from a source so concealed,
and has its seat in the profound recesses of the soul.
The very stupendousness of the relationship staggers

our belief. To be fully assured of our divine adoption demands other than the testimony either of our own feelings, or the opinion of men. Our feelings—sometimes excited and visionary—may mislead; the opinion of others—often fond and partial—may deceive us. The grand, the Divine, and only safe testimony is, "the Spirit itself beareth witness with our spirit." There exists a strong combination of evil tending to shake the Christian's confidence in the belief of his sonship. *Satan* is ever on the watch to insinuate the doubt. He tried the experiment with our Lord. "*If* thou be the Son of God."* In no instance would it appear that he actually denied the truth of Christ's divine relationship; the utmost that his temerity permitted was the suggestion to the mind of a doubt, leaving it there to its own working. Our blessed Lord thus assailed, it is no marvel that his disciples should be exposed to a like assault. The *world*, too, presumes to call it in question. "Behold what manner of love the Father hath bestowed upon us, that we should be called the sons of God: therefore *the world knoweth us not*, because it knew him not."† Ignorant of the Divine Original, how can it recognise the divine lineaments in the faint and imperfect copy? It has no vocabulary by which it can decipher the "new name written in the white stone." The sons of God are in the midst of a crooked and perverse nation, illumining it with their light, and preserving it by their grace, yet disguised from its

* Matt. iv. 6. † 1 John iii. 1.

knowledge, and hidden from its view. But the strongest doubts touching the validity of his adoption are those gendered in the believer's own mind. Oh, there is much there to generate and foster the painful misgiving. We have said that the very greatness of the favour, the stupendousness of the relationship, startles the mind, and staggers our faith. "What! to be a child of God! God my Father! Can I be the subject of a change so great, of a relationship so exalted? Who am I, O LORD GOD, and what is my house, that thou shouldest exalt me to be a king's son? Is this the manner of men, O Lord God?" And, then, there crowd upon the believer's mind thoughts of his own sinfulness, and unworthiness of so distinguished a blessing. "Can it be? With such depravity of heart, such carnality of mind, such rebellion of will, such a propensity to evil each moment, and in everything such backslidings and flaws, does there yet exist within me a nature that links me with the Divine? It seems impossible!" And when to all this are added the varied dispensations of his Heavenly Father, often wearing a rough garb, assuming an aspect sombre, threatening, and crushing, oh, it is no marvel that, staggered by a discipline so severe, the fact of God's love to him, and of his close and tender relation to God, should sometimes be a matter of painful doubt. That thus he should reason—"If his child, reposing in his heart, and sealed upon his arm, why is it thus? Would he not have spared me this heavy stroke? Would not this cup have passed my lips? Would he have asked me to slay my Isaac, to resign my Benjamin? All these things are against me." And thus are the children of God constantly tempted to question the fact of their adoption.

But the Lord has graciously and amply provided for this painful part of Christian experience in the Witness of the Spirit. The perfect competence of the Spirit is assumed. Who can reasonably question it? Is *verity* essential to a witness? Then is he most competent, for he is the "Spirit of *truth*." Essentially Divine, his testimony is to be received as of one whose truthfulness cannot be impeached. If he witness to us that we are born from above, and belong to the one family, then we may safely credit his testimony, and receive the comfort it imparts. Is it essential that he should *know the fact* whereof he affirms? Who so competent to authenticate the work of the Spirit in the heart as the Spirit himself? We, then, may safely confide in the truthful and intelligent testimony which the Spirit of God bears to our being the sons of God.

As to the great truth thus witnessed to by the Spirit, we are not to suppose that the testimony is intended to make the fact itself more sure; but simply to confirm our own minds in the comfortable assurance of it. Our actual adoption cannot be more certain than it is. It is secured to us by the predestinating love of God, and the everlasting covenant of grace; is confirmed by our union with the Lord

Jesus, and is sealed by the Holy Spirit of promise. " Having predestinated us unto the adoption of children by Jesus Christ to himself, according to the good pleasure of his will."* But the testimony which the Spirit bears is designed to meet the phase of Christian experience just adverted to—the painful uncertainty to the children of God themselves, by which this truth is often enshrouded. It is not for the benefit of our fellow-creatures, still less for the satisfaction of God himself, but for the assurance and comfort of our own hearts, that the Spirit bears witness with our spirits that we are the children of God. The testimony is for the confirmation of our own faith, and the consolation of our own hearts.

But the question arises, What is the mode of his testimony? In attempting to supply an answer, we must acknowledge that we have no certain data to guide us. Sufficient light, however, beams from his work in general, to assist us in forming an intelligent and correct idea of his operations. How, then, may we suppose the Spirit witnesses with our spirit? Not by visions and voices; not by heats and fancies; nor by any direct inspiration, or new revelation of truth. Far different from this is the mode of his testimony. We may gather from the measure of light vouchsafed, that he first implants within the soul the germ of spiritual life, which beneath his culture produces the " fruits of love, joy, peace, long-suffering, gentleness, goodness, faith, meekness, temperance." From these

* Ephes. i. 5.

we are left to draw the rational deduction of our adoption. If, for example, a child of God, with all lowliness of spirit, and after much prayerful inquiry, discover that, more or less, some of these effects of the Spirit's operation are developed in his experience, then it is no presumption in that individual, honestly and humbly to conclude that he is a child of God. This is the Spirit's witness, and he cannot gainsay it without wilful blindness, nor reject it without positive sin. The breathing of the renewed heart after holiness, supplies another illustration of the mode of the Spirit's testimony. The panting after Divine conformity is the Spirit's inspiration. Where, therefore, it exists, the deduction is, that the individual is a child of God. Thus, by begetting in us the Divine nature—by producing in us spiritual fruits—and by breathing in our souls a desire for holiness, the Spirit conducts us to the rational conclusion that we are born of God. By shedding abroad God's love in the soul—by sprinkling the conscience with the atoning blood—by endearing the Saviour to our hearts—by leading us more simply to rest in his finished work, yea, to rest in himself—by creating and increasing love to the members of the one family, and fellowship with whatever is holy, and heavenly, and useful, he thus testifies to our divine relationship.

Nor would we pass by the harmony which subsists between the Bible and the experience of the sanctified heart, by which the Spirit witnesses that we are born of God. Whatever may be the mode of his testimony, it never contradicts the word of truth, but always is in perfect agreement with, and fully sustains it. As it is by the truth he quickens, and through the truth he sanctifies, so with the truth he witnesses. If our sentiments, and feelings, and actions are invariably and unequivocally opposed to God's revealed word, we may vaunt ourselves as we will of our divine relationship, we yet are self-deceived, and are " bastards and not sons."   Is there in our lives a correspondence of Christian experience and revealed truth ?   " I could not, without making my own doctrine outstrip my own experience, vouch for any other intimation of the Spirit of God, than that which he gives in the act of making the word of God clear unto you, and the state of your own heart clear unto you. From the one you draw what are its promises—from the other what are your own personal characteristics; and the application of the first to the second may conduct to a most legitimate argument, that you personally are one of the saved—and that not in tardy or elaborate argument either, but with an evidence quick and powerful as the light of intuition.   By a single deposition of conscience, for example, I may know that I do indeed hunger and thirst after righteousness ; and by a single glance with the eye of my understanding, I may recognise a Saviour's truth, and a Saviour's tenderness in the promise that all who do so shall be filled; and without the intervention of any lengthened process of reasoning, I may confidently give to the general announcement in the gospel such a specific application to myself, as to convey my own distinct and assured hope of a particular interest therein. Thus there is no whisper of the Spirit distinct from the testimony of the word. Thus there is no irradiation, but that whereby the mind is enabled to look reflexly and with rational discernment upon itself. And hence there is no conclusion, but what comes immediately and irresistibly out of promises which are clear to me, while they lie hid in deepest obscurity from other men: and all this you will observe with the rapidity of thought—by a flight of steps so few, as to be got over in an instant of time—by a train of considerations strictly logical, while the mind that enjoys and is impressed with all this light is not sensible of any logic,—and yet withal by the Spirit of God, for it is he who hath brought the word nigh, and given it weight and significancy to my understanding, and it is he who hath manifested to me the thoughts and intents of my own heart, and evinced some personal characteristic within that is coincident with the promise without, and it is he who sustains me in the work of making a firm and confident application. In all this he utters no voice. The word of God made plain to my convictions, and his own work upon me made plain to my conscience—these are the vocables, and I do imagine the only vocables, by which he expresses himself; but enough to furnish any Christian with a reason of the hope that is in him, and better than articulation itself to solace and to satisfy the inquiring spirit of its relationship to the family of God." *

Nor is the *comfort* which the Spirit imparts the least evidence of our adoption. As our chastenings are marks of our sonship, equally so are our consolations. The kindly view the Spirit gives of our Father's dispensations—the meek submission of the will—the cordial acquiescence of the heart—and the entire surrender of the soul to God, which he creates, supplies us with indisputable ground for drawing a conclusion favourable to the reality of our being the children of God. There is a depth of sympathy and a degree of tenderness in God's comforts, which could only flow from the heart of a *Father*—that Father, God himself. " *As a father* pitieth his children, so the Lord pitieth them that fear him." Sweet to know that the correction and the consolation, the wounding and the healing, flow from the same heart—come from the same hand, and bear each a message of love, and a token of sonship. Is the God of all comfort sustaining, soothing, and quieting your oppressed, chafed, and sorrowful heart? Oh, it is the Spirit's witness to your adoption. Bending to your grief, and associating himself with every circumstance of your sorrow, he seeks to seal on your softened heart the deeper, clearer impress of your filial interest in God's love. And oh, if this overwhelming bereavement—if this crushing stroke—if the bitterness and gloom of this

* Chalmers.

hour be the occasion of the Spirit's gentle, gracious
lifting you from the region of doubt and distress, as
to your sonship, into the serene sunlight of your
Father's love, so that you shall question, and doubt,
and deny no more your acceptance in the Beloved,
and your adoption into his family, will you not kiss
the rod, and love the hand, and bless the heart that
has smitten? One word in conclusion. Forget not
that the inward seal of adoption is testified by the outward seal of sanctification, and that if the Spirit of
Christ is in your heart, the fruits of the Spirit will
be exhibited in your life. Then, thus meek, and
gentle, and lowly, like the Saviour; separated from
the world, that you live not and joy not, as the world
does,—in the secret chamber of your soul you shall
often hear the voice of God, saying, "I will be a
Father unto you, and ye shall be my sons and daugh-
ters, saith the Lord Almighty."

CHAPTER XVII.

THE CHRISTIAN'S JOINT HEIRSHIP.

" And if children, then heirs ; heirs of God, and joint-heirs with
Christ."—ROMANS viii. 17.

It is a natural and graceful transition this from a
consideration of the believer's relationship to God,
and the nature of the evidence which makes it certain, to a consideration of his heirship, and the nature
of the inheritance to which that relationship links
him. "If children, then heirs." The first truth that
demands our attention is a vast and comprehensive
one—GOD himself the inheritance of his people. Not
only are they begotten by God as his children, and
by a sovereign act of his most free mercy, have become the heirs of an inheritance—but subjectively,
they are made the heirs of himself. "Heirs *of God*."
Not only are all things in the covenant theirs, but the
God of the covenant is theirs. This is their greatest
mercy. "I am thy part and thine inheritance," are
his words addressed to all his spiritual Levites. Not
only are they put in possession of all that God has—
a boundless wealth ; but they are in present possession
of all that God is—an infinite Portion. And what

an immense truth is this, "I will be their God, and they shall be my people!" Take out this truth from the covenant of grace, were it possible, and what remains? It is the chief wealth and the great glory of that covenant that God is our God. This it is that gives substance to its blessings, and security to its foundation. So long as faith can retain its hold upon the God of the covenant, as our God, it can repose with perfect security in expectation of the full bestowment of all the rest. Here lies our vast, infinite, and incomputable wealth. What constitutes the abject poverty of an ungodly man? His being without God in the world. His earthly possessions may be boundless; he may look out from the crystal windows of his castellated mansion upon a far-spreading and magnificent domain, and exclaim, "This is all my own"—yet is he poor! and when death relaxes his grasp, and summons him to the account of his stewardship, he closes his eyes upon all his proud possessions, and his only portion, and that for ever, is the "worm that never dies, and the fire that is never quenched." Be you, my reader, rich or poor, high or low in this world, *without God*, you are undone to all eternity. It is but of trivial moment whether you pass in rags and meanness, or move in ermine and pomp to the torments of the lost—those torments will be your changeless inheritance, living and dying without God, and without Christ, and without hope. But contrast this with the state of the poorest child of God. The universe is not only his—

"for all things are yours"—but the God of the universe is his—"The Lord is my portion, saith my soul, therefore will I hope in him." We have a deathless interest in every perfection of the Divine nature. Is it Wisdom? It counsels him. Is it Power? It shields him. Is it Love? It soothes him. Is it Mercy? It upholds him. Is it Truth? It cleaves to him. "As the mountains are round about Jerusalem, so *the Lord* is round about his people, from henceforth, even for evermore." What more can we ask than this? If God be ours, we possess the substance and the security of every other blessing. When the Lord appeared to Abraham, with what truth did he seek to win his confidence, and ask his obedience! "I am the Almighty God." And then follows the precept, "Walk before me and be thou perfect." And this is just the truth with which God would preface every blessing, and comfort us in all our tribulation. "They shall be my people, and I will be their God." He would bring us to an absolute trust in an absolute God. Winning us to an entire relinquishment of all expectation from any other source, he would allure us to his feet with the language of the Church breathing from our lips—"Behold we come unto thee, for thou art the Lord our God. Truly in vain is salvation hoped for from the hills, and from the multitude of mountains: truly *in the Lord our God* is the salvation of Israel." * And again, "Asshur shall not save us, we will not ride upon

* Jer. iii. 22, 23.

horses; neither will we say any more to the work of our hands, Ye are our gods: for *in thee* the fatherless findeth mercy." * Only in the Lord our God is our salvation—only in him does the orphan find the mercy that soothes, provides, and encompasses him as a shield. Nor the fatherless only: is he not equally the covenant God of the *widow?* " I am married unto you," † saith God. And again, " Thy Maker is thy husband (the Lord of hosts is his name)." ‡ And yet again, " Let thy widows trust in me." Thus does he by words the most persuasive, and by imagery the most touching, seek to endear himself to us as our Portion. It is in the heart of our God to give us the chiefest and the best. Had there been a greater, and a better, and a sweeter, and a more satisfying portion than himself, then that portion had been ours. But since there is not, nor can be, a greater than he, the love, the everlasting, changeless love that he bears to us, constrains him to give himself as our God, our Portion, our All. And have we not experienced him to be God all-sufficient? Have we ever found a want or a lack in him? May he not justly challenge us, and ask, " Have I been a wilderness unto Israel? a land of darkness?"§ Oh no! God is all-sufficient, and no arid wilderness, and no dreary land have we experienced him to be. There is in him an all-sufficiency of love to comfort us; an all-sufficiency of strength to uphold us; an all-sufficiency of

---

* Hos. xiv. 3.   † Jer. iii. 14.
‡ Isa. liv. 5.   § Jer. ii. 31.

power to protect us; an all-sufficiency of good to satisfy us; an all-sufficiency of wisdom to guide us; an all-sufficiency of glory to reward us; and an all-sufficiency of bliss to make us happy here, and happy to all eternity. "This God is our God for ever and ever, and he will be our guide even unto death." "In thy presence there is fulness of joy, and at thy right hand there are pleasures for evermore." Such is the inheritance to which, as children of God, we are the heirs.

"Joint-heirs with Christ." This must be understood in a limited, though still in a very enlarged sense. In its highest meaning—touching the Essential Deity of our Lord—he is the Heir of all things. All worlds and all souls are his. All things were created by, and for him. Heaven is his throne, and earth is his footstool. To participation in *this* heirship we cannot be admitted. Nor can there be any conjointure with Christ in the *merit* that purchased our redemption. Here again he is alone, no creature aiding the work, or dividing the glory. But, mediatorially, in consequence of the union subsisting between Christ and his people, they become heirs with him in all the privileges and hopes appertaining to his kingdom. Our union to the Lord Jesus brings us into the possession of vast and untold blessings. On the basis of his atonement we build our claim. He merits all, and we possess all. All the immunities and glories of our present and reversionary inheritance flow to us through Christ. "*In whom* also we have

obtained an inheritance." *   " If a son, then an heir
of God *through Christ*." †   We cannot lay too great
stress on this truth.   We possess nothing—we receive nothing—we expect nothing but *through Christ*.
All is given to us in consideration of a Righteousness
which upholds and honours the Divine Government.
Jesus is the meritorious Recipient, and we receive
only through him.   " If ye be Christ's, then are ye
Abraham's seed, and heirs according to the promise."   " Knowing that of the Lord ye shall receive
the reward of the inheritance." ‡   And yet again,
alluding to our right to, and our possession of, our
inheritance, the Apostle traces both to the atonement
of the Son of God—" And for this cause he is the
Mediator of the new testament, that *by means of
death*, for the redemption of the transgressions that
were under the first testament, they which are called
might receive the promise of eternal inheritance." §
Thus it is alone through the " meetness " imparted
by Christ, the merit he substitutes in our behalf, and
the righteousness he imputes to us, that we become
" partakers of the inheritance of the saints in light."
Blessed Redeemer! to what dignity and honour, to
what privilege and blessing, to what hope and glory
our union with thee has advanced us! We were fallen,
and thou hast lifted us up; we were poor, and
thou hast enriched us; we were naked, and thou
hast clothed us; we were aliens, and thou hast made
us children; we were bankrupts, and thou hast made

* Eph. i. 10.   † Gal. iv. 7.   ‡ Col. iii. 24.   § Heb. ix. 15.

us heirs; we lost all from fatal union with the first Adam, we receive all, and infinitely more, by our glorious union with thee, the Second Adam. Oh for a heart to love thee! Oh for grace to glorify thee! Be thou increasingly precious to us, and may we be increasingly devoted to thee!

But observe in what this joint-heirship consists— suffering, and glory.

"If so be that we suffer with him." It is first an heirship of *suffering*. "If so be," or, as it has been rendered, "Seeing that we suffer with him;" thus removing any seeming idea of suffering being a meritorious cause of glory. As Christ is the Head, and we the body, there is a fellowship of condition, a sympathy of suffering of the closest character. Most assuredly there is a sense in which we could have no actual participation in the sufferings of our Lord— the sense in which those sufferings were *expiatory*. But mystically, the church suffered with the Head. And having begun in suffering, suffering more or less, tracks our course to glory. "If any man will come after me," says Christ, "let him deny himself, and take up his cross, and follow me."* "If we be dead with him, we shall also live with him: if we suffer, we shall also reign with him."† Suffering in inseparable from true godliness. "All that will live godly in Christ Jesus, shall suffer persecution."‡ Thus our very union with Christ involves suffering with Christ. We are joint-heirs with the "Man of sorrows." We

* Matt. xvi. 24.   † 2 Tim. ii. 11, 12.   ‡ 2 Tim. iii. 12.

are united to a crucified Head. We cannot assert
any valid claim to a union with Christ, and plead
exemption from trial. Our fellowship with him in
his sufferings is the seal of our heirship with him in
his glory. See you a professed disciple of the Lord
Jesus exempt from all sorrow—from that sorrow, we
mean, peculiar to the chastened and disciplined sons
of God? you see him lacking one of the strongest
and most valid evidences of sonship. "For if ye be
without chastisement, whereof all are partakers, then
are ye bastards and not sons."* Suffering is the
beaten path to heaven. A public avowal of adherence
to Christ—allegiance to his authority—fidelity to his
truth—separation from the world as a professed disciple of Jesus—will often entail suffering of a most
humiliating and painful character. But let us not
overlook the alleviations. It is not, as in the case of
our Lord, unmixed suffering—suffering borne alone.
When he sorrowed in the garden, his disciples slept.
When he was accused at Pilate's bar, one of them
denied him. When suspended upon the cross, all of
them forsook him. He was *alone* in suffering. But
when we suffer, it is a suffering *with Christ*. In all
our affliction he is afflicted. He suffers with us.
There is an outflow of the purest, tenderest human
sympathy. Our spirit is never oppressed, our heart
is never sad, our love is never wounded, our principles
are never assailed, our persons are never persecuted,
but Christ is with us in the closest alliance. "Saul,

* Heb. xii. 8.

Saul, why persecutest thou *me ?*" With such a fellow-sufferer at our side, why should we fret and murmur and repine? " Unto us it is given in the behalf of Christ, not only to believe on him, but also to suffer for his sake."* We must, if his true disciples, drink of the cup that he drank of, and be baptized with the baptism that he was baptized with; for " Christ also suffered for us, leaving us an example that we should follow his steps."   Oh, sweet words !   " If so be that we *suffer with him*."   Not as he suffered.   Oh, no ! there is no curse, no wrath, no hell in the cup of sorrow which we drink.   All these ingredients composed his bitter draught.   Yet he suffers with us, and permits our afflictions to be called the " afflictions *of Christ*."   He is with you on that bed of sickness; he is with you on that couch of languishing ; he is with you in that darkened room ; he kneels with you at that coffin ; and he weeps with you by the side of that sepulchre.   Oh, may it not reconcile us to all the suffering we have ever endured, or may yet be called to endure, to feel the perfect oneness, the presence, the sympathy, the succourings of such a Saviour ? Who would wish to shun the obloquy of his cross, the scorn of his name, the lowliness of his kingdom, the self-denial of his religion, allied in the tenderest sympathy at every step with this illustrious Martyr— this Prince of sufferers—this Brother born for adversity ?   Blessed school of heavenly training !   By this afflictive process, oh, of what profounder teaching,

* Phil. i. 29.

what deeper purification have we become the favoured subjects! It is good for us to have been afflicted. Now have we, like our Lord, learned obedience by the things which we have suffered; and like him, too, are being made perfect through suffering. The heart has been emptied of its self-confidence—the shrine has been despoiled of its idol—the affections that had been seduced from God, have returned to their rest—the ties that bound us to the vanities of a world, perishing in its very using, have become loosened—the engagements that absorbed our sympathies, and secularized our minds, have lost their fascination and their power—the beguiling and treacherous enjoyments that wove their spell around us, have grown tasteless and insipid—and thus, by all these blessed and hallowed results of our trial, the image of the earthy has become more entirely effaced, and the image of the heavenly more deeply engraven, and more distinctly legible.

"That we may be glorified together." As suffering precedes glory, so glory assuredly follows suffering. Thus was it with our Lord. " Ought not Christ to have *suffered* these things, *and to enter into his glory?*"* The Apostle speaks of himself as a *"witness* of the *sufferings* of Christ, and also a *partaker of the glory* that shall be revealed."† Our Lord is in glory. The head that once bowed in death, pale and bleeding, is now raised in life, encircled with a glory brighter than ten thousand suns. The humanity

* Luke xxiv. 26.   † 1 Pet. v. 1.

that was despised from the meanness of its birth, that was mocked, and scourged, and spit upon, and slain, is now, from its indissoluble union with the Deity, exalted far above principalities and powers, glorified with the glory he had with the Father before the world was. Having purged our sins, he is set down on the right hand of the Majesty on high. To that glory which belongs to him as the Mediator of the Church, each suffering confessor of Christ shall be exalted—the body with the Head, and each part of that body with the whole. A joint-heirship of suffering, it is now a joint-heirship of glory: "We shall be *glorified* together *with Christ.*" Still the onenesss is manifest, and never so clearly seen as now. Glory bathes it in its light, and eternity impresses it with its seal. It is an undimmed and changeless glory. And Christ acknowledges their right to this oneness in glory. As they were not ashamed of him amongst men, he is not now ashamed of them amongst angels. As they linked themselves to his cross, he binds them to his throne. As they confessed him before the world, he now confesses them before his Father. "Glorified together." Wondrous words! Elevated to his side—leaning upon his bosom—gazing on his beauty—listening to his voice—entering into his joy —at home, and for ever with the Lord. Now is answered in its fulness, the prayer mingled with tears, and breathed from the scene of his suffering below— "Father, I will that they also whom thou hast given me, be with me where I am; that they may behold my glory."* Welcome the suffering, succeeded by such glory. Welcome the cross, followed by such a crown.

Let us learn to regard our present tutorage as preparatory to our future inheritance. "The heir as long as he is a child, differeth nothing from a servant, though he be lord of all; but is under tutors and governors until the time appointed of the father."† Thus is it with us. But soon we shall attain our majority and come into possession of our estate. Ere long we shall have done with governors and tutors, and need no more the lessons of the school, and the discipline of suffering. Oh, let us live in its near anticipation. To the poor of Christ's flock how animating the prospect! "Hath not God chosen the poor of this world, rich in faith, and heirs of the kingdom which he hath promised to them that love him?"‡ What though straitened resources, what though pinching poverty, what though absolute want, be your present allotment, lift up your heads with joy, for you have a joint-heirship with Christ in a kingdom which your Heavenly Father will give. Confide in its security. It is made sure to you by Divine oath:—"Wherein God willing more abundantly to show unto the heirs of promise the immutability of his counsel, confirmed it by an oath."§ Thus inalienably is it secured. Death, which robs the earthly heir of his inheritance, puts you in possession of

---

* John xvii. 24.   † Gal. iv. 1, 2.
‡ James ii. 5.   § Heb. vi. 17.

yours. Your estate comes not to you robed in mourning, for your Father never dies. No succession awaits you, for your inheritance is yours for ever. "Blessed be the God and Father of our Lord Jesus Christ, which according to his abundant mercy hath begotten us again unto a lively hope, by the resurrection of Jesus Christ from the dead, to an inheritance incorruptible, and undefiled, and that fadeth not away, reserved in heaven for you, who are kept by the power of God through faith unto salvation, ready to be revealed in the last time."

CHAPTER XVIII.

PRESENT SUFFERING WEIGHED WITH FUTURE GLORY.

" For I reckon that the sufferings of this present time are not
worthy to be compared with the glory which shall be revealed
in us."—ROMANS viii. 18.

How forcible are the words, and how powerful is
the influence, of an experienced man of God! In
listening to his testimony, we feel the deep conviction
that he believes and therefore speaks; that he testifies, not from what others have described, but from
what he has himself felt. Such is the testimony of
Paul. Who, of mere men, could so well expatiate
upon suffering—its varied forms, its appropriate
soothings, and its hallowed results, as he? "I will
show him how great things he shall suffer for my
name's sake," * were the words of the Saviour as he
predicted his future history, dating it from his mira-
culous conversion, to his glorious martyrdom. Having
affirmed of the Christian's sufferings that they were
endured in alliance with the Saviour, and would be
succeeded by a glory again to be shared with him,

* Acts ix. 16.

the Apostle proceeds to contrast those sufferings
with that glory, and concludes by summing up the
vast disproportion of the one to the other—" I reckon
that the sufferings of this present time are not worthy
to be compared with the glory which shall be revealed
in us."

Dismissing any further minute reference to the
sufferings of the believer, he contents himself, in the
present instance, with simply alluding to their temporary existence. He characterizes them as the " sufferings of this *present time*." That the sufferings of
the believer are bounded by the limits of the present
state, is a truth replete with soothing to the Christian
mind.   Earth is the " house of our pilgrimage." The
present life is the " time of our sojourning." " Here
we have no continuing city." Alas ! how we forget
that we are but strangers and pilgrims on the earth ;
that we are journeying to our home, and will soon be
there !   And yet we would not pen a sentence tending to lessen the dignity and importance of our present existence, or calculated to engender a spirit of
dissatisfaction and distrust with our present allotment.   There is much folly, nay, much infidelity in
a remark common to many—" It will be all the same
a hundred years hence." Not so. The relation of
the present to the future is causal ; it is a relation of
the closest character, and of the most solemn results.
Time is the infant of eternity. It is its commence-
ment ; and is, in a sense, its most momentous part.
Shaded with grief, linked with suffering, and transient

in its stay, yet all the future receives its complexion
and its character from the present. The life that now
is, casts its light or its shade upon the life that is to
come. Eternity will be bright or gloomy, joyous or
sad, happy or miserable, as time shall impart to it its
complexion and its shape. Each individual of the
human race is training for the future; and as a man
soweth so shall he reap. Will you, then, my reader,
in view of this statement of truth, persist in believing
that, regarding any given act of your life, when that
life shall have passed away, with it will have passed
all the accountability, and all the traces of that act;
and that a century hence it will be as though it had
not been? Away with the fatal fallacy! If it
be true, as philosophers assert, that sounds once
awakened, vibrate through eternity, what shall be
said of the moral actions of a rational, responsible,
and accountable being, but that they form links in an
interminable chain, each quivering with indescribable
agony, or thrilling with unspeakable pleasure through
an endless existence!

And still the sufferings of the children of God are
but the sufferings of the present time. That world
where Satan's seat is, and overshadowed by his
gloomy reign, *must* be a world of suffering. " Satan,
whence comest thou?" was the inquiry of God.
" Then Satan answered the Lord and said, From
going to and fro in the earth, and from walking up
and down in it." * The world where not a spot is

* Job i. 7.

found unscathed by the curse *must* be a world ot su.
fering. The world where sin holds its universal empire, tainting every object, and beclouding every scene,
must be a world of suffering. The world where the
spirit is wounded, and the heart is broken, and reason
is dethroned, and hope languishes, and the eye weeps,
and the nerve trembles, and sickness wastes, and
death reigns, must needs be a world of suffering.
From none of these forms of woe does Christianity
exempt its believers. But with this truth, on the
other hand, it soothes and reconciles—they are the
sufferings of the *present time*. They are but momentary, will soon be over—and for ever. We live
in a dying world—a world that is passing away. Time
is short—is ever on the wing—and we are ever on
the wing of time, borne each moment by its sweeping
pinion nearer and still nearer our Father's house; of
whose occupants it is said, " God shall wipe away all
tears from their eyes; and there shall be no more
death, neither sorrow, nor crying, neither shall there
be any more pain : for the former things are passed
away." Oh, how gentle is the admonition—" Arise,
and depart, for this is not your rest, it is polluted."
Then comes the glory,—" The glory which shall be
revealed in us." What word could more appropriately
express the future condition of the saints? The
world claims the title, but has no claim to the reality.
What is the glory of science—of learning—of rank—
of wealth, but a tinselled pageant, a meteor blazing
for a moment, and then disappearing in eternal

night? But the glory that awaits the suffering Christian, is a real, a substantial glory. At present it is veiled. The world sees it not; the believer only beholds it through faith's telescope. But the day of its full, unclouded revelation awaits us. It draweth near. It will be a glory *revealed in us*. This truth may be startling to some. " What ! " they exclaim, " a glory to be revealed *in me?* In me, who can scarcely reflect a solitary ray of light ! In me, so dark, so sinful, living at so remote a distance from communion with the Father of lights! Can it be that *in me* this glory will be revealed ? " So affirms the word of our God. If a child of the light, dwelling it may be, in the world's shade, and often called to walk in great darkness, you shall one day outshine the brightness of the firmament, and the stars for ever and ever. But in what respects will it be a glory revealed *in us ?* It will be the glory of *perfect knowledge*. " Now we see through a glass darkly ; but then face to face : now I know in part ; but then shall I know even as also I am known." * Oh, what an orb of intellectual light will be each glorified mind ! What capacity of understanding will it develop—what range of thought will it compass—what perfection of knowledge will it attain ! How will all mysteries then be unravelled, and all problems then be solved, and all discrepancies then be reconciled ; and every truth of God's revelation, and every event of God's providence, and every decision of God's government, stand out more trans-

* 1 Cor. xiii. 12.

parent and resplendent than ten thousand suns! Do you, in your present search for spiritual knowledge, deplore the darkness of your mind, the feebleness of your memory—the energy of your mental faculties impaired, dimmed, and exhausted? Oh, rejoice in hope of the glory that is to be revealed in you, when all your intellectual powers will be renewed as the eagle's strength; developed, sanctified, and perfected, to a degree outvying the mightiest angel in heaven. Then shall we know God, and Christ, and truth, and providence, and ourselves, even as now we are known.

It will also be a glory in us of *perfect holiness*. The kingdom within us will then be complete. The good work of grace will then be perfected. It will be the consummation of holiness, the perfection of purity. No more sin! The conscience no more sullied—the thoughts no more defiled—the affections no more ensnared—but a glory of holiness, dazzling and resplendent, beyond an angel's, revealed in us. "It doth not yet appear what we shall be: but we know that when he shall appear, *we shall be like him*." *

The glory of perfect *happiness* will be the certain effect of perfect sanctity. The completeness of Christ is the completeness of moral purity. With reverence be it spoken, God himself could not be a perfectly happy, were he not a perfectly holy Being. The radiance of the glorified countenance of the saints will be the reflection of holy thoughts and holy feelings glowing within. Joy, and peace, and full satis-

* 1 John iii. 2.

faction will beam in every feature, because every faculty, and feeling, and emotion of the soul will be in perfect unison with the will, and in perfect assimilation to the image of God. Who can paint the happiness of that world from whence everything is banished that could sully its purity, disturb its harmony, and ruffle its repose? Where everything is included that comports with its sanctity, harmonizes with its grandeur, and heightens its bliss. Oh, yes! it will be a glory revealed *in us*. The glory of the Father's adoption,—the glory of Christ's atonement, —the glory of the Spirit's regeneration, radiating from a poor, fallen son of Adam,—a sinner redeemed, renewed, and saved. And what is each present ray of heavenly light—and each thrill of Divine love— and each victory of indwelling grace—and each glimpse of the upper world, but the foreshadowings of the glory yet to be revealed in us?

Suffering and glory thus placed side by side, thus contrasted and weighed, to what conclusion does our Apostle arrive? "I reckon that the sufferings of this present time *are not worthy to be compared* with the glory which shall be revealed in us." No, not worthy of a comparison. Do we measure their relative *duration?* Then, "our light affliction is but for *a moment,*" while our glory is a "far more exceeding and *eternal* weight." Ere long all suffering and sorrow will for ever have passed away—a thing of history and of memory only—while glory will deepen and expand as eternity rolls on its endless ages. Do we *weigh* them? What comparison has the weight of the cross, with the weight of the crown? Place in the scales the present "light affliction," and the future "exceeding and eternal weight of glory," which is the lightest? are they worthy to be compared? Oh, no! One second of glory will extinguish a lifetime of suffering. What were long years of toil, of sickness, of battle with poverty, and persecution, and sorrow in every form, and closing even with a martyr's death, weighed with one draught of the river of pleasure at Christ's right hand—with one breath of Paradise—with one wave of heaven's glory —with one embrace of Jesus, with one sight of God?

Oh, what are the pangs of present separation, in comparison with the joy of future reunion? What the pinchings of poverty now, with the untold riches then? What the suffering, and gloom, and contempt of the present time, with the glory that is to be revealed in us? We can go no further. Tell us, ye spirits of just men made perfect, if it be lawful, if it be possible, what the glory that awaits us is! Tell us what it is to be an unclothed spirit—to dwell in the bosom of Jesus—to see God—to be perfectly holy— to be supremely happy! Wait, my soul! ere long it will be all revealed!

CHAPTER XIX.

THE EARNEST EXPECTATION OF THE RENEWED CREATURE.

" For the earnest expectation of the creature waiteth for the manifestation of the sons of God. For the creature was made subject to vanity, not willingly, but by reason of him who hath subjected the same in hope. Because the creature itself also shall be delivered from the bondage of corruption into the glorious liberty of the children of God."

ROMANS viii. 19—21.

WE have now arrived at what has been regarded as, perhaps, the most remarkable and difficult passages in this chapter. It would answer no purpose, but to perplex the reader's mind, were we to quote the various, conflicting, and often extremely fanciful interpretations which they have received from critics of equal learning and piety.* Rejecting at once the interpretations of the term " creature" which restrict it to the Gentile nations in opposition to the Jews— to unconverted men in distinction from the sons of

* PROFESSOR STUART, in his Exegetical Commentary on the Epistle to the Romans, enumerates eleven different renderings which have been given to the term κτίσις, " creature," in these verses.

God—to mankind in general—and lastly, to the irrational creation, we at once propose for the acceptance of the reader, as being to our own mind the most fair and correct meaning of the term, that interpretation which predicates it of the *renewed creature*—the Christian in his regenerate state. A slight examination of the connexion in which the passages stand will, we think, justify and sustain this view. What appears to be the scope and design of the Apostle in the verses immediately preceding those under consideration? He had been addressing himself to *suffering* believers in Christ. His aim was to fortify their minds under trial by arraying before them the strong consolations of the Gospel, and by unveiling to their view the animating prospect of a certain and glorious deliverance—the "manifestation of the sons of God." To whom could all this correctly and appropriately apply, save to the *renewed* creature? Let it be considered, too, what the nature of this prospect is, for which the "creature" is represented as "waiting" in the posture of "earnest expectation." Is it not most spiritual, holy, and glorious? Does it not seem a lowering of the dignity, and a shading of the lustre of that prospect, to represent either the animal creation, or the unregenerate mass of mankind, as waiting with outstretched neck, and panting desire, and earnest expectation, the period of its arrival? Of whom can all this be reasonably predicated but of the renewed creature? And thus is the believer frequently called. "If any man be in Christ, he is *a new creature*."* "In Christ Jesus neither circumcision availeth anything, nor uncircumcision, but a *new creature*."† It is, then, of the *new man*, "created in Christ Jesus," that we, without hesitation, interpret the term "creature," as employed in these remarkable verses. Read the passages once more with this rendering, and we think that both their meaning and their beauty will be instantly apparent. Having thus explained the sense in which we propose to use the term, let us now proceed to open the text.

The present state of the renewed creature is described as one of *humiliation*. "The creature was made subject to vanity." The vanity here referred to is opposed to the state of glory in anticipation, and therefore expresses the condition of corruption and trial in the midst of which the renewed creature dwells, and to the assaults of which it is incessantly exposed. The world through which the Christian is passing to his rest may be emphatically called a state of vanity. How perpetually and forcibly are we reminded of the King of Israel's exclamation, "Vanity of vanities, all is vanity and vexation of spirit."‡ "Surely every man walketh in a vain show."‖ His origin, the earth; his birth, degenerate; his rank, a bauble; his wealth, but glittering dust; his pomp, an empty pageant; his beauty, a fading flower; his pursuits, an infant's play; his honours, vexations of

* 2 Cor. v. 17.   † Gal. vi. 15.
‡ Eccles. i. 2.   § Psa. xxxix. 6.

spirit; his joys, fleeting as a cloud; his life, transient as a vapour; his final home, a grave. "Surely man in his best estate is altogether vanity."* And what is his religion but vanity? His native holiness, a vain conceit; his natural light, Egyptian darkness; his human wisdom, egregious folly; his religious forms, and rites, and duties, "a vain show in the flesh;" his most gorgeous righteousness, "filthy rags." In the impressive language of Scripture, of him it may be said, "That man's religion is vain." "Lord! what is man that thou art mindful of him, or the son of man that thou regardest him?" Truly, "vanity" is inscribed in legible characters on each created good. How, then, can the renewed creature escape its influence? He is "subject to vanity." Dazzled by its glare, captivated by its fascinations, ensnared by its promises, he is often the victim of its power. But it is not a voluntary subjection on the part of the renewed creature. "For the creature was made subject to vanity, *not willingly*." It is not with him a condition of choice. He loves it not, he prefers it not, he glories not in it. From it he would fain be freed, beyond it he would gladly soar. "For we who are in this tabernacle do groan, being burdened: not for that we would be unclothed, but clothed upon, that mortality might be swallowed up of life."† His prayer is, "Turn away mine eyes from beholding vanity; and quicken thou me in thy way."‡ He pants for a holier and a happier state,—a state more

* Psa. xxxix. 5   † 2 Cor. v. 4.   ‡ Psa. cxix. 37.

congenial with his renewed nature. Like the Israelites under the Egyptian bondage, he is a most unwilling servant, groaning beneath his galling yoke, and sighing for the glorious liberty of the children of God." Ah, yes! God has given you another will, O renewed creature! and your present subjection to this poor, vain world, is an involuntary subjection of the divine nature within you. Why God should have subjected the renewed creature to vanity does not appear; we well know that he could have transferred us to heaven the moment that he renewed us on earth. But may we not infer that in sending his people into the world, after he had called them by his grace, and, in a sense, taken them out of it, that in subjecting them for so many years to this state of vanity, he has best consulted his own glory and their good? The school of their heavenly teaching, the scene of their earthly toil, and the theatre of their spiritual conflict, they are kept in this world for a season; "made subject to vanity, not willingly, but by reason of him who hath subjected the same in hope." Hearken to the words of their great Intercessor, when breathing forth his prayer for them on earth:—" These are in the world, and I come to thee. I pray not that thou shouldest take them out of the world, but that thou shouldest keep them from the evil. As thou hast sent me into the world, even so have I also sent them into the world."* Not into the solitude of the desert— not into the calm, but selfish repose of the domestic

* John xvii. 11, 15, 18.

circle—not into the hallowed but restricted fellowship of the church—but *into the world*—encircling them, for a season, by its vanity, and subjecting them to its trials. And what is their mission? That they should love the world? comport with the world? fraternize with the world? Oh, no! Not for this were they sent into it. An object more worthy of His wisdom who sends, and more in harmony with their high calling who are sent, is before them. They are sent into the world that their lives should be a constant, uncompromising, and solemn protest against its vanities and its sins. Mark again the words of Christ :—"*As* thou hast sent me into the world, *even so* have I also sent them into the world." Christ was commissioned to testify of the world that the works thereof were evil. He came to labour for the world—to bless the world—to honour his Father in the world. And, oh, it was the glory of the world that the Son of God was sent into it—that he made it for a while the place of his temporary abode, and the scene of his stupendous redemption. It was the glory of the earth that he trod upon its turf. It was the glory of the ocean that he sailed upon its bosom. It was the glory of the sun that it beamed upon his head. It was the glory of the air that it fanned his brow. It was the glory of the waters that they quenched his thirst. It was the glory of the flowers that they perfumed his path. It was the glory of the sky that it spread above him its blue canopy. What planet has been so honoured as this? What world so visited, so distinguished, so blest? Such is the Christian's pattern. Why has Christ placed you in the position you now occupy? Why are you begirt with so much folly, and trial, and danger? You are converted in the midst of the world—your family is in the world—your associates are in the world—your calling is in the world. Why is it so? Even that like your Lord and Master you might by your unworldly, unearthly, heavenly life testify of the world that the works thereof are evil, and only evil, and evil continually.

One more phrase completes this picture of our present humiliation: "The bondage of corruption." There is nothing in these words that disproves a declaration of the same Apostle in another place, "Sin shall not have dominion over you." And yet it must be admitted of the believer that he is under the "bondage of corruption." Who of the family of God is exempt? Imprisoned and fettered by the inherent corruption of his fallen nature, the renewed creature exclaims with the Apostle, "That which I do I allow not: for what I would, that do I not; but what I hate, that do I. If then I do that which I would not not, I consent unto the law that it is good. Now then it is no more I that do it, but sin that dwelleth in me. For I know that in me (that is, in my flesh,) dwelleth no good thing: for to will is present with me; but how to perform that which is good I find not. For the good that I would I do not: but the evil which I would not, that I do. Now if I do that I would not, it is no more I that do it, but sin that dwelleth in me. I find then a law, that, when I would do good, evil is present with me. For I delight in the law of God, after the inward man: but I see another law in my members, warring against the law of my mind, and bringing me into captivity to the law of sin which is in my members. O wretched man that I am! who shall deliver me from the body of this death?" * It is the bondage of corruption, and yet the bondage of those whom Christ has made free, and to whom there is " now no condemnation."

But painful and humiliating as is the present condition of the renewed creature, it is yet one of earnest expectation and of hope: " Who hath subjected the same *in hope.*" From this state of vanity, and bondage of corruption, the believer is expecting and hoping to be delivered. His gesture is most expressive—it is that of earnest expectation. And are we not in truth earnest expectants? Would we live alway here? Could we be content that this state of vanity should be our condition for ever? Ah, no! we expect a better and a holier state than this. With outstretched neck we are looking for the sunny coast towards which we are voyaging. With earnest expectation we are watching for the signs of his approach, who will restore all things: " Looking for that blessed hope, and the glorious appearing of the great God, and our Saviour Jesus Christ."† ' Hope,' too, rises like the day-spring from on high in our souls. If we are in the bondage of corruption, we yet are

* Rom. vii. 15—25.   † Tit. ii. 13.

"prisoners of hope." Not always shall we be thus fettered. Not for ever shall we look out from the bars of our prison, and exclaim, "Why are his chariot wheels so long in coming?" Oh, no! hope, building upon the atoning work of Christ—hope, springing from his open grave—hope, beaming down from the throne in heaven, within whose veil as an anchor it is cast—"hope that maketh not ashamed" sheds its lustre upon all the future, clothing its landscape with verdure, and silvering it with beauty. Prisoner of hope! lift up your head and rejoice, for your redemption draweth nigh. "Wherefore gird up the loins of your mind, be sober, and hope to the end for the grace that is to be brought unto you at the revelation of Jesus Christ."†

The great consummation toward which this expectation and hope tendeth is the "manifestation of the sons of God." The sons of God are at present *incognito*. Unknown to the world, often veiled, in a great degree, to the brotherhood, and sometimes ignorant of their own divine relation, the Church of God is anything but a visible body. But it will not be always so. There is fast hastening a day of perfect manifestation. The sons of God shall be known. Their relationship will be manifest—their principles will be manifest—their glory will be manifest before the universe. Emerging from the obscurity of the wilderness into which she had been driven, throwing off the sackcloth in which she had so long prophesied,

* 1 Pet. i. 13.

the Church of God, the adoption of the Father, will stand forth before an astonished and admiring world clothed in all the glories of the manifested sons of God. More than this—they will be manifested to themselves. Self-disguise will no longer prompt the trembling inquiry, "Am I a child of God?" That question will now be answered by a testimony to the fact, clear and convincing as the noontide light, before whose brightness every gloomy doubt and slavish fear will vanish as the morning grey, with all the objects looming in its mist, vanish before the uprising sun. For this the renewed creature is in the posture of earnest expectation. "We through the Spirit wait for the hope of righteousness by faith."*

Connected with this blessed condition there is yet another not less so : "Because the creature itself also shall be delivered from the bondage of corruption into the glorious liberty of the children of God." They are already in possession of a liberty most costly and precious. Is it no true liberty to stand before God accepted in the Beloved? Is it no liberty to draw near to him with all the confidence of a child reposing in the boundless affection of a loving father? Is it no liberty to travel day by day to Jesus, always finding him an open door of sympathy the most exquisite, of love the most tender, and of grace the most overflowing? Is it, in a word, no real liberty to be able to lay faith's hand upon the everlasting

* Gal. v. 5.

covenant, and exclaim, "There is *now* no condemnation?" Oh, yes! This is the liberty wherewith Christ *hath* made us free. But the *glorious* liberty of the children of God is yet to come. Glorious it will be because more manifest and complete. Including all the elements of our present freedom, it will embrace others not yet enjoyed. We shall be emancipated from the body of sin and of death. Every fetter of corruption will be broken, and every tie of sense will be dissolved. All sadness will be chased from our spirit, all sorrow from our heart, and all cloud from our mind. Delivered from all sin, and freed from all suffering, we shall wander through the many mansions of our Father's house, and tread the star-paved streets of the celestial city, and repose beneath the sylvan bowers of the upper Paradise, and drink of the waters, clear as crystal, that flow from beneath the throne—our pure, and blissful, and eternal home—exulting in the "glorious liberty of the children of God."

In conclusion—how striking and solemn is the contrast between the present and the future state of the believer and the unbeliever! Yours, too, unregenerate reader, is a state of vanity. But, alas! it is a most *willing* subjection, and the bondage of corruption which holds you is uncheered by one ray of hope of final deliverance. What a terrible and humiliating bondage, a willing slave to sin and Satan! All is vanity which you so eagerly pursue. "The Lord knoweth the thoughts of men that they

are vanity." Were it possible for you to realize all
the schemes of wealth, and distinction, and pleasure,
and happiness which now float in gorgeous visions
before your fevered fancy, still would your heart utter
its mournful and bitter complaint, "All is vanity
and vexation of spirit." Oh, turn you from these
vain shadows to Jesus, the substance of all true
wealth, and happiness, and honour. That fluttering
heart will never find repose until it rests in him.
That craving soul will never be satisfied until it be
satisfied with Christ. At his feet, then, cast you
down, and with the tears of penitence, and the reliance of faith, and the expectation of hope, ask to be
numbered amongst the adopted, who shall ere long be
delivered from the bondage of corruption into the
glorious liberty of the children of God.

CHAPTER XX.

A SUFFERING WORLD IN SYMPATHY WITH SUFFERING MAN.

"For we know that the whole creation groaneth and travaileth in
pain together until now."—ROMANS viii. 22.

FROM the ruin of man, our Apostle naturally turns
his consideration to the ruin in which the apostasy of
man plunged the whole creation—animate and inanimate. If another link were wanting to perfect the
chain of evidence demonstrating the existence of the
Divine curse for man's sin, this passage would seem to
supply it. We read of no blight resting on the
material world, of no suffering in the brute creation,
prior to the period of Adam's transgression. The
present is just the reverse of the original constitution
of the world. When God made all things he pronounced them very good. We delight to look back
and imagine what this world was when, like a new-
born planet, it burst from the Fountain of Light, all
clad with beauty, radiant with holiness, and eloquent
with praise. The winds blew not rudely then—the
verdure withered and died not then—the flowers

drooped and faded not then. There were no tornadoes, no earthquakes, no volcanoes, no electric clouds. All the materials and elements of nature were harmless, and in harmony, because all were sinless. Innocence and happiness reigned over the irrational creation. The whole world was at rest, because man was at peace with God, at peace with his fellows, at peace with himself. There was nothing to darken, to hurt, or destroy in all God's holy mountain. Man was in "league with the stones of the field, and the beasts of the field were at peace with him." * Oh, what a world of love, and what a picture of loveliness was our pure creation then! But what is it now? "The whole creation groaneth and travaileth in pain." Speak we of the material world? What is our earth, but a globe of volcanic fire, smouldering in its centre, ever and anon bursting forth and burying smiling villages and magnificent cities beneath its torrents of flame? What is the wind, but a fierce sirocco, bearing pestilence and death upon its sweeping wings? And what is the sea, but a vast cemetery, its mountain waves the crested monuments of the millions it has ingulfed in its yawning abyss? Yea, what are earth, and air, and water, but agents of destruction, messengers of death to man, as if in vengeance for his sin? Speak we of the brute creation? How does it groan and travail in pain! To what suffering, what cruelty, what death is it subject! Yea, every creature that we meet, and

* Job v. 23.

every object we behold, supplies an evidence of man's
fall, and bears the frown of God's curse. One loud,
agonizing, and universal wail of mourning, lamenta-
tion, and woe bursts from the *whole* creation, as it
groans and travails in pain, from the first moment of
the apostasy until now.

Let us pause and contemplate this overpowering
evidence of sin. Why is the ground cursed? Why
is this once beautiful and fertile earth sown with
briers and noxious weeds? so that, were the labourer
to withdraw his hand, the richest and loveliest
spot would be abandoned to the spontaneous and
luxuriant growth of the deadly nightshade, and the
poisonous nettle, and unpruned trees, and wild
forests—the haunt of every savage beast, and the
abode of man yet more savage. Why this ferocity
and deadly enmity in the brute creation—tribe warring
with tribe, and animal the prey and food of animal?
Because of man's transgression. Oh, Sin, what hast
thou done! Thus closely is a suffering world linked
with suffering man. Thus the *whole* creation—
material and animal—sympathizes with the weight of
woe that crushes our race to the earth. When man
fell, God cursed the ground, and cursed the brutes of
the field, for man's sake; and now the whole creation
groans and travails in pain until the time of the
restitution of all things shall arrive.

It will not, we trust, be considered either inap-
propriate to, or beneath the dignity of our subject,
if we, in this connexion, point out the proper feeling

of sympathy with which the sufferings of the brute
creation should be regarded by man, the author of
those sufferings. We have already adverted to the
fact of the origin of all woe—man's sin. And yet,
clear as this is, how fearfully is the suffering of
inferior tribes, first occasioned by human transgression, aggravated and increased by human cruelty!
It is impossible to open the eye without seeing the
fact, or to contemplate it, when seen, without horror.
The dominion and authority which God gave man
over the beasts of the field contained no clause
whatever giving him a right or power to subject
them to the exercise of unnecessary suffering and
barbarity. We find the terms of the original grant
to be, " The fear of you and the dread of you shall
be upon every beast of the earth, and upon every
fowl of the air, upon all that moveth upon the earth,
and upon all the fishes of the sea; into your hand
are they delivered."* But is not the authority over
the irrational creature with which man is here
invested, a restricted authority ? Unquestionably. Is
he warranted by the terms of the grant to exercise
the plenitude of power thus given, arbitrarily,
ferociously, inhumanly ? Is it a liberty to use the
brute creation as he pleases ? By no means. It is
the authority of man made in the similitude of Him
who is love, extending over brute dependants, and not
the authority of demons over their helpless victims.
It is impossible, too, to contemplate the natural con-

* Gen. ix. 2.

dition of the animal world—their susceptibility of
pain, and their sense of kindness, gratefully and un-
mistakeably shown, without tracing a strong resemblance to ourselves. "These poor animals,"
remarks an eloquent and benevolent writer, "just
look and tremble, and give forth the very indications
of suffering that we do. Theirs is the distinct cry of
pain—theirs is the unequivocal physiognomy of pain
—they put on the same aspect of terror on the
demonstration of a menaced blow—they exhibit the
same distortions of agony after the infliction of it.
The bruise, or the burn, or the fracture, or the deep
incision, or the fierce encounter with one of equal or
inferior strength, just affects them similarly to ourselves. Their blood circulates as ours—they have
pulsations in various parts of the body like ours—
they sicken and they grow feeble with age, and finally
die just as we do—they possess the same feelings, and
what exposes them to like suffering from another
quarter, they possess the same instincts with our own
species. The lioness robbed of her whelps, causes
the wilderness to ring aloud with the proclamation of
her wrongs; and the bird whose little household has
been taken, fills and saddens all the grove with
melodies of the deepest pathos. All this is palpable
even to the general and unlearned eye; and when the
physiologist lays open the recesses of their system by
means of that scalpel under whose operation they
just shrink and are convulsed as any living subject of
our own species, there stands forth to view the same

sentient apparatus, and furnished with the same con-
ductors for the transmission of feeling to every
minutest pore upon the surface. Theirs is unmixed
and unmitigated pain—the agonies of martyrdom,
without the alleviation of the hopes and the sentiments whereof they are incapable. When they lay
them down to die, their only fellowship is with
suffering; for in the prison-house of their beset and
bounded faculties, there can no relief be afforded
of communion with other interests or other things.
The attention does not lighten their distress, as it
does that of man, by carrying off his spirit from
that existing pungency and pressure which might
else be overwhelming. There is but room in their
mysterious economy for one inmate, and that is the
absorbing sense of their own single and concentrated
anguish. And so in that bed of torment, whereon
the wounded animal lingers and expires, there is a
depth and intensity of suffering, which the poor
dumb animal itself cannot tell, and against which it
can offer no remonstrance; an untold and unknown
amount of wretchedness, of which no articulate
voice gives utterance. But there is an eloquence in its
silence, and the very shroud which disguises it, only
serves to aggravate its horrors!"* To say nothing
of the spirit and the precepts of Christianity, where
is the humanity that from sinister motives can over-
work, or from a love of sport can wantonly and
cruelly abuse the jaded and suffering, yet noble

* Dr. Chalmers.

brute, placed in our power, contributing to our convenience, and over whom God has constituted us not the lord but the guardian—not the tormentor, but the friend? And who can think of the pastime of the pit, and the sports of the field, and the needless torture of the slaughter-house, without a cheek burning with indignation? But God, the infinitely great God, has a tender regard for the irrational part of his creation. He commands us to be their advocate against heartless cruelties: "Open thy mouth for the dumb."* And he will, hating nothing that he has created, make inquisition for blood; he will redress their wrongs, and visit their merciless taskmasters and inhuman oppressors with tokens of his just displeasure. How striking and touching is his tender regard for the inferior race as exhibited in his word!—"Thou shalt not muzzle the ox when he treadeth out the corn." "Thou shalt not see thy brother's ass or his ox fall down by the way, and hide thyself from them. Thou shalt surely help them, to lift them up again." "Thou openest thy hand and suppliest the want of every living thing." "He giveth to the beast his food, and to the young ravens when they cry." The regard which we pay to the brute creation must always be considered a test of disposition and character. "A righteous man regardeth the life of his beast."† No individual can be trusted for his humane feeling to his own species who is not humane in his feelings towards the inferior

* Prov. xxxi. 8.   † Prov. xii. 10.

tribes. It is recorded, that when an ancient senate of the Areopagites were assembled in the open air, a small bird, to escape a larger one of prey, took refuge in the bosom of one of the senators, who, being of a cruel disposition, hurled it from him so rudely, that he killed it. On which the senate instantly banished him from their presence, declaring that he who was destitute of humanity, even to a helpless and confiding bird, was unworthy the honour of a seat in their body. An indulged propensity of cruelty to insects, or larger animals, as Hogarth has finely illustrated, has often ended in the perpetration of crimes of the deepest dye. Those who have wantonly sported with life in inferior creatures, have come to sport with life in beings of a higher and nobler order. The author, then, as man is, of all the evil which afflicts the irrational world, let us learn to sympathize with its sufferings, and its travail; and thus lessen, and soothe, and hush, as far as God gives us influence and power, the curse we entailed, the pang we inflicted, and the sign we awoke.

Sad as is this picture of a suffering creation, dark and gloomy as is its colouring, it is not without its bright and cheering hues. Hope casts upon the sombre canvas a strong and steady light. The Bible teaches that there is coming a day—oh, speed its dawning!—of millennial blessedness, when peace and repose shall be restored to this disordered world, and the groaning of the creation shall cease, its sighs be hushed, and its sufferings be terminated for ever.

When that period arrives we are told that the " wolf shall dwell with the lamb, and the leopard shall lie down with the kid; and the calf, and the young lion, and the fatling together, and a little child shall lead them. And the cow and the bear shall feed; their young ones shall lie down together: and the lion shall eat straw like the ox. And the sucking child shall play on the hole of the asp, and the weaned child shall put his hand on the cockatrice' den. They shall not hurt nor destroy in all my holy mountain: for the earth shall be full of the knowledge of the Lord, as the waters cover the sea."* Then when the Restorer of all things shall come, there will be a " new heavens and a new earth, wherein dwelleth righteousness."† Such is the beauteous light with which this dark picture is clothed. Let us pray for its coming, and instrumentally hasten its approach ; remembering that the world is to be filled with the knowledge of the Lord through the sanctified agency of the church.

* Isa. xi. 6—9. † 2 Pet. iii. 13.

CHAPTER XXI.

THE FIRST-FRUITS OF THE SPIRIT, AN EARNEST OF THE FULL REDEMPTION.

"And not only they, but ourselves also, which have the first-fruits of the Spirit, even we ourselves groan within ourselves, waiting for the adoption, to wit, the redemption of our body."
ROMANS viii. 23.

FROM his natural and impressive digression, the Apostle again returns to the renewed creature of whom he had previously been speaking. Having adverted to the suffering of the whole animate creation, he proceeds to show that this condition was not peculiar or solitary,—that not only in the heart of the irrational creature, but even in the heart of the renewed Christian there were the intense throbbings of a woe, and the deep groanings of a burden, from which it sighed and hoped to be delivered. Let us take each section in its order, of this remarkable passage.

"Ourselves also, which have the first-fruits of the Spirit." It had been the earnest aim of the Apostle broadly and distinctly to draw the great line of demarcation between the state of nature and the state of grace. What distinctive feature more illustrative of the Christian character could he have selected than this?—" Who have the first-fruits of the Spirit." The figurative allusion is to a familiar law of the Jewish economy. It will be recollected that, under the Levitical dispensation, the Lord commanded that the first-fruits, in the form of a single sheaf, should be sickled, and waved before him by the priest; and that this wave-offering was to be considered as constituting the herald or the pledge of a ripened and full harvest.* And not only should it be an earnest and a pledge, but it should represent the nature and character of the fruit which, ere long, in luxuriant abundance would crowd with its golden sheaves, and amidst shouts of gladness, the swelling garner. When, therefore, it is said that believers in Jesus have the "first-fruits of the Spirit," the meaning clearly is, that they have such communications of the Spirit now, as are a pledge and foretaste of what they shall possess and enjoy in the great day of the coming glory. " In whom also after that ye believed, ye were sealed with that Holy Spirit of promise, which is the earnest of our inheritance, until the redemption of the purchased possession, unto the praise of his glory."† We remark, in general terms, that if we are believers, then are we partakers of that grace which is the earnest of glory. Do we partake of the grace of *life?* It is the same life which beats in the

* Lev. xxiii. 10, 11.   † Eph. i. 13, 14.

souls of the glorified. In us its pulsations are faint and fluctuating; in them they are deep and unfluttering—yet the life is the same. And if we have the Spirit of life dwelling in us now, then have we the first-fruits of the life which is to come. Have we the Spirit of *adoption?* What is it but the earnest and the seal of our certain reception into our Father's house? The love to God which overflows our hearts, the yearnings of those hearts to be at home, are the first-fruits of our consummated and glorified sonship. Thus might we travel the entire circle of the Christian graces which go to form, sanctify, and adorn the Christian character, illustrating the truth, that each grace wrought by the Spirit in the heart on earth is the germ of glory in heaven, and that the perfection of glory will be the perfection of each grace. The present character and tutelage of the child of God are preparatory to a higher state of being—yea, it is an essential part of that being itself. Oh, it is a holy and inspiriting thought, that every development of grace, and every aspiration of holiness, and every victory of faith, and every achievement of prayer, and every gleam of joy in the soul here below, is the earnest-sheaf of the golden ears of happiness and glory garnered for the saints on high. "He that goeth forth weeping, bearing precious seed, shall doubtless return again with joy, bringing his sheaves with him."

"Even we ourselves groan within ourselves." In these words the expectant of glory is represented as sympathizing, in a certain degree, with the general condition of present misery, and expectation of future good.   But we must distinguish the emotion here described, from the somewhat kindred depression beneath which the whole creation is bowed.   It is the groaning of those who have the "first-fruits of the Spirit"—consequently it is the emotion of a living soul.   In the one case, the groaning is the throb and the throe of death; in the other case it is the evidence and the breathing of life.   To what causes may it be traced?   We groan within ourselves on account of sin—its innate principle, and its practical outbreakings.   Over what do our tears flow the bitterest and the fastest?   The winged riches?   The heart's treasure wrenched from our grasp by ruthless death, and which the cruel grave has hid from our view?   Ah, no! but the sin which lays us in penitence and grief at the Saviour's feet, with David's confession and prayer breathing from our lips—"Against thee, thee only, have I sinned, and done this evil in thy sight."   Oh, what a mercy to know that the "sacrifices of God are a broken spirit: that a broken and contrite heart he will not despise!"   There is also the groaning arising from external trial.   Of this cup, which all alike drink, none quaff so deeply as those to whom are imparted the "first-fruits of the Spirit."   The path of sorrow is the path to glory, and the "bread and the water of affliction" is the aliment of all the "prisoners of hope."   But spring from what cause it may, this groaning of the servants of God confirms

the affecting truth, that the believer possesses but the
"*first-fruits* of the Spirit;" and that, consequently,
his present condition, being one of but partial sanctification, must of necessity be one of but limited happiness. And yet we would not fail to remind the
reader of the truth, that the deeper his sanctification
the keener will be his sense of indwelling corruption,
and the heavier his groaning because of it. So that,
so long as he is still the tenant of a tabernacle of sin
and death—an unwilling subject of vanity—and so
long as he grows in grace, he will "groan being
burdened," and will the more deeply sigh, and the
more intensely long for the uncaging of his spirit,
that frees him entirely for ever from its oppressiveness
and its thraldom.

But, oh, there is music in the groaning of those
who have the "first-fruits of the Spirit!" The chain
they wear is not the manacle of a slave of sin, shaking
his galling fetters in deep and dark despair. The
captivity that confines him is not the subjection of a
voluntary vassal of Satan, crouching beneath the
burden, and trembling at the lash of a hard task-
master. Oh, no! it is the sensibility, the consciousness, the groaning of the Christian. It tells of the
Spirit's indwelling. It betokens the hope of glory.
Those inward heavings of the soul are the pantings of
a life divine; those deep groanings of the heart are
the muffled chimings of heaven. They are the in-
dices of a nature which God will ere long lift to its
native home; they are the discordant notes of an

anthem, which soon will fill heaven with its swelling and entrancing music.

" Waiting for the adoption, to wit, the redemption of the body." The terms " adoption," " redemption," must here be taken in a restricted sense. Our present adoption into God's family is as perfect as God can make it. We shall not in reality be more the children of God in heaven than we are now. Dwell upon this truth, beloved. Press it in faith and gladness to your sighing, groaning heart. Is God's hand uplifted? Oh, tremble not! It is a Father's hand. Say not that it presses heavily upon you— it is the pressure of love. Oh, think not that there is one throb of affection less towards you in his heart. " Beloved, *now* are we the sons of God," and all the immunities and blessings of a *present* sonship are ours. Equally as complete is our redemption from all that can condemn. When Jesus exclaimed, " It is finished!" by one offering he perfected for ever the salvation of his church. Then did he entirely roll away the curse from his people. Then did he hurl their sins into an infinite depth. Then did he complete the work the Father gave him to do. For the finishing of that work, thanks be to God, the saints do not "wait"!

And still, all believers are the expectants of an " adoption " to be confirmed, and of a " redemption " to be perfected. Their adoption now is concealed,— their adoption then will be visible. Their present adoption is limited in its privileges,—their future adoption

will introduce them to all the riches of their inheritance and to all the splendours of their Father's house.
For this unveiled, this manifest, this full adoption
they are " waiting." And so, too, of "redemption."
The ransom price is paid, but the body is not yet
fully redeemed. It still is fettered, and cribbed,
and cabined by a thousand clinging corruptions and
infirmities. But the day of its complete redemption
draweth nigh. In virtue of its ransom it will spring
from the dust, its last link of corruption entirely and
for ever dissolved. " Our conversation is in heaven;
from whence also we look for the Saviour, the Lord
Jesus Christ: who shall change our vile body, that it
may be fashioned like unto his glorious body." Like
unto Christ's glorious body! Oh, then, no deformity
will mar its symmetry! no infirmity will impair its
strength! no sickness, no faintings, no nervousness,
no pangs of suffering or throes of death will ever
assail and torment it more! For this "redemption
of the body" the sons of God are waiting. Our
heavenly Father has adopted it. Our divine Saviour
has redeemed it. The Holy Spirit, our Comforter,
has sealed it. Oh, yes! The first-fruits of the
" first resurrection " bloom on the grave of the holy
dead. Plant not above their heads the flowers that
fade. There are flowers blooming there, plucked from
the amaranthine bowers of immortality, and they will
never die.

This page may arrest the eye of a sufferer, not
soothed in his grief, or cheered in his loneliness by

such prospects as these. There is coming a day when the irrational creation, of whom we have been speaking, will suffer no more. " The spirit of a beast goeth downwards." But no such annihilation awaits suffering man. Oh, melancholy condition! Oh, dreary prospect! Suffering in this life, and suffering in the life to come! to pass from a fire that is temporary, to a fire that is eternal—from the agonies and throes of the first death, to the power and the pangs of the second! But there still is hope. Jesus died for *sinners*, and there is mercy even for the *chief*. Blessed suffering, hallowed sorrow, if now, in the agony of your grief, you are led to the Saviour to learn, what in the sunny hour of prosperity and gladness you refused to learn, that God only can make you happy, and that God in Christ is prepared to make you happy. Oh, heaven-sent affliction! sweet messenger of love! beautiful in thy sombre robes, bearing to my soul a blessing so divine, so precious as this!

Have you the " first-fruits of the Spirit?" Guard them with tender, sleepless care. Nature in her richest domain yields no such fruits or flowers as these. Employ all the means and appliances within your reach to keep verdant and fruitful the sacred garden of your soul. Unveil it to the sun's light, to the gentle showers, and the soft gales of heaven. Let your incessant prayer be, " Awake, O north wind; and come, thou south; blow upon my garden, that the spices thereof may flow out. Let my beloved come into his garden, and eat his pleasant fruits."

Oh, guard those precious "first-fruits!" Soon the glory they foreshadow will be revealed. The autumnal tints are deepening, the golden ears are ripening, the reaper's sickle is preparing, and ere long we shall join in the song of the angels' harvest-home, "Grace, grace unto it!"

CHAPTER XXII.

SAVED BY HOPE.

"For we are saved by hope: but hope that is seen is not hope; for what a man seeth, why doth he yet hope for? But if we hope for that we see not, then do we with patience wait for it."—ROMANS viii. 24, 25.

WE have been contemplating the present state of the renewed creature as one rather of expectancy than of attainment,—not of realization, but of hope. We have seen him in his lofty position, as he stands in Christ Jesus, towering above the storm and thunder-cloud of sin, the curse and condemnation, tinted with the first beams of opening day, and waving the first golden sheaves of the ripening harvest. The description and the argument now approach their climax. As if these trembling rays and these first-fruits might fail to assure the believing heart of the certain day, and the actual harvest, our Apostle, in yet stronger language, meets the misgiving, and quells the fear, by declaring that we are "*saved* by hope." Affirming this, he then proceeds tenderly to exhort the believer to a patient waiting its certain and full realization. There are, in these passages, some points of the deepest interest. May the Holy Spirit unfold and apply them!

" We are saved by hope."   The phrase, as employed
by the Apostle, does not imply the instrument by
which we are saved, but the condition in which we are
saved.   The condition of the renewed creature is one
of *hope*.   Salvation by the atonement of Christ—faith,
and not hope, being the instrument of its appropriation
—is a complete and finished thing.   We cannot give
this truth a prominence too great, nor enforce it with
an earnestness too intense.   We cannot keep our eye
too exclusively or too intently fixed on Jesus.   All
salvation is in him—all salvation proceeds from him—
all salvation leads to him, and for the assurance and
comfort of our salvation we are to repose believingly
and entirely on him.   Christ must be all.   Christ the
beginning—Christ the centre—and Christ the end.
Oh, blessed truth to you who sigh and mourn over
the unveiled abominations that crowd and darken the
chamber of imagery !   Oh, sweet truth to you who
are sensible of your poverty, and vileness, and insuffi-
ciency, and the ten thousand flaws and failures of
which, perhaps, no one is cognizant but God and your
own soul !   Oh, to turn and rest in Christ—a full
Christ—a loving Christ—a tender Christ, whose heart's
love never chills, from whose eye darts no reproof,
from whose lips breathes no sentence of condemnation !
But as it regards the complete effects of this salvation
in them that are saved, it is yet future.   It is the
" hope laid up for us in heaven."   It would seem
utterly incompatible with the present economy that
the renewed creature should be in any other condition

than one of hopeful expectation. The constitution towards which he tends, the holiness for which he looks, the bliss for which he pants, and the dignity to which he aspires, could not for a moment exist in the atmosphere by which he is here begirt. His state must of necessity be one of hope, and that hope must of necessity link us with the distant and mysterious future. The idea, "*saved* by hope," is illustrated by the *effects* of Christian hope. It is that divine emotion which buoys up the soul amidst the conflicts, the trials, and the vicissitudes of the present life. So that we are cheered and sustained, or 'saved' from sinking amidst the billows, by the 'hope' of certain deliverance and a complete redemption. "In hope of eternal life, which God that cannot lie, promised before the world began."*

The Christian's state, then, is one of hope. Around this single subject how much of Scripture light gathers! A remarkable reference to it is found in these words of the Apostle, "Now the God of hope fill you with all joy and peace in believing, that ye may abound in hope, through the power of the Holy Ghost."† Well might Tertullian exclaim in view of a passage so rich as this, "Adoro Scripturæ plenitudinem."‡ God is here portrayed as the "God of hope"—what a glorious title! The believer is then described as the subject of hope—what a blissful being! We are then exhorted to abound in hope—

---

* Titus i. 2.   † Rom. xv. 13.
‡ "I adore the fulness of the Scriptures."

what a precious privilege! This magnificent bow spans the whole horizon of our splendid future. We do not yet realize our heaven—but we *hope* for it. We do not yet see Jesus—but we *hope* to see him. We do not yet exult in our emancipation from corruption—but we *hope* to be free. We do not yet drink of the river of pleasure that is at God's right hand, nor bathe in the sea of glory that rolls around the throne—but we *hope* to do. "We hope for that we see not." But what is the character, and what the foundation of Christian hope?

It is emphatically a "*good* hope."* In every point of view it sustains this scripture character. The hope of heaven fostered by an unrenewed mind is baseless and illusory. There exists not a single element of goodness in its nature. It is the conception of a mind at enmity against God. It is the delusion of a heart in covenant with death, and in agreement with hell. It is the inspiration of the wind. It is the night-vision that plays around the slumbering pillow. It is the meteor-light that flashes upon the tomb. It is the treacherous beacon that decoys the too confiding but deluded voyager to the rock-bound shore. Unscriptural, unreal, and baseless, it must eventually cover its possessor with shame and confusion of face. But not such is the believer's hope. Begotten with his second nature— the in-breathing of the Spirit of God—an element of the renewed mind, and based upon the atonement of

* 2 Thess. ii. 16.

the Saviour, it must be essentially a *good* hope.
Cleansed from moral impurity, not in the laver of
baptism, but with the blood of Christ; justified, not
by the ritual of Moses, but by the righteousness of
the Incarnate God; sanctified, not by sacramental
grace, falsely so called, but by the in-being of the
Holy Ghost,—the believer's hope of heaven is as
well founded as the throne of the Eternal. Moreover,
it is " a good hope *through grace.*" The first and the
last lesson we learn in our Christian course is, that
" by grace we are saved." Lord! dost thou require
of me one thought of stainless purity, one throb of
perfect love, one deed of unsullied holiness, upon
which shall hinge my everlasting happiness? Then
am I lost for ever! But since thou hast provided a
Righteousness that justifies me from all things, that
frees me from all condemnation,—and since this
righteousness is thy free, unpurchased gift, the
bestowment of sovereign grace, I clasp to my
trembling yet believing heart the joyous hope this
truth inspires. It is a *blessed* hope. " Looking for
that blessed hope." Its object is most blessed. The
heaven it compasses is that blissful place where the
holy ones who have fled from our embrace are reposing in the bosom of the Saviour. They are the
blessed dead. The day of their death was to them
better than the day of their birth. The one was the
introduction to all sorrow, the other is a translation
to all joy. Blessed hope! the hope of being for
ever with the Lord. No more to grieve the Spirit

that so often and so soothingly comforted our hearts; no more to wound the gentle bosom that so often pillowed our head. No more to journey in darkness, nor bend as a bruised reed before each blast of temptation. To be a pillar in the temple of God, to go no more out for ever. And what a *sanctifying* hope is it! This, to the spiritual mind, is its most acceptable and elevating feature. " Every man that hath this hope in him purifieth himself even as he is pure." It detaches from earth, and allures to heaven. Never does it glow more brightly in the soul, nor kindle around the path a lustre more heavenly, than when it strengthens in the believer a growing conformity of character to that heaven towards which it expands its wings and soars. It is, in a word, a *sure* hope. Shall the worm undermine it? shall the tempest shake it? shall the waters extinguish it? Never. It *saves* us. It keeps, preserves, and sustains us amidst the perils and depressions of our earthly pilgrimage. And having borne us through the flood, it will not fail us when the last surge lands us upon the shore of eternity. "That by two immutable things, in which it was impossible for God to lie, we might have a strong consolation, who have fled for refuge to lay hold upon the hope set before us: which hope we have as an anchor of the soul, both sure and stedfast, and which entereth into that within the veil, whither the Forerunner is for us entered, even Jesus."*

* Heb. vi. 18—20.

"Therefore do we with patience wait for it." This is our true posture—a patient waiting its fruition. This grace is called the "patience of hope."* "We through the Spirit wait for the hope of righteousness by faith."† We wait the Bridegroom's coming. We wait the descent of the chariot. We wait the Father's summons to our home. We wait the Master's call to our rest. We wait the uncaging of the spirit, that it may fly. The desire to depart is ardent, but patient. The longing to be with Christ is deep, but submissive. For the full realization of a hope so sublime, so precious, and so sure, we can patiently wait. The theatre of suffering is the school of patience : " And patience worketh experience, and experience hope ;" and hope in the depth of the trial, and in the heat of the battle, looks forward to the joy of deliverance, and to the spoils of victory. It is well remarked by Calvin, that " God never calls his children to a triumph till he has exercised them in the warfare of suffering." Thus all who shall eventually wear the palm, must now wield the sword. For the consummation of this hope, then, let us diligently labour, meekly suffer, and patiently wait. Living beneath the cross, looking unto Jesus, toiling for Jesus, testifying for Jesus, and cultivating conformity to Jesus, let us "be always ready to give a reason of the hope that is in us ;" and be always ready to enter into the joy and fruition of that hope, the substance and security of which is—"Christ in you the hope of glory."

* 1 Thess. i. 3.   † Gal. v. 5.

CHAPTER XXIII.

THE SYMPATHY OF THE SPIRIT WITH THE INFIRMITY
OF PRAYER.

" Likewise the Spirit also helpeth our infirmities : for we know
not what we should pray for as we ought ; but the Spirit
itself maketh intercession for us with groanings which
cannot be uttered."—ROMANS viii. 26.

THE condition of the Church of God has ever been
one of weakness and infirmity. Her brightest and
palmiest days were the first and the earliest of her
history. Yet no sooner were the saints of God
gathered into Christian communities, and planted as
churches in each province, and in every land, than
the infirmity of the body began to appear, in the
heresies, divisions, and parties which sprung up, while
yet the Apostles lived to intercede for them with their
prayers, and to teach and admonish them by their
epistles. From that period until now, the history of
the church of God has presented an unbroken chain
of evidence to the truth of the same affecting fact.
A body yet but partially renewed, a church but
imperfectly sanctified, it must of necessity be so.
But let us leave the consideration of the church as a

society, and contemplate it in its individual relation. Each member of that church is the subject of infirmity. It were marvellous were it not so. We have seen that the present condition of the believer is a state of vanity. That it is one of hope rather than of realization. Binding in his bosom the green first-fruits of glory, there yet cling to him a thousand grievous infirmities, the sighs of which, the foretastes of heaven cannot stifle. Encompassed with infirmities, weary and heavy laden, he journeys homeward, amidst the fluctuations of hope and fear, joy and sorrow; sometimes foiled, then overcoming; often mourning, and anon praising; yet ever deeply conscious that the present home of his renewed and heavenly nature is a body of humiliation and death—constituting a perpetual and oppressive clog to the heaven-ascending tendency of his sanctified affections. But we need not extend our classification. The infirmities of the believer are as varied as they are numerous. Some are weak in faith, and are always questioning their interest in Christ. Some, superficial in knowledge, and shallow in experience, and are ever exposed to the crudities of error, and to the assaults of temptation. Some are slow travellers in the divine life, and are always in the rear; while yet others are often ready to halt altogether. Then there are others who groan beneath the burden of bodily infirmity, exerting a morbid influence upon their spiritual experience. A nervous temperament—a state of perpetual depression and despondency—the constant corrodings of mental disquietude—physical ailment—imaginary forebodings a facile yielding to temptation—petulance of spirit—unguardedness of speech—gloomy interpretations of providence—an eye that only views the dark hues of the cloud, the sombre shadings of the picture. Ah! from this dismal catalogue how many, making their selection, may exclaim, "This is *my* infirmity!" But be that infirmity what it may, let it endear to our hearts the grace and sympathy of Him who for our sake was encompassed with infirmity, that he might have compassion upon them that are alike begirt. All the fulness of grace that is in Jesus is for that single infirmity over which you sigh.

But it is one specific infirmity of the Christian to which the passage restricts our attention—*the infirmity of Prayer.* Of this, all the children of God in different degrees partake. A more holy and solemn engagement enlists not the thoughts, and feelings, and time of the believer, than the engagement of PRAYER. In proportion, then, to the spirituality of a duty will be its keen sense of the opposition it meets from either the mental or physical frailties which encompass the Christian. The Apostle thus defines this infirmity—"We know not what we should pray for as we ought." How shall we describe it? With what feature shall we begin? There is first the difficulty which some feel in reference to the *nature* of prayer. Simple as prayer is, we see how even an apostle could be perplexed, for he includes himself in this general description of the saints. Three times did he urge a petition the granting of which would have proved a curse rather than a blessing. " What am I to pray for?" is the earnest inquiry of some. " Am I to limit my requests in petitioning for spiritual blessings, and may I include in my petitions blessings that are temporal?" "And what is real prayer?" is the yet more earnest question of another. " I fear mine is not true prayer. May I characterize by such a holy and significant term the cold effusions of my closet, the feeble ejaculations of the wayside, the wandering devotions of the sanctuary, the moanings of a spirit wounded, the sighs of a heart oppressed, the upward glancings of a mind beclouded, the breathings of a soul whose spiritual exercises are at times so opposite and contradictory? Is *this* prayer?" And, then, there is the infirmity of the act of prayer. The vagrancy of thought—the coldness of affection——the intrusion of low cares—the consciousness of unreal petitions, of unfelt confessions, of undesired desires,—the felt oppressiveness of a distasteful task, rather than the felt luxury of a precious privilege— the slovenliness of the performance—the little solemnity of mind—all mark the infirmity which attaches to this transcendently spiritual employment.

Then as to the *mode* of prayer; this also is felt to be a source of painful embarrassment by some. There are many Christians who find it difficult, if not impossible to give expression to the heart's utterances, in what is termed *free* prayer. Compelled, through an infirmity they cannot conquer, to restrict themselves to a liturgical form of devotion, while others pour out their souls to God in unfettered breathings, in unrestricted communion, they are, at times, perplexed to know whether they are acquainted with the reality and power of true prayer. And thus many a saint of God, whose wants are not the less real, whose desires are not the less spiritual, and whose breathings are not the less fervent and divinely acceptable, may, through this his infirmity, be much cast down and discouraged. But who, whatever be his mode of prayer, is free from *some* clinging infirmity, interfering with the sanctity and power of this hallowed engagement? Who is not mournfully sensible, that of all his spiritual privileges, this, his highest, most sacred, and solemn, is the most encompassed with, and marred and fettered by, the deep corruptions of his fallen and depraved nature? That after all his rigid observance of the duty, his many devotional engagements, public and private, there should yet be so little felt nearness to God, so little confidential communion—in a word, so little *real* prayer. Oh, how much *prayerless prayer* do we have to mourn over! How little brokenness of heart; how little sense of sin; how faint a taking hold of the atoning blood; how imperfect a realization of God's relation to us as a Father; how little faith in his promise to hear, in his ability to aid, in his readiness to bless us! Such are some of the many infirmities associated with prayer. But there is encouragement—let us contemplate it.

"Likewise the Spirit also helpeth our infirmities." The word here rendered "helpeth," properly means to take part with. It implies, not merely sympathy with, but a personal participation in our infirmity. The Spirit helps our infirmities by sharing them with us. Now take the general infirmities of the believer —infirmities which, unaided by another and a superior power, must crush and overwhelm—and trace the help thus afforded by the Spirit. We are taught to adore the love of the Father, from whence each rill of mercy has its rise. We delight to dwell upon the love of the Son, through whose channel all redemption-blessing flows. And shall we overlook the love of the Holy Ghost? Shall we forget his affection, his grace, his succourings? Forbid it, thou eternal and blessed Spirit! Thy essential Deity—thy personal subsistence—thy tender love—thy Divine power—thy efficacious grace—thy sovereign mercy—thy infinite patience—thy exquisite sympathy—all demand our deepest love, and awake our loftiest praise. But how is this sympathy of the Spirit expressed? Seeing the soul bound with an infirmity, all his compassion is awakened. Approaching, he takes hold of the burden. Constrained by a love which no thought can conceive, moved by a tenderness no tongue can describe, he advances, and places the power of his Godhead beneath the pressure—and thus he helpeth our infirmity. Doubt you this? We summon you as a witness to its truth. Why are you not a ruin and a wreck? Why has not *your* infirmity long since dethroned reason, and annihilated faith, and extinguished hope, and clad all the future with the pall of despair? Why have you ridden serene and secure upon the crest of the billow, smiling calmly upon the dark and yawning surges dashing and foaming around you? Why have you, when your heart has been overwhelmed, found relief in a sigh, in a tear, in an uplifted glance, in one thought of God? Oh, it has been because the Spirit, all silent and invisible, was near to you, sympathizing, helping, bearing your infirmities. Because around you the power of his Deity was placed. And when you have staggered, and turned pale, and have well nigh given up all for lost, resigning yourself to the broodings of despair, that Spirit has approached, all-loving and powerful, and helped, by sharing your infirmity. Some appropriate and precious promise has been sealed upon your heart—some clear and soothing view of Christ has been presented to your eye—some gentle whisper of love has breathed upon your ear—and you have been helped. The pressure has been lightened, the grief has been assuaged, the weakness has been strengthened, and you have risen superior to the infirmity that bowed you to the dust. Oh, it was the Spirit that helped you. Grieved, and wounded, and slighted a thousand times over though he has been, receiving at your hands the unkindest requital for the tenderest love, yet when your infirmity bowed you to the earth, and the sword entered your soul, he drew near, forgetting all your base ingratitude, and administered wine to your dejected spirit and oil to your bleeding wound, and placed beneath you the encircling arms of his everlasting love.

But we are yet to contemplate the aid afforded by the Spirit in the especial infirmity of prayer.

" We know not what we should pray for as we ought; but the Spirit itself maketh intercession for us with groanings which cannot be uttered." The Holy Spirit is here represented in the character of a pleader, or advocate for the saints. To form a vivid conception of this truth, we have but to imagine an anxious and embarrassed client prosecuting some important suit, or, perchance, battling for his life in a court of justice. At his side stands his counsellor, thoroughly acquainted with the nature of his case, and deeply versed in the bearings of the law. He is there to instruct the suppliant how to shape his course, with what arguments to support, with what pleas to urge, with what words to clothe his suit. Such is the advocacy and such the aid of the Spirit in the matter of prayer. We stand in the presence of the Lord—it may be to deprecate a deserved punishment, or to plead for a needed blessing. " We know not what we should pray for as we ought." How shall we order our cause before the Great Judge? With what feelings, with what language, with what arguments shall we unburden our heart, unveil our sorrow, confess our sin, and make known our request? How overcome the remembrance of past ingratitude, and the conviction of present guilt, and the pressure of deep need, and the overwhelming sense of the Divine Majesty? How wake the heart to feeling, how rouse the dull, sluggish emotions of the soul, how recall the truant affections, and how concentrate the mind upon the holy and awful engagement? But our Counsellor is there! "The Spirit itself maketh intercession for us." And how does he this? He *indites the prayer.* Think not that that spiritual petition which breathed from your lips and rose as an incense-cloud before the mercy-seat was other than the inditing of the Holy Ghost. He inspired that prayer, he created those desires, and he awoke those groanings. The form of your petition may have been ungraceful—your language simple, your sentences broken, your accents tremulous, yet was there an eloquence and a power in that prayer which reached the heart and moved the arm of God. It overcame the Angel of the Covenant. And whose eloquence and whose power was it?—The interceding Spirit. He also teaches us *what to pray for.* Many and urgent as our wants are, we only accurately know them as the Spirit makes them known. Alas, what profound ignorance of ourselves must we cherish when we know not what we should ask God for as we ought! But the Spirit reveals our deep necessity, convinces us of our emptiness, poverty, and need, and teaches us what blessings to ask, what evils to deprecate, what mercies to implore. He sympathizes, too, with our infirmity in prayer, by portraying to our view the parental character of God. Sealing on our hearts a sense of adoption, he emboldens us to approach God with filial love and child-like confidence. He leads us to God as a *Father*. Nor must we overlook the skill with which the Spirit enables us to urge in our approaches to God the sinner's great plea—the atoning blood of Jesus. This is no small part of the divine aid we receive in our infirmity. Satan, the accuser of the saints, even follows the believer to the throne of grace to confront and confound him there. When Joshua stood before the Angel of the Lord, Satan stood at his right hand to resist him. But the Spirit, too, is there! He is there in the character and to discharge the office of the praying soul's Intercessor. He instructs the accused suppliant what arguments to use, what pleas to urge, and how to resist the devil. He strengthens the visual organ of the soul so that it clearly discerns the blood upon the mercy-seat within the veil, on which it fixes the eye in simple faith. Oh, it is the delight of the Spirit to take of the things of Jesus— his love, his work, his sympathy, his grace, his power, —and show them to the soul prostrate in prayer before the throne of grace.

Thus does the Spirit "make intercession for us with groanings which cannot be uttered." These groanings are those of the believer, yet inspired by the Spirit. They are the inarticulate utterances of a heart overshadowed by the Holy Ghost. No language can adequately express them. They "cannot be uttered." It is the soul's hidden communion with

God. Nay, it is possible that even to the petitioner himself these groanings present but vague and indefinite conceptions of the heart's deep desires, of the soul's yet deeper wants. He is conscious of a need, but he can scarcely define its nature, or suggest its supply. He is sensible of a lack, but what it is, or how it may be met, he is perplexed to know. He inwardly, deeply groans, but these emotions utter a language which even he cannot interpret. But there is One who can. Be that need, be that lack what it may, Christ knows it, Christ sympathizes with it, Christ meets it. He in whom dwelt all the fulness of the Godhead bodily, is prepared to supply all our need. There riseth not a groan of the Spirit from the soul of a sinner, the meaning of which God cannot understand, and the prayer of which God will not answer. To the soul who breathes it, it may appear, as were many of the predictions of the ancient prophets, unintelligible and meaningless; yet, like those prophetic utterances, they have a sense and a language clear and articulate to Him who inspired them. Oh blessed, eloquent groanings in the heart of a poor sinner, which human words fail to utter! God hears them—Jesus understands them—the Spirit creates them—and not one shall be uttered in vain. Whether it be the groaning from a pressure of sin, or from a sense of desire, or from a conviction of want, or from the smiting hand of God himself, that groaning ascends to heaven, and bears to the throne of the

Etérnal, whose ear bends to the softest whisper, and hearkens to the gentlest sigh of his child, a confession, or a request, which shall not be unheard, unheeded, or forgotten.

In conclusion, overlook not the fitness of the Lord Jesus to meet all the infirmities of his people. There are two touching and expressive passages bearing on this point. "Himself took our *infirmities*, and bare our sicknesses."* Wondrous view of the Incarnate God! That very infirmity, Christian reader, which now bows you to the earth, by reason of which you can in no wise lift up yourself, your Saviour bore. Is it sin? is it sorrow? is it sickness? is it want? It bowed him to the dust, and brought the crimson drops to his brow. And is this no consolation? Does it not make your infirmity even pleasant, to remember that Jesus once bore it, and in sympathy bears it still? The other passage is—"We have not an high priest which cannot be touched with the feeling of our *infirmities*."† *Touched* with my infirmity! What a thought! I reveal my grief to my friend. I discern the emotions of his soul. I mark the trembling lip, the sympathizing look, the moistened eye—my friend is *touched* with my sorrow. But oh, what is this sympathy—tender, soothing, grateful as it is—to the sympathy with which the great High Priest in heaven enters into my case, is moved with my grief, is touched with the feeling of my infirmity?

* Matt. viii. 17.   † Heb. iv. 15.

Let us learn more tenderly to sympathize with the infirmities of our brethren. "We that are strong ought to bear the *infirmities* of the weak, and not to please ourselves."* Oh for more of this primitive Christianity! The infirmity of a Christian brother should, by a heartfelt sympathy, become in a measure our own. We ought to *bear it*. The rule of our conduct towards him should be the rule of our conduct towards our own selves. Who would feel bound or disposed to travel from house to house, proclaiming with trumpet tongue and with evident satisfaction his own weaknesses, failings, and infirmities? To God we may confess them, but no divine precept enjoins their confession to man. We unveil them to his eye, and he kindly and graciously veils them from all human eyes. Be this our spirit and our conduct towards a weak and erring brother. Let us rather part with our right hand than publish his infirmity to others, and thus wound the Head by an unkind and unholy exposure of the faults and frailties of a member of his body, and by so doing cause the enemies of Christ to blaspheme that worthy name by which we are called.

Honour and glorify the Spirit who thus so graciously and so kindly sympathizes with our infirmities. Pay to him divine worship, yield to him divine homage, and let your unreserved obedience to his commands, and your jealous regard for his honour,

* Rom. xv. 1.

and your faithful hearkening to the gentle accents of his "still, small voice" manifest how deeply sensible you are of his love, his grace, and faithfulness in sympathizing with your sorrows, in supplying your need, and in making your burdens and infirmities all and entirely his own.

CHAPTER XXIV.

THE INTERCESSION OF THE SPIRIT IN THE SAINTS.

"And he that searcheth the hearts, knoweth what is the mind of
  the Spirit, because he maketh intercession for the saints,
  according to the will of God."—ROMANS viii. 27.

WE are here presented with another and a deeper
unfolding of the work of the Spirit in relation to
prayer. Having shown to us in what way he aids
the infirmity of this holy exercise, chiefly by im-
parting the spirit of grace and of supplication, the
Apostle now reminds us how those inditings, thus
originating with the Holy Spirit, are in perfect harmony with the will of God. The whole subject is
based upon one of the most solemn views of the
Divine Being presented in the Bible. Having contemplated this, we shall then proceed to open up the
Spirit's work of intercession in the saints.

"He that searcheth the hearts." This is, and this
only can be, the prerogative of God. It is not in the
power of man or angel to look within the human
heart. It is the awfully solemn prerogative of God

only. Thus is the truth declared: "The Lord seeth not as man seeth; for man looketh at the outward appearance, *but the Lord knoweth the heart.*"* "The Lord *searcheth all hearts,* and understandeth all the imaginations of the thoughts."† "The fining pot is for silver, and the furnace for gold: *but the Lord trieth the hearts.*"‡ And what a solemn declaration of this truth is put forth by the prophet Jeremiah! "The heart is deceitful above all things, and desperately wicked: who can know it? *I the Lord search the heart,* I try the reins."§ With a most emphatic enunciation of this truth does the sacred canon of Scripture close: "And all the churches shall know that I am he *which searcheth the reins and hearts:* and I will give unto every one of you according to your works."‖ We find the same divine prerogative ascribed to the Lord Jesus, thus forming one of the strongest evidences of his essential Deity: "Then there arose a reasoning among them which of them should be greatest. And Jesus, *perceiving the thought of their heart,* took a child, and set him by him."¶ Again, "But Jesus did not commit himself unto them, because he knew all men. And needed not that any should testify of man; *for he knew what was in man.*"** How could Jesus perceive the thoughts of their heart, and how could he know what was in man —what thoughts were revolving, what schemes were

---

* 1 Sam. xvi. 7.   † 1 Chron. xxviii. 9.   ‡ Prov. xvii. 3.
§ Jer. xvii. 9, 10.   ‖ Rev. ii. 23.   ¶ Luke ix. 46, 47.
** John ii. 24, 25.

planning, what intrigues were plotting in the deep
recesses of the soul, were he not absolutely God?
But solemn as is this view of the Divine character,
the believing mind finds in it sweet and hallowed
repose. What more consolatory truth, in some of
the most trying positions of a child of God, than
this—the Lord knoweth the heart? The world condemns, and the saints judge—but God knoweth the
heart. And to those who have been led into deep
discoveries of the heart's hidden evil, to whom have
been made unveilings startling and distressing, how
precious is this character of God—"he that searcheth
the heart!" Is there a single recess of our hearts
we would veil from his penetrating glance? Is there
a corruption we would hide from his view? Is there
an evil of which we would have him ignorant? Oh
no! Mournful and humiliating as is the spectacle,
we would throw open every door, and uplift every
window, and invite and urge his scrutiny and in-
spection, making no concealments, and indulging in
no reserves, and framing no excuses when dealing
with the great Searcher of hearts—exclaiming,
"Search me, O God, and know my heart: try me,
and know my thoughts: and see if there be any
wicked way in me, and lead me in the way everlasting."* And while the Lord is thus acquainted
with the evil of our hearts, he most graciously conceals that evil from the eyes of others. He seems to
say, by his benevolent conduct, "I see my child's

* Psa. cxxxix. 23, 24.

infirmity "—then covering it with his hand, exclaims
—" but no other eye shall see it save my own !" Oh,
the touching tenderness, the loving-kindness of our
God! Knowing, as he does, all the evil of our
nature, he yet veils that evil from human eye, that
others may not despise us as we often despise ourselves. Who but God could know it—who but God
would conceal it? And how blessed, too, to remember that while God knows all the evil, he is as
intimately acquainted with all the good that is in the
hearts of his people! He knows all that his Spirit
has implanted, that his grace has wrought. Oh,
encouraging truth! That spark of love, faint and
flickering,—that pulsation of life, low and tremulous,
—that touch of faith, feeble and hesitating,—that
groan, that sigh, that low thought of self that leads
a man to seek the shade,—that self-abasement that
places his mouth in the dust, oh, not one of these
sacred emotions is unseen, unnoticed, by God. His
eye ever rests with infinite complaisance and delight
on his own image in the renewed soul. Listen to his
language to David: "Forasmuch as it was in thine
heart to build an house for my name, thou didst well,
in that it was in thine heart." *

"Knoweth what is the mind of the Spirit." It
would appear by these words, that in prayer the
great interpreter of the heart is the Spirit. And
when it is declared that our Father in heaven knows
what is the mind of the Spirit, it means that he is

* 2 Chron. vi. 8.

essentially acquainted with all the inditings and breathings of the Spirit in the heart. With what powerful and irresistible attractions does this truth invest the throne of grace! To remember that in prayer we draw near to that God who knows all the desires of the heart, which, though they be clothed with no diction, and are inarticulate in their accents, are yet known to, and understood by, him. Yea, before that thought is conceived, or that feeling is inspired, and when actually conceived and inspired, is, perhaps, to us confused, and indefinite, and meaningless, leaving nothing to repose in but the bare consciousness of sincere desire and real earnestness; yet he who knows what is the mind of the Spirit, understands it altogether. To him it has a voice, to him a language, and to him a meaning. He knows the mind of the Spirit in his saints. Oh, sweet encouragement to prayer! It is not your voice that speaks, but the Spirit's, when you draw near to God.

"Because he maketh intercession for the saints according to the will of God." We are wont to read in the Bible of one Intercessor, and of one advocacy. "There is one Mediator between God and men, the man Christ Jesus." * "If any man sin, we have an Advocate with the Father, Jesus Christ the righteous." † But the believer has two courts with which prayer has to do. In the court below, where prayer is offered, the Spirit is his Intercessor. In

* 1 Tim. ii. 5.   † 1 John ii. 1.

the court above, where prayer is presented, Jesus is his Intercessor. Then, what an honoured, what a privileged man is the praying man! On earth—the lower court—he has a Counsellor instructing him for what he should pray, and how he should order his suit. In heaven—the higher court—he has an Advocate presenting to God each petition as it ascends, separating from it all that is ignorant, and sinful, and weak, and pleading for its gracious acceptance, and asking for its full bestowment. Here, then, is our vast encouragement in prayer. The inditings of the Spirit—the Intercessor on earth—are always in agreement with the mind of God. In prayer we need just such a Divine counsellor. Is it temporal blessing that we crave? We need not be taught how to graduate our request to our necessity, and how to shape our necessity to our heavenly calling. Supplication for temporal good is, we think, limited. And this is the limit: "Having food and raiment, let us therewith be content." What child of God is warranted in asking worldly wealth, or distinction, or rank? And what child of God, in a healthy state of soul, would ask them? "But," says the Apostle, "my God shall supply all your *need*, according to his riches in glory by Christ Jesus."* Should God, in his providence, send either of these temporal things undesired, unasked, and unexpected, receive it as from him, and use it as to him. But with regard to spiritual blessings, our grant is illi-

* Phil. iv. 19.

mitable, our requests may be boundless. Here we may quit the shore we have so long been hugging, and boldly launch out into the deep—even the depths of God's love, and of the Saviour's grace. "Ask what thou wilt," is the broad, unrestricted warrant. When we ask to be perfected in the love of God, we ask for that which is in accordance with the will of God—for "God is love." When we ask for an increase of faith, we ask for that which is in accordance with the will of God—for "without faith it is impossible to please him." When we ask for more divine conformity, we ask for that which is in harmony with God's will—for he hath said, "Be ye holy, for I am holy." And when we ask for comfort, we plead for that which is in his heart to give—for he is the "God of all comfort." Oh, to possess a Divine counsellor, dwelling in our hearts, who will never indite a wrong prayer, nor suggest a weak argument, nor mislead us in any one particular, in the solemn, the important, the holy engagement of prayer; who is acquainted with the purpose of God; who knows the mind of God; who understands the will of God; who reads the heart of God; yea, who is God himself. What encouragement is this, to more real prayer! Are you moved to pray? While you muse does the fire burn? Is your heart stirred up to ask of God some especial blessing for yourself, or for others? Are you afflicted? Oh, then, rise and pray—the Spirit prompts you—the Saviour invites you—your heavenly Father waits to answer you.

With such an Intercessor in the court on earth—so divine, so loving, and so sympathizing; and with such an Intercessor in the court in heaven — so powerful, so eloquent, and so successful—" let us come boldly unto the throne of grace, that we may obtain mercy, and find grace to help in time of need."

CHAPTER XXV.

ALL THINGS WORKING FOR GOOD.

" And we know that all things work together for good to them
that love God, to them who are the called according to his
purpose."—ROMANS viii. 28.

WHAT a glorious Being must our God be, who
from the direst evil can educe the greatest good!
Having, by an exercise of power the most divine, and
by an act of grace the most stupendous, " turned the
curse into a blessing," he is still, in the exercise of
the same divine and beneficent power, employed in
overruling the daily consequences of man's original
woe for the greater promotion of his present happiness. The interesting passage now about to engage
our thought, seems an amplification of a truth the
inspired writer had previously advanced—that, though
this were the suffering state of the Church of God,
yet was it a palmy state; for, from those very sufferings were extracted some of the richest blessings of
the Christian,—that, by the active combination of all
the events of his history, there is working out a great
and a present good. The leading point that arrests

the eye in this remarkable verse is the beautiful portrait which it sketches of the believer's character. Let this be our first feature of contemplation.

"Them that love God." Surely it is no small mercy belonging to the Church of Christ, that, composed as it is of all people and tongues, its members as "strangers scattered abroad," and its essential unity deeply obscured, and its spiritual beauty sadly disfigured by the numerous divisions which mar and weaken the body of Christ, there yet is an identity of character in all, by which they are not only known to God, but are recognised by each other as members of the one family—"them that love God."

Love to God, then, is the grand distinctive feature of the true Christian. The reverse marks all the unregenerate. Harmonious as their nature, their creed, their church, may be, *no love to God* is their binding, assimilating feature, their broad distinctive character. But the saints are those who *love God.* Their creeds may differ in minor shades, their ecclesiastical relations may vary in outward forms,—as rays of light, the remoter their distances from the centre, the more widely they diverge from each other. Yet in this one particular there is an essential unity of character, and a perfect assimilation of spirit. They love one God and Father; and this truth— like those sundered rays of light returning to the sun, approximate to each other—forms the great assimilating principle by which all who hold the Head, and love the same Saviour, are drawn to one centre, and in which they all harmonize and unite. The regeneration through which they have passed has effected this great change. Once they were the children of wrath, even as others, at enmity with God. Ah! is not this a heart-affecting thought? But now they love him. The Spirit has supplanted the old principle of enmity by the new principle of love. They love him as revealed in Christ, and they love him for the gift of the Revealer,—the visible image of the invisible God. Who, as he has surveyed the glory and realized the preciousness of the Saviour, has not felt in his bosom the kindling of a fervent love to him who, when he had no greater gift, commended his love to us by the gift of his dear Son? They love him, too, in his paternal character. Standing to them in so close and endearing a relation, they address him as a Father,— they confide in him as a Father,—they obey him as a Father. The Spirit of adoption takes captive their hearts, and they love God with a child's fervent, adoring, confiding affection. They love God, too, for all his conduct. It varies, but each variation awakens the deep and holy response of love. They love him for the wisdom, the faithfulness, the holiness of his procedure—for what he withholds, as for what he grants—when he rebukes, as when he approves. For his frown, they know it to be a Father's frown; for his smile, they feel it to be a Father's smile. They love him for the rod that disciplines as for the sceptre that governs,—for the wound that bleeds, as for the balm that heals. There is nothing in God, and there is nothing from God, for which the saints do not love him. Of one truth—the source of this feeling—let us not lose sight: "We love him because he first loved us." Thus the motive of love to God as much springs from him, as the power to love him.

"Who are the called according to his purpose." Another characteristic of the children of God is this. The calling here referred to, is that inward, effectual calling of which the same apostle speaks in another place. "Among whom are ye also the called of Jesus Christ: to all that be in Rome, beloved of God, called to be saints."* Oh what a glorious vocation is this! To have heard the Holy Spirit's divine yet gentle voice in the deep recesses of the soul—to have felt the drawings of the Saviour's love upon the heart—to have listened to a Father's persuasive assurance of a love that has forgotten all our enmity, forgiven all our rebellion, and that remembers only the kindness of our youth, and the love of our espousals,—called to be saints, God's holy ones,—called to be sons, the Father's adopted ones,—oh this were a vocation worthy indeed of God, and demanding in return our supremest, deepest affection! The principle upon which this call proceeds is said to be, " according to his purpose." Thus it is a calling over which we have no control, either in originating or frustrating it, and therefore there is no ground of self-boasting. "In whom also we have obtained an inheritance,

* Rom. i. 6, 7.

being predestinated according to the purpose of him who worketh all things after the counsel of his own will."* It excludes all idea of merit on the part of the called. "Who hath saved us, and called us with an holy calling, not according to our works, but according to his own purpose and grace, which was given us in Christ Jesus before the world began."† Oh, yield your heart to the full belief and holy influence of this truth. Does it clash with your creed?— then your creed is defective. Does it awaken the opposition of your heart?—then your heart is not right. Are you really among the "called of God?" —then ascribe it to his eternal purpose, and believe that you have no ground of boasting, in the possession of a favour so distinguished, save in the sovereign will and most free grace of the holy Lord God who has called you. Has this call reached you, my reader? Ministers have called you,—the Gospel has called you, —providences have called you,—conscience has called you,—but has the Spirit called you with an inward and effectual vocation? Have you been called, spiritually called, from darkness to light,—from death to life,—from sin to holiness,—from the world to Christ,—from self to God? Examine your heart and ascertain. Oh, it is a matter of the greatest moment that you know that you are *truly* converted, that you are called of God. Has the thrilling, life-inspiring music of that call sounded and reverberated through all the chambers of your soul?

* Ephes. i. 11.   † 2 Tim. i. 9.

We now come to consider the exalted privilege which appertains to this holy character of those who love God, and who are the called according to his purpose.

"All things work together for good." The comprehensiveness of this privilege is boundless. "All things" under the righteous government of God must necessarily be a working out of *good*. "Thou art good, and doest good." In him there is no evil, and consequently nothing can proceed from him that tendeth to evil. But lest the great scope of this subject should lead us from the point directly before us, we confine our illustration of this truth to the experience of the individual Christian. Here it is palpably clear and emphatically true that all that occurs in the Lord's government of his people conspires for, and works out, and results in, their highest happiness, their greatest good. The passage supposes something antagonistic to the well-being of the believer in God's conduct at times. He would appear to place himself in an attitude of hostility to those who love him, to stand in their path as with a drawn sword in his hand. And yet, to no single truth does the Church bear a stronger testimony than to this, that the darkest epochs of her history have ever been those from which her brightest lustre has arisen; and that those very elements which wore an aspect so portentous and threatening, by a mutual and concurrent influence, under the guiding hand of God, have evolved purposes and plans, have developed thoughts and feelings, and have terminated in results and ends, all seeking and advancing the best welfare, the highest good, of the Church of Christ. But let us pass within the individual circle of the Church. Shall we take the gloomiest and most painful circumstances in the history of the child of God? The word declares that these identical circumstances, without a solitary exception, are all conspiring, and all working together, for his real and permanent good. As an illustration of this, take tribulation as the starting-point. Thus says the Apostle: "We glory in tribulation, knowing that tribulation worketh patience"—the grace that shines with such surpassing lustre in the furnace; "and patience experience"—apart from which all religious profession is vain; "and experience hope "—the pole-star of the believer voyaging homeward; "and hope maketh not ashamed "—but confirms and realizes all that it expected. And yet, from whence this flow of precious blessing—serene patience, vital experience, and beaming hope?—all flow from the sombre cloud of *tribulation!* That tribulation was, perhaps, of the most mysterious character—of the most humiliating nature—of the most overpowering force—yet behold the blessings it flung from its dark bosom! Who with a finite prescience could have predicted, still less have commanded, that from a bud so bitter and un-sightly, a flower so sweet and fair should have blown? —that a cloud so dark and foreboding should have unbosomed a blessing so brilliant and so precious?

The Bible is rich in its illustrations of this principle of the Divine government. Take for example the case of Jacob. Heavy and lowering was the cloud now settling upon his tabernacle. Severe was the test, and fearful the trembling of his faith. His feet were almost gone. The sad recollection of his bereavement still hovered like clinging shadows around his memory; gaunt famine stared him in the face; and a messenger with tidings of yet heavier woe lingered upon the threshold of his door. And when those tidings broke upon his ear, how touching the expression of his grief!—"Me have ye bereaved of my children: Joseph is not, and Simeon is not, and ye will take Benjamin away: all these things are against me."* But lo! the circumstances which to the dim eye of his faith wore a hue so sombre, and an aspect so alarming, were at that moment developing and perfecting the events which were to smooth his passage to the grave, and shed around the evening of his life the halo of a glorious and a cloudless sunset. All things were working together for his good! Joseph, too, reviewing the past of his chequered and mysterious history, arrives at the same conclusion, and confirms the same truth. Seeking to tranquilize his self-condemning brothers, he says, "But as for you, ye thought evil against me; but God meant it unto good, to bring to pass, as it is this day, to save much people alive."† The envy of his brethren, his being sold as a slave, his imprisonment, were all working

* Gen. xlii. 36.   † Gen. l. 20.

out God's purpose and plan of wisdom and love.
And yet, who could have foreseen and predicted, that
from those untoward events the exaltation, power, and
wealth of Joseph would spring? Yet all things were
working together for good. Thus is it, too, in the
history of the Lord's loving corrections. They are
all the unfoldings of a design, parts of a perfect whole.
From these dealings, sometimes so heart-crushing,
what signal blessings flow! "Thou hast chastised
me, and I was chastised." And what was the result?
It awoke from Ephraim this precious acknowledgment
and prayer: "Surely after that I was turned, I
repented; and after that I was instructed, I smote
upon my thigh: I was ashamed, yea, even confounded,
because I did bear the reproach of my youth."* Oh,
who can compute the good, the real, the permanent
good that results from the trying dispensations of
God?—from the corrections of a Father's love? The
things that appear to militate against the believer,
unfolding their heaven-sent mission, turn out rather
for the furtherance of his best welfare and his highest
interest.

But observe the unity of operation. They "work
together,"—not singly and separately, but conjointly,
—as adjunct causes and mutual helps. Therefore it
is that we often mark a plurality of trial in the
calamity which befals the Christian. Seldom does
affliction come solitary and alone—the gentle wavelet
upon the surface forebodes the agitation of the waters

* Jer. xxxi. 19.

and is often the precursor of the mountain billow, and the billow in its turn is often the herald of the huge waterspout. Storm rises upon storm, cloud on cloud. One messenger of woe is quickly succeeded by another, burdened with tidings of yet heavier sorrow. Trace the wisdom, nor the wisdom only, but the love of thy God, O child of suffering, in ordaining your path to heaven through "*much* tribulation*," and in weaving around you *many* trials. Single and alone, the good they are charged to convey were but partially accomplished, and the evil they were designed to meet but imperfectly cured. It is the compounding of the ingredients in the recipe that constitutes its sanative power. Extract any one ingredient, and you impair the others and destroy the whole. We may not understand the chemistry of the process; we do not see how one element acts upon the properties of the others, nor how, by the combination of all, the cure is effected. Yet, confiding in the skill of the compounder, and submitting our reason to our faith, we take the remedy and receive the benefit. So, with the Divine dispensations, they work, but "work together." How assuredly would the curative process of trial be impaired, if but one of the several sent were wanting! How would the adjustment, harmony, and symmetry of God's arrangement be destroyed, if one dark dispensation were lacking of, perhaps, the many which lour upon our horizon! It is the combination of sound, the harmony of many, and often discordant

notes, that constitute music. Oh, how imperfectly
are we aware, not of the necessity of trial only, but
of a plurality of trial, in order to wake from our lips
the sweetest, loftiest anthem of praise and thanksgiving to God! Thus it is that the most deeply tried
believers are the most skilful and the most melodious
choristers in God's church. They sing the sweetest
on earth, and they sing the loudest in heaven, who are
passing through, and who have come out of, *"great
tribulation."* Then, Christian, count it all joy when
you fall into divers trials; be not terrified if wave
responds to wave—if cloud caps cloud—if storm rises
on storm—if your Joseph has been taken, and now
your Benjamin be demanded. The greater the accumulation of trial, the richer the freight it bears.
Then it is that the interposition, the wisdom, and
love of our God appear the most conspicuous
and wonderful. Having delivered us out of six
troubles, we see him hastening to our rescue in the
seventh. Then it is, the experience of the sweet
singer of Israel awakes an echo in our heart: "He
sent from above, he took me, he drew me out of
many waters." It has been well observed, "The
mechanism of providence is made up of so many parts,
as often to baffle the comprehension of man; yet all
is clear to the eye and under the sovereign hand of
Him who works it; and when we are lost in the
bewilderments of a history that we cannot scan;
when we are entangled among the mazes of a
labyrinth that we cannot understand, it is well to

be told that all is ordered, and that all worketh for good."

And let us not forget that it is a *present* working. It says not that all things *have* worked together for good, though this is most true. It says not that all things *shall* work together for good, though this is equally certain. But it says that all things *do now work* together for good. It is not a past, nor a future, but a *present* process. They are *always* working for good. The operation may be as invisible and noiseless as the leaven fermenting in the meal, and yet not less certain and effectual. The kingdom of God cometh not into our souls with observation, nor does it grow in our souls with observation. And whether the good thus borne upon the raven-wing of trial, thus embosomed in the louring cloud of some crushing providence, be immediate or remote, it matters little; sooner or later it will accomplish its benign and heaven-sent mission, and then trial will expand its dark pinions and fly away; and sorrow will roll up its sombre drapery and disappear. The painful and inexplicable dispensations, which at the present moment may be thickening and deepening around your path, are but so many problems in God's government, which he is working out to their certain, satisfactory, and happy results.

Safely, then, may the Apostle rest his appeal with us: "*We know* that all things work together for good." We know it, because God has said it. We know it, because others have testified to it. Best of all, we know it, because we have experienced it ourselves. We can set our seal to the truth that all things under the government of an infinitely great, all-wise, righteous, and beneficent Lord God, both in the world, and in the church, and in the history of each member of the church, work together for good. What that good may be, the shape it may assume, the complexion it may wear, the end to which it may be subservient, we cannot tell. To our dim view it may appear an evil, but to God's far-seeing eye it is a positive good. His glory is secured by it, and, that end accomplished, we are sure it *must* be good. Oh, truth most divine! Oh, words most consolatory! How many whose eye traces this page, it may be whose tears bedew it, whose sighs breathe over it, whose prayers hallow it, may be wading in deep waters, may be drinking bitter cups, and are ready to exclaim—" All these things are against me! " Oh no, beloved of God, all these things are for you! "The Lord sitteth upon the flood." " The voice of the Lord is upon the waters." " He maketh the clouds his chariot." Be not, then, afraid! Christ restrains the flood upon whose heaving bosom he serenely sits. Christ controls the waters, whose sounding waves obey the mandate of his voice. Christ's cloudy chariot is paved with love. Then, fear not! Your Father grasps the helm of your storm-tossed bark, and through cloud and tempest will steer it safely to the port of endless rest. " There is none like unto the God of Jeshurun, who rideth upon the heavens in thy help, and in his excellency on the sky. The Eternal God is thy refuge, and underneath are the everlasting arms." Again, learn instruction from analogy. All the beauty, and fragrance, and music of nature, spring from a union and blending of opposites. So is it in that kingdom which is within you. The beauty of holiness with which God adorns you—the perfume of grace which he flings around you—the melody of praise which he wakes from your lips—are the result of " *all* things " in your history conspiring, combining, and working together for your good.

> " Love thou thy sorrow ? Grief shall bring
> Its own excuse in after years.
> The rainbow—see how fair a thing
> God hath built up from tears ! "

Oh, calmly stay your faith, then, on this divinely assured truth, that " all things work together for good to them that love God." Will it not be a *good*, if your present adversity results in the dethronement of some worshipped idol—in the endearing of Christ to your soul—in the closer conformity of your mind to God's image—in the purification of your heart— in your more thorough meetness for heaven ? Will it not be a real good if it terminate in a revival of God's work within you—in stirring you up to more prayer—in enlarging your heart to all that love the same Saviour—in stimulating you to increased activity for the conversion of sinners, for the diffusion of the truth, and for the glory of God? Oh yes! good, real good, permanent good *must* result from *all* the Divine dispensations in your history. Bitter repentance shall end in the experienced sweetness of Christ's love. The festering wound shall but elicit the healing balm. The overpowering burden shall but bring you to the tranquil rest. The storm shall but quicken your footsteps to the Hiding-place. The *north* wind and the *south* wind shall breathe together over your garden, and the spices shall flow out. In a little while—oh, how soon!—you shall pass away from earth to heaven, and in its clearer, serener light shall read the truth,

" Oft read with tears before,"

"ALL THINGS WORK TOGETHER FOR GOOD TO THEM THAT LOVE GOD."

" Oh, what a load of struggle and distress
  Falls off before the Cross ! The feverish care ;
  The wish that we were other than we are :
  The sick regrets ; the yearnings numberless ;
  The thought, 'This might have been,' so apt to press
  On the reluctant soul ! even past despair,
  Past sin itself,—all—all is turn'd to fair,
  Ay, to a scheme of order'd happiness,
  So soon as we love God, or rather, know
  That God loves us ! . . Accepting the great pledge
  Of His concern for all our wants and woe,
  We cease to tremble upon danger's edge,
  While varying troubles form and burst anew,
  Safe in a Father's arms, we smile as infants do !" *

* Chauncy Hare Townshend.

CHAPTER XXVI.

" For whom he did foreknow, he also did predestinate to be
conformed to the image of his Son, that he might be the
firstborn among many brethren."—ROMANS viii. 29.

IN directing the reader's attention to the preceding
verse, of which the present would seem to be an
amplification, it was our endeavour to show, that
under the government of an infinitely righteous Lord
God, especially as that government extended to the
Church of Christ, all circumstances and events re-
lating to man, both as a society and as an individual,
constituted a vast confederacy, a perfect machinery,
for the working out of results the most wise and
beneficent. We remarked, further, that much of the
spiritual dejection and despondency of which so many
of God's people are the subjects, may be traced to
a forgetfulness of the great and obvious truth, that
the Lord Jesus has so completely answered all the
claims of God's moral government, that nothing can
transpire in his providential dispensations but what
evidences his love to, and illustrates his character
towards, his people, as a most kind and gracious

Father. Were this truth more distinctly recognised and remembered—were the cross more simply dealt with, each dispensation in the experience of the child of God, sombre though were its garb, and harsh though were its tones, would be interpreted, not as a terrifying agent of evil, but as a heaven-sent messenger of good. Then would the beautiful thought be realized, that

> " Every cloud that spreads above,
> And veileth love, *itself is love*." *

Guided by the latter clause of the preceding verse, we were led to advert to the settled purpose and plan of God as it related to the conversion of his people. The passage under present consideration carries forward the same argument another step, and shows that the doctrine thus clearly enunciated is not a crude and speculative dogma of the schools, which some suppose, but is a truth of distinct revelation, divine in its origin, experimental in its nature, and sanctifying and comforting in its effects. Let us, then, divesting our minds of all prejudice, address ourselves to its consideration, in prayerful reliance upon the teaching of the Spirit, and with the earnest simplicity of children desiring to come to a knowledge of the truth, and to stand complete in all the will of God.

"Whom he did foreknow." In this place the word "foreknow" assumes a particular and explicit

---

* Tennyson.

meaning. In its wider and more general application it must be regarded as referring not simply to the Divine prescience, but more especially to the Divine pre-arrangement. For God to foreknow is, in the strict meaning of the phrase, for God to fore-ordain. There are no guesses, or conjectures, or contingencies with God as to the future. Not only does he know all, but he has fixed, and appointed, and ordered "all things after the counsel of his own will." In this view there exists not a creature, and there transpires not an event, which was not as real and palpable to the Divine mind from eternity as it is at the present moment. Indeed, it would seem that there were no future with God. An eternal Being, there can be nothing prospective in his on-looking. There must be an eternity of perception, and constitution, and presence; and the mightiest feature of his character —that which conveys to a finite mind the most vivid conception of his grandeur and greatness — is the simultaneousness of all succession, and variety, and events to his eye. "He is of one mind; and who can turn him?" But the word "foreknow," as it occurs in the text, adds to this yet another, a more definite, and, to the saints, a more precious signification. The foreknowledge here spoken of, it will be observed, is limited to a particular class of persons who are said to be "conformed to the image of God's Son." Now this cannot, with truth, be predicated of all creatures. The term, therefore, assumes a particular and impressive signification. It includes

the everlasting love of God to, and his most free
choice of, his people, to be his especial and peculiar
treasure. We find some examples of this — "God
hath not cast away his people whom he did *foreknow.*" * Here the word is expressive of the two
ideas of love and choice. Again, "Who verily was
fore-ordained (Greek, foreknown) before the foundation of the world." † "Him, being delivered by the
determinate counsel and foreknowledge of God." ‡
Clearly, then, we are justified in interpreting the
phrase as expressive of God's especial choice of, and
his intelligent love to, his church—his own peculiar
people. It is a foreknowledge of choice—of love—
of eternal grace and faithfulness.

"He also did predestinate." This word admits
of but one natural signification. Predestination, in
its lowest sense, is understood to mean the exclusive
agency of God in producing every event. But it
includes more than this: it takes in God's predeter-
minate appointment and fore-arrangement of a thing
beforehand, according to his divine and supreme will.
The Greek is so rendered,—"For to do whatsoever
thy hand and thy counsel determined before to be
done." § Again, "Having predestinated us unto
the adoption of children by Jesus Christ to himself,
according to the good pleasure of his will."‖ It is
here affirmed of God, that the same prearrangement
and predetermination which men in general are

* Rom. xi. 2.　　† 1 Pet. i. 20.　　‡ Acts ii. 23.
§ Acts iv. 20.　　　　　‖ Eph. i. 5.

agreed to ascribe to him in the government of matter, extends equally, and with yet stronger force, to the concerns of his moral administration. It would seem impossible to form any correct idea of God, disassociated from the idea of predestination. "The sole basis of predestination is the practical belief that God is eternal and infinite in and over all. And the sole aim of its assertion should be, as the sole legitimate effect of that assertion is, to settle down the wavering and rebel soul from the vague, and sceptical, and superstitious inapplicabilities of a peradventure as to this world's history, unto the living, and overwhelming, and humbling practicality of conviction, that, just because God sees all things, provides all things, and has power over all things, therefore man must act as if he believed this to be true. The first and the last conviction of every honest inquirer must be, that God is, and is Lord over all—and the whole of Scripture bears testimony to the fact of his infinitude." And yet how marvellously difficult is it to win the mind to a full, unwavering acquiescence in a truth which, in a different application, is received with unquestioning readiness! And what is there in the application of this law of the Divine government to the world of matter, which is not equally reasonable and fit in its application to the world of mind? If it is necessary and proper in the material, why should it not be equally, or more so, in the spiritual empire? If God is allowed the full exercise of a sovereignty in the one, why should he be excluded from an unlimited sovereignty in the other? Surely it were even more worthy of him that he should pre-arrange, predetermine, and supremely rule in the concerns of a world over which his more dignified and glorious empire extends, than that in the inferior world of matter he should fix a constellation in the heavens, guide the gyrations of a bird in the air, direct the falling of an autumnal leaf in the pathless desert, or convey the seed, borne upon the wind, to the spot in which it should fall. Surely if no for-tuitous ordering is admitted in the one case, on infinitely stronger grounds it should be excluded from the other. Upon no other basis could Divine foreknowledge and providence take their stand than upon this. Disconnected from the will and purpose of God there could be nothing certain as to the future, and consequently there could be nothing certainly foreknown. And were not Providence to regulate and control persons, things, and events,— every dispensation, in fact,—by the same precon-structed plan, it would follow that God would be exposed to a thousand contingencies unforeseen, or else that he acts ignorantly, or contrary to his will. What, then, is predestination but God's determining will?

Now all this will apply with augmented beauty and force to the idea of a predestinated church. How clearly is this doctrine revealed! "Whom he fore-knew, them he also did predestinate." "According as he hath chosen us in him before the foundation of the world."* "And as many as were ordained to eternal life believed.",† "Knowing, brethren beloved, your election of God."‡ "We are bound to give thanks unto God always for you, brethren, beloved of the Lord, because God hath from the beginning chosen you to salvation."§ "Whose names are written in the book of life from the foundation of the world."‖ "Who hath saved us, and called us with an holy calling, not according to our works, but according to his own purpose and grace, which was given us in Christ Jesus before the world began."¶ "Elect according to the foreknowledge of God the Father."** "Come, ye blessed of my Father, inherit the kingdom prepared for you from the foundation of the world."†† What an accumulation of evidence in proof of a single doctrine of Scripture! Who but the most prejudiced can resist, or the most sceptical deny its overwhelming force? Oh, to receive it as the word of God! To admit it, not because reason can understand, or man can explain it,—for all truth flowing from an Infinite source must necessarily transcend a finite mind,—but because we find it in God's holy word. But it is not so much our province to establish the truth of this doctrine, and explain its reasonableness and the harmony of its relations, as to trace its sanctifying tendency and effect. Predestination must be a divine verity, since it stands essen-

* Eph. i. 4.   † Acts xiii. 48.   ‡ 1 Thess. i. 4.
§ 2 Thess. ii. 13.   ‖ Rev. xvi. 8.   ¶ 2 Tim. i. 9.
** 1 Pet. i. 2.   †† Matt. xxv. 34.

tially connected with our conformity to the Divine image. "Predestinated to be conformed to the image of his Son." Addressing ourselves to this deeply interesting and important branch of our subject, let us first contemplate the believer's model.

"The image of his Son." No standard short of this will meet the case. How conspicuous appears the wisdom and how glorious the goodness of God in this—that in making us holy, the model or standard of that holiness should be Deity itself! God would make us holy, and in doing so he would make us like himself. But with what pencil—dipped though it were in heaven's brightest hues—can we portray the image of Jesus? The perfection of our Lord was the perfection of holiness. His Deity, essential holiness—his humanity without sin, the impersonation of holiness, all that he was, and said, and did, was as coruscations of holiness emanating from the Fountain of essential purity, and kindling their dazzling and undying radiance around each step he trod. How lowly, too, his character! How holy the thoughts he breathed, how pure the words he spake, how humble the spirit he exemplified, how tender and sympathizing the outgoings of his compassion and love to man!—"the chief among ten thousand, the altogether lovely." Such is the believer's model. To this he is predestinated to be conformed. And is not this predestination in its highest form? Would it seem possible for God to have preordained us to a greater blessing, to have chosen us to a higher distinction? In choosing us in Christ before the foundation of the world, that we should be holy, he has advanced us to the loftiest degree of honour and happiness to which a creature can be promoted—assimilation to his own moral image. And this forms the highest ambition of the believer. To transcribe those beauteous lineaments which, in such perfect harmony and beautiful expression, blended and shone in the life of Jesus, is the great study of all his true disciples. But in what does this conformity consist? The first feature is, a conformity of *nature*. And this is reciprocal. The Son of God, by an act of divine power, became human;—the saints of God, by an act of sovereign grace, become divine. " Partakers of the divine nature." This harmony of nature forms the basis of all conformity. Thus grafted into Christ, we grow up into him in all holy resemblance. The meekness, the holiness, the patience, the self-denial, the zeal, the love, traceable —faint and imperfect indeed—in us, are transfers of Christ's beauteous and faultless lineaments to our renewed soul. Thus the mind that was in him is in some measure in us. And in our moral conflict, battling as we do with sin, and Satan, and the world, we come to know a little of fellowship with his sufferings, and conformity to his death. We are here supplied with a test of Christian character. It is an anxious question with many professors of Christ, " How may I arrive at a correct conclusion that I am amongst the predestinated of God?—that I am included in his purpose of grace and love?—that I have an interest in the Lord's salvation?" The passage under consideration supplies the answer— conformity to the image of God's Son. Nothing short of this can justify the belief that we are saved. No evidence less strong can authenticate the fact of our predestination. The determination of God to save men is not so fixed as to save them be their character what it may. Christ's work is a salvation *from* sin, not *in* sin. "According as he hath chosen us in him before the foundation of the world, *that we should be holy*."* In other words, that we should be conformed to the Divine image. That we should be like Christ—like Christ in his Divine nature— like Christ in the purity of his human nature —like Christ in the humility he exemplified, in the self-denial he practised, in the heavenly life he lived. In a word, in all that this expressive sentence comprehends,—"conformed to the image of his Son." And as we grow day by day more holy, more spiritually minded, more closely resembling Jesus, we are placing the truth of our predestination to eternal life in a clearer, stronger light, and consequently the fact of our salvation beyond a misgiving and a doubt. In view of this precious truth, what spiritual heart will not breathe the prayer, "O Lord! I cannot be satisfied merely to profess and call myself thine. I want more of the power of vital religion in my soul. I pant for thine image. My deepest grief springs

* Eph. i. 4.

from the discovery of the little real resemblance which I bear to a model so peerless, so divine,—that I exemplify so little of thy patience in suffering; thy meekness in opposition; thy forgiving spirit in injury; thy gentleness in reproving; thy firmness in temptation; thy singleness of eye in all that I do. Oh, transfer thyself wholly to me. What were this world, yea, what were heaven itself, without thee? A universe of creatures, the fondest, the holiest, could not be thy substitute to my yearning, longing soul, O Lord! Come, and occupy thine own place in my heart. Wake it to thy love. Sweep thou its chords with thy gentle hand, and it shall breathe sweet music to thy dear name."

> "I love thee, Saviour, for my soul craves joy!
> I want Thee, without hope I cannot live!
> I look for thee; my nature pants to give
> Its every power a rapture and employ;
> And there are things which I would fain destroy
> Within my bosom; things that make me grieve;
> Sin, and her child, Distrust, that often weave
> About my spirit darkness and annoy:
> And none but Thou canst these dissolve in light;
> And so I long for Thee, as those who stay
> In the deep waters long for dawning day!
> Nor would I only have my being bright,
> But peaceful, too: so ask Thee if I might
> My head on Thy dear bosom lean alway."*

"That he might be the firstborn among many brethren." The Son of God sustains to us the relation of the Elder Brother. He is emphatically the

---

* Townshend.

"Firstborn." In another place we read, "Forasmuch then as the children are partakers of flesh and blood, he also likewise took part of the same." He is the "Brother born for adversity." Our relation to him as our Brother, is evidenced by our conformity to him as our Model. We have no valid claim to relationship which springs not from a resemblance to his image. The features may be indistinctly visible, yet one line of holiness, one true lineament, drawn upon the heart by the Holy Ghost, proves our fraternal relationship to him, the "Firstborn." And how large the brotherhood!—"many brethren." What the relative proportion of the church is to the world,—how many will be saved, —is a question speculative and profitless. But this we know,—the number will be vast, countless. The one family of God is composed of "*many* brethren." They are not all of the same judgment in all matters, but they are all of the same spirit. The unity of the family of God is not ecclesiastical, nor geographical; it is spiritual and essential. It is the "unity of the Spirit." Begotten of one Father, in the nature of the Elder Brother, and through the regenerating grace of the one Spirit, all the saints of God constitute one church, one family, one brotherhood—essentially and indivisibly one. Nor is this relationship difficult to recognise. Take an illustration. Two brethren in the Lord of widely different sections of the church, and of much dissonance of sentiment on some points of truth, meet and converse together. Each wonders that, with the Word of God in his hand, the other should not read it as he reads it, and interpret it as he interprets it. But they drop the points of difference, and take up the points of agreement. They speak of Christ —the Christ who loves them both, and whom they both love. They talk of the one Master whom they serve; of their common labours, and infirmities, and trials, and temptations, and discouragements, and failures, and success; they talk of the heaven whither they are journeying; of their Father's house, in which they will dwell together for ever; they kneel in prayer; they cast themselves before the cross; the oil of gladness anoints them; their hearts are broken, their spirits are humbled, their souls are blended; they rise, and feel more deeply and more strongly than ever, that they both belong to the same family, are both of the "many brethren," of whom the Son of God is the "Firstborn," the Elder Brother. Oh, blessed unity! What perfect harmony of creed, what strict conformity of ritual, what sameness of denominational relation, is for a moment to be compared with this? Have you, my reader, this evidence that you belong to the "many brethren?"

We purpose concluding this chapter by briefly showing how encouraging is the doctrine it teaches to the soul in sincere and earnest seeking of Christ, and by tracing some of the peculiar blessings which flow from it to the saints of God. There is a class of individuals, unhappily a large one, over whose spiritual feelings the doctrine of Divine predestination would seem to have cast a deep and settled gloom. We refer to those who are wont to regard this truth with deep antipathy, if not with absolute horror, as constituting, in their view, one of the most formidable and insurmountable obstacles to their salvation. But the validity of this objection we by no means admit. There can be nothing in the Bible adverse to the salvation of a sinner. The doctrine of predestination is a revealed doctrine of the Bible; therefore, predestination cannot be opposed to the salvation of the sinner. So far from this being true, we hesitate not most strongly and emphatically to affirm, that we know of no doctrine of God's Word more replete with encouragement to the awakened, sin-burdened, Christ-seeking soul than this. What stronger evidence can we have of our election of God than the Spirit's work in the heart? Are you really in earnest for the salvation of your soul? Do you feel the plague of sin? Are you sensible of the condemnation of the law? Do you come under the denomination of the "weary and heavy laden?" If so, then the fact that you are a subject of the Divine drawings—that you have a felt conviction of your sinfulness—and that you are looking wishfully for a place of refuge, affords the strongest ground for believing that you are one of those whom God has predestinated to eternal life. The very work thus begun, is the Spirit's first outline of the Divine image upon your soul—that very image to which the saints are predestinated to be conformed. But whilst we thus vindicate this doctrine as being inimical to the salvation of the anxious soul, we must, with all distinctness and earnestness declare, that in this stage of your Christian course, you have primarily and mainly to do with another and a different doctrine. We refer to the doctrine of the Atonement. Could you look into the book of the Divine decrees, and read your name inscribed upon its pages, it would not impart the joy and peace which one believing view of Christ crucified will convey. It is not essential to your salvation that you believe in election; but it *is* essential to your salvation that you believe in the Lord Jesus Christ. In your case, as an individual debating the momentous question how a sinner may be justified before God, your first business is with Christ, and Christ exclusively. You are to feel that you are a lost sinner, not that you are an elect saint. The doctrine which meets the present phase of your spiritual condition is, not the doctrine of predestination, but the doctrine of an atoning Saviour. The truth to which you are to give the first consideration, and the most simple and unquestioning credence is, that " Christ died for the ungodly,"— that he came into the world to save sinners,—that he came to call, not the righteous but sinners to repentance,—that in all respects, in the great business of our salvation, he stands to us in the relation of a

Saviour, while we stand before him in the character of a sinner. The mental conflict into which you have been brought touching this doctrine, is but a subtle and dexterous stroke of the enemy to divert your thoughts from Christ. Your soul is at this moment in what may be termed a transition state. A crisis in your history has been reached. How momentous the result! Shall we portray your present feelings? You are sensible of your sinfulness; are oppressed by its guilt, and are in dread of its condemnation. You have no peace of mind, no joy of heart, no hope of heaven. Life with you has lost its charm, society its attractions, and pleasure its sweetness. A sombre hue paints every object, and insipidity marks every engagement. Whence this marvellous revolution? this essential and wondrous change? We answer, it is the Spirit of God moving upon your soul. And what truth, think you, meets the case? Predestination? Election? Oh, no! These are hidden links in the great chain of your salvation, upon which in your present state, you are not called to lay your hand in grasping that chain. But there are other and intermediate links, visible, near, and within your reach. Take hold of them, and you are saved; " This is a faithful saying, and worthy of all acceptation, that Christ Jesus came into the world to save sinners." " God so loved the world that he gave his only begotten Son, that whosoever believeth in him should not perish, but have everlasting life." " The blood of Jesus Christ his Son cleanseth us from all sin." "Come unto me, all ye that labour and are heavy laden, and I will give you rest." "Him that cometh unto me I will in no wise cast out." "Whoever will, let him take of the water of life freely." "Being justified freely by his grace through the redemption that is in Christ Jesus." "Ho, every one that thirsteth, come ye to the waters." "In whom we have redemption through his blood, the forgiveness of sins, according to the riches of his grace." "By grace are ye saved, through faith, and that not of yourselves, it is the gift of God." "Wherefore he is able to save them to the uttermost that come unto God by him." "Believe in the Lord Jesus Christ, and thou shalt be saved." Grasp, in simple faith, each or any one of these golden links, and from that moment for you there is no condemnation. But what is the real difficulty? It is not predestination. Travel into the inmost recesses of your heart and ascertain. May there not be some defect in your actual conviction of sin? Were you thoroughly convinced of your lost and ruined condition as a sinner, would you cavil and demur at any one revealed doctrine of Scripture? Would this, of all doctrines, prove a real stumblingblock in your way? Would the question of election give you a moment's serious thought? Would it interpose a true and valid objection to your coming to Christ to be saved by him? Suppose, to illustrate the idea, you were roused from sleep in the dead hour of night by the approach of flames kindling fiercely around you. One avenue of escape presented itself. Would you pause for an instant upon its threshold to debate the question of your predestinated safety? Would you not at once decide the question in your favour, by an instant retreat from the devouring element, through the only door that proffered you deliverance? Most assuredly. To a matter so momentous as your salvation apply the same reasoning. Were it not folly, yea, insanity itself, to hesitate for a moment to consider whether you are predestinated to escape the wrath to come, when, if you do not escape, that wrath will assuredly overwhelm you? One refuge alone presents itself. One avenue only invites your escape. Let no other doctrine but faith in the Lord Jesus Christ occupy your thoughts at this juncture of your religious course. Diverging from this path, you will be plunged into a sea of perplexities, you know not how inextricable, which may land you, you know not where. For they who have

> "Reasoned high
> Of providence, foreknowledge, will, and fate,
> Fixed fate, freewill, foreknowledge absolute,
> Have found no end in wandering mazes lost."

O let one object fix your eye, and one theme fill your mind—Christ and his salvation. Absorbed in the contemplation and study of these two points, you may safely defer all further inquiry to another and a more advanced stage of your Christian course. Remember that the fact of your predestination, the certainty of your election, can only be inferred from your conversion. We must hold you firmly to this truth. It is the subtle and fatal reasoning of Satan, a species of atheistical fatalism, to argue, " If I am elected I shall be saved whether I am regenerated or not." The path to eternal woe is paved with arguments like this. Men have cajoled their souls with such vain excuses until they have found themselves beyond the region of hope! But we must rise to the fountain by pursuing the stream. Conversion and not predestination, is the end of the chain we are to grasp. We must ascend from ourselves to God, and not descend from God to ourselves in settling this great question. We must judge of God's objective purpose of love concerning us, by his subjective work of grace within us. One of the martyr reformers has wisely remarked, " We need not go about to trouble ourselves with curious questions of the predestination of God; but let us rather endeavour ourselves that we may be in Christ. For, when we be in him, then are we well: and then we may be sure that we are ordained to everlasting life. When you find these three things in your hearts, repentance, faith, and a desire to leave sin, then you may be sure your names are written in the book, and you may be sure also, that *you* are elected and predestinated to eternal life." Again he observes, " If thou art desiring to know whether thou art chosen to everlasting life, thou mayest not begin with God, for God is too high, thou canst not comprehend him. Begin with Christ, and learn to know Christ, and wherefore he came; namely, that he came to save sinners, and made himself subject to the law, and a fulfiller of the law, to deliver us from the wrath and danger thereof. If thou knowest Christ, then thou mayest know further of thy election." And illustrating his idea by his own personal experience, he says, "If I believe in Christ alone for salvation, I am certainly interested in Christ; and interested in Christ I could not be, if I were not chosen and elected of God." * In conclusion, we earnestly entreat you to lay aside all fruitless speculations, and to give yourself to prayer. Let reason bow to faith, and faith shut you up to Christ, and Christ be all in all to you. Once more we solemnly affirm that, CONVERSION, and *not* Predestination, is the doctrine with which, in your present state of inquiry, you have to do. Beware that you come not short of true conversion—a changed heart, and a renewed mind, so that you become "a new creature in Christ Jesus." And if as a poor lost sinner you repair to the Saviour, all vile, and guilty, and unworthy, and weak as you are, he will receive you, and shelter you within the bosom that bled on the cross to provide an atonement and an asylum for the very chief of sinners. Intermeddle not, therefore, with a state which you can only ascertain to be yours by the Spirit's work upon your heart. "Your election will be known by your interest in Christ; and your interest in Christ by the sanctification of the Spirit. Here is a chain of salvation; the beginning of it is from the Father; the dispensation

* Latimer.

of it through the Son; the application of it by the
Spirit. In looking after the comfort of election, you
must look inward to the work of the Spirit in your
heart; then outward to the work of Christ on the
cross; then upward to the heart of the Father in
heaven." Oh, let your prayer be—urged until that
prayer is answered in the assurance of full pardon
sealed upon your conscience by the Holy Ghost—
" God be merciful to me a sinner ! " Thus knocking
at mercy's door, the heart of God will fly open, and
admit you to all the hidden treasures of its love.*

We can but group some of the great blessings
which flow from this truth to the saints of God. The
doctrine of predestination is well calculated to confirm and strengthen the true believer in the fact and
certainty of his salvation through Christ. Feeling,
as he does, the plague of his own heart, experiencing
the preciousness of the Saviour, looking up through
the cross to God as his Father, exulting in a hope
that maketh not ashamed, and remembering that
God the Eternal Spirit only renews those who are
chosen by God the Father, and are redeemed by God
the Son, this doctrine is found to be most comforting
and confirming to his faith. The faintest lineaments
of resemblance to God, and the feeblest breathing of
the Spirit of adoption he discovers in his soul, is to
him an indisputable evidence of his predestination to

---

* The reader to whom this appeal is especially made, is re-
quested to read carefully, and with prayer, the succeeding chapter
of this volume.

Divine sonship and holiness.* Another blessing accruing from the doctrine, is the sweet and holy submission into which it brings the mind under all afflictive dispensations. Each step of his pilgrimage, and each incident of his history, the believer sees appointed in the everlasting covenant of grace. He recognises the discipline of the covenant to be as much a part of the original plan as any positive mercy that it contains. That all the hairs of his head are numbered; that affliction cometh not out of the earth, and therefore is not the result of accident or chance, but is in harmony with God's purposes of love; and, thus ordained and permitted, must work together for good;—not the least blessing resulting from this truth, is its tendency to promote personal godliness. The believer feels that God hath " chosen us to salvation through *sanctification* and belief of the truth;"† that he hath " chosen us *that we should be holy* and without blame before him in love ;"‡ that we are " his workmanship, created in Christ Jesus unto *good works,* which God hath before *ordained* that we should walk in them."§ Thus the believer desires to " give all diligence to make his calling and

* The Sixteenth Article of the Church of England thus appositely expresses the same idea: " The goodly consideration of Predestination and our election in Christ, is full of sweet, pleasant, and unspeakable comfort to godly persons, drawing up their minds to high and heavenly things; because it doth greatly establish and confirm their faith of eternal salvation to be enjoyed through Christ, fervently kindling their love towards God," &c.

† 2 Thess. ii. 13. ‡ Eph. i. 4. § Eph. ii. 10.

election sure," or undoubted, by walking in all the ordinances and commandments of the Lord blameless, and standing complete in all the will of God. And what doctrine more emptying, humbling, and therefore sanctifying, than this? It lays the axe at the root of all human boasting. In the light of this truth, the most holy believer sees that there is no difference between him and the vilest sinner that crawls the earth, but what the mere grace of God has made. Such are some of the many blessings flowing to the Christian from this truth. The radiance which it reflects upon the entire history of the child of God, and the calm repose which it diffuses over the mind in all the perplexing, painful, and mysterious events of that history, can only be understood by those whose hearts have fully received the doctrine. Whatever betides him—inexplicable in its character, enshrouded in the deepest gloom, as may be the circumstance— the believer in this truth can "stand still," and, calmly surveying the scene, exclaim: "This also cometh forth from the Lord of Hosts, who is wonderful in counsel, and excellent in working. He who worketh all things after the counsel of his own will hath done it, and I am satisfied that it is well done."

In conclusion—Saints of God, have close relations and intimate dealings with your Elder Brother. Repose in him your confidence, yield to him your affections, consecrate to him your service. He regards you with ineffable delight. With all your interests he is identified, and with all your sorrows he sympathizes. He may, like Joseph, at times speak roughly to his brethren, in the trying dispensatious of his providence; yet, like Joseph, he veils beneath that apparent harshness a brother's deep and yearning love. Seek a closer resemblance to his image, to which, ever remember, you are predestinated to be conformed. In order to this, study his beauty, his precepts, his example, that with "open face, beholding as in a glass the glory of the Lord, you may be changed into the same image, from glory to glory, even as by the Spirit of the Lord."

CHAPTER XXVII.

"Moreover whom he did predestinate, them he also called."

ROMANS viii. 30.

THE truth of God must necessarily be a perfect whole, a chain of doctrines in which not a single link is wanting to connect together the different parts binding and weaving them into a beautiful and harmonious system. To a mind not thoroughly skilled in the deep things of God, this chain may appear broken and incomplete, because to such an individual there may appear truths which are either irreconcileable or are invisible altogether. But this apparent discrepancy and invisibility of truth forms no real evidence of an actual want of continuity or harmony, any more than a chain thrown across the channel of a river would be regarded as broken and incomplete simply because some of its links were submerged beneath the stream, or its two extremes were invisible to the eye. A beautiful chain of truth is presented to our view in the present verse. The first and extreme link has already been examined.

The second, a sequence from the first, is now to engage our attention; the effectual vocation of those who are predestinated.

"Whom he predestinated, them he also CALLED." While we maintain that the vocation here referred to is a particular and effectual vocation, we yet as strenuously maintain that there is an external call lying at the door of every individual who hears the Gospel. Recognizing human responsibility, the Gospel meets man as a sinful and accountable being. It lifts up its voice in silver tones, and exclaims, "Unto you, O men, I call; and my voice is to the sons of men." When our Lord returned from his grave, he enlarged the commission of his apostles, and placed the call of the Gospel upon a broader basis. "Go ye into all the world, and preach the gospel to *every creature*." Thus to every creature the external call of the Gospel is to be addressed. Who will dare to limit and circumscribe what God has made as wide and boundless as man's moral necessity? "Many are called." Oh, it is a real and a solemn call, the call of the Gospel. He who hears it is brought beneath a responsibility the most tremendous. From its obligations nothing can ever release him. For every summons he has had to repent, to lay down his arms, to give up his enmity, to turn to the Lord, to believe in Christ, to escape from the wrath to come, he will be called to an account when all shall appear before the judgment seat of Christ. Dear reader, has the music of this call, breaking so sweetly and so solemnly upon your external ear, penetrated your soul, echoing through the chambers of your heart, and awaking a response of love, surrender, and obedience? Or,—solemn conclusion!—or, are you wilfully turning from the sound "like the deaf adder that stoppeth her ear; which will not hearken to the voice of charmers, charming never so wisely?"*

But the call here referred to is the especial call of the Gospel—the secret, effectual call which has found its way to the heart by the power of the Holy Ghost. The connexion of these two truths—an especial people, and an especial call—is thus conclusively shown—"And that he might make known the riches of his glory in the vessels of mercy, which he had afore prepared unto glory, even us, whom he hath called."† "Who hath saved us, and called us with an holy calling, not according to our works, but according to his own purpose and grace, which was given us in Christ Jesus, before the world began."‡ "Them that are sanctified by God the Father, and preserved in Christ Jesus, and called." § Honoured Church! Happy people! Called to be saints. Oh, to have the Divine testimony that we are amongst them!

But from what, and into what, are the Lord's people called? The Apostle answers—"That ye should show forth the praises of him who hath

* Psa. lviii. 4, 5.   † Rom. ix. 23, 24.   ‡ 2 Tim. i. 9.
§ Jude 1.

called you out of darkness into his marvellous light."* It is indeed "marvellous light;" and marvellous grace, that calls us out of a deeper than Egyptian darkness, to see and rejoice in the glory of God beaming in the face of Jesus Christ. We find it, too, a calling into liberty. "Brethren, ye have been called unto liberty."† Bond-slaves to sin and Satan, we become Christ's freemen, those whom his Spirit and truth have made free. It is also a call into fellowship. "God is faithful, by whom ye were called unto the fellowship of his Son Jesus Christ our Lord;"‡ called into a oneness with Christ, privileged to open the heart to him in all the confidence and affection of a child, while in return he reveals the secret of the Lord to us.

And what are some of the attributes of this calling? It is *holy*. "Who hath saved us, and called us with an *holy calling*."§ They who are the subjects of this call desire to be holy. Their direst evil is sin. It is, in their experience, not a silken chain, but a galling fetter, beneath whose weight they mourn, and from whose bondage they sigh to be delivered. It is a *high* and *heavenly* calling. "I press toward the mark for the prize of the high calling of God in Christ Jesus."‖ "Wherefore, holy brethren, partakers of the heavenly calling."¶ How does this calling elevate a man—his principles, his character, his aims, his hopes! It is emphatically

* 1 Pet. ii. 9. † Gal. v. 13. ‡ 1 Cor. i. 9.
§ 2 Tim. i. 9. ‖ Phil. iii. 14. ¶ Heb. iii. 1.

a "high vocation." So heavenly is it, too, it brings something of heaven into the soul. It imparts heavenly affections, heavenly joys, and heavenly aspirations. It leads to heaven. Could he look within the veil, each called saint would see a prepared mansion, a vacant throne, a jewelled crown, a robe, and a palm, all ready for the wearing and the waving, awaiting him in glory. Thus it is a call from heaven and to heaven. It is an *irrevocable* calling. "The gifts and calling of God are without repentance." God has never for a moment repented that he chose, nor has the Saviour repented that he redeemed, nor has the Spirit repented that he called, any of his people. Not all their wanderings, nor failures, nor unfruitfulness, has ever awakened one regret in the heart of God that he has called them to be saints. "I knew that thou wouldest deal treacherously." "He will visit their transgressions with his rod, and their iniquities with his stripes, but his lovingkindness he will not take from them, nor suffer his faithfulness to fail." "Faithful is he that calleth you."

Nor must we overlook the Divine sovereignty which appears so illustrious in this especial calling. All ground of human boasting is removed, and God has secured to himself, from eternity, the entire glory of his people's salvation. So conspicuously appears the sovereignty of God in this effectual calling, that all foundation of creature-glory is annihilated. And if it be asked by the disputers of this truth, why one is called and another is left? Why Jacob, and not Esau? Why David, and not Saul? Why Cornelius the Gentile, and not Tertullus the Jew? Why the poor beggars in the highway, and not the bidden guests? Why the woman who laved with her tears the Saviour's feet, and not Simon, in whose house the grateful act was performed? The answer is, "He will have mercy upon whom he will have mercy." To this acquiescence in the sovereignty of the Divine Will our Lord was brought when he beheld the mysteries of the Gospel veiled from the wise of this world: "I thank thee, O Father, Lord of heaven and earth, that thou hast hid these things from the wise and the prudent, and hast revealed them unto babes. Even so, Father, for so it seemeth good in thy sight." To this precious truth let us bow; and if the efficacious grace of God has reached our hearts, let us ascribe its discriminating choice to the sovereign pleasure of that Divine and supreme Will, which ruleth amongst the armies of heaven, and amongst the inhabitants of earth, and to which no creature dare say, "What doest thou?"

But let us pass for a moment to a more experimental and practical view of this subject.

The question has often been asked by the trembling lip, "How may I be assured of an interest in the eternal purpose and everlasting love of God? By what evidence may I conclude that I am one 'whom he predestinated?'" Listen to the words of the

Apostle, addressed to the Thessalonian saints—
"Knowing, brethren beloved, your election of God."*
But how did he know this? Had he read their
names in the Lamb's book of Life? No! See how
he solves the mystery: "For our Gospel came not
unto you in word only, but also in power, and in the
Holy Ghost, and in much assurance."† .By this he
knew their election of God. And by a similar test
you must bring the question to an issue. Has the
Gospel come to your heart by the Holy Ghost? In
other words, have you been called by the inward call?
Have you fled as a poor sinner to Christ, and is he
all your salvation and all your desire? Assume the
truth of nothing, take nothing for granted as to your
salvation, until this is the case. We recur to a
thought advanced in the preceding chapter, that it is
with the fact of your open call, and not with the fact
of your secret predestination, that you have mainly
to do. It is this central and visible link in the chain
that you must grasp. Secret things belong to God.
The things revealed belong to us. You are assuming
an attitude of the most appalling temerity in attempting to force your way into the secret counsels of the
Most High, plunging into the fathomless depths of a
past eternity, and intruding into those mysteries,
veiled and unsearchable, upon whose awful threshold
an angel's foot dare not tread. But oh, how near,
how visible, how precious, the truth with which you
have to do,—God standing in the most impressive

* 1 Thess. i. 4. † 1 Thess. i. 5.

and winning attitude of a gracious, sin-pardoning
God—inviting you, imploring you, all guilty, and burdened, and sorrowful as you are, to accept his mercy,
to avail yourself of his forgiveness, to believe in his
Son; and thus by grasping the outstretched hand, by
heeding the earnest call, and accepting the gracious
invitation, you may set for ever at rest the question of
your salvation.   Oh, let the great, the all-absorbing
question with you be, "What shall I do to be saved?"
Postpone every other question, adjourn every other
debate, until this is met and fairly settled, that you
are the *called* of God.   Take hold of the full and free
invitations of the Gospel—and Christ, and salvation,
and heaven are yours.

And for your encouragement we would say, that
the feeblest puttings forth of grace in the soul are indisputable evidences of the inward and effectual call
of the Spirit.   If in the spring-time I mark the
gentle buddings of the costly plant, I rejoice, yet
with trembling.   The cold wind may blow and the
hoar frost may light upon those buds, and so nip and
kill them that they shall never burst into the beautiful
and fragrant flower.   But when I trace the buddings
of grace in the heart of a poor sinner, when I descry
the evidence of the Spirit's operation in the soul, I
feel no misgiving, I cherish no fear, for I am assured
that He who hath begun the good work will carry it
on and perfect it in glory.   No worm shall kill its
root, no frosts shall nip its leaf, no winds shall scatter
its fruit, it shall never, *never* be destroyed.   God will

complete the work to which he puts his hand. Oh, precious truth, replete with encouragement to the sorrow-stricken, sin-burdened, Christ-seeking soul! Sweeter music is not heard in heaven than chimes in these words addressed to you—"Him that cometh unto me I will in no wise cast out."

Are we called? Then let us heed the earnest entreaty of the Apostle, "I therefore, the prisoner of the Lord, beseech you that ye *walk worthy* of the vocation wherewith ye are called."* Let the lowliest and the highest vocation of life be dignified and sanctified by the heavenly calling. Wherever you are, and in whatever engaged, forget not your high calling of God. You are called to be saints; called to a separation from the world; called to a hcly, heavenly life; called to live for God, to labour for Christ; and soon will be called to be with the Lord for ever!

* Eph. iv. 1.

CHAPTER XXVIII.

FREE JUSTIFICATION.

"And whom he called, them he also justified."

ROMANS viii. 30.

SUCH is the third link in this golden chain of heavenly truth. Those whom God appoints unto salvation, he as certainly calls by his effectual grace; and those whom he thus calls by his Spirit, he as certainly justifies through his Son. As we are not composing a treatise on the doctrine of Justification, we must assume it as divinely revealed, restricting ourselves, in the present instance, to a simple and brief presentation of the truth, as it forms an essential step in the believer's progress from condemnation to glory. "Whom he called, *them he also justified.*"

Of the *necessity* of justification, we need not speak at great length. If there is no condemnation where justification is attained, it follows that where there is not the condition of justification, the law must be left to take its full effect. But the very provision proves the necessity. Had it been possible for our fallen race to have recovered their former state of

holiness and consequent Divine acceptance by an
expedient of their own invention, think we that God
would have provided a way of justification so costly
or so stupendous as that which the Gospel reveals?
The utter incapacity of the sinner to justify himself,
left the way open for the display of God's infinite
wisdom, holiness, and grace. The theatre was prepared for the development of his great and grand
expedient of justifying the sinner, and yet remaining
truly, unbendingly, and unimpeachably just. But
not upon man's inability to justify himself rests alone
the necessity of a Divine method of justification, but
mainly upon the nature of God's moral government.
As a holy God, he can only consistently pardon and
justify upon the basis of a righteousness which fully
sustains the purity of his nature, the majesty of his
law, and the glory of his entire moral government.
Here are the two extremes of being—the holy, condemning Lord God, and the unholy and condemned
sinner. It is proposed that they should meet as upon
an equal footing, and that perfect reconciliation and
peace should eternally be established between them.
But upon what basis? Without a mediating plan,
how shall this be effected? God is under a most
free necessity to maintain the dignity of his throne,
the holiness of his nature, and the righteousness of
his law. Should he justify the sinner upon the ground
of mere mercy, apart from a full satisfaction to the
Divine government, what would become of his justice
and his holiness? and with what truth could it be

affirmed that "he is of purer eyes than to behold evil, and cannot (not will not, but *cannot*) look on iniquity?"* If, then, man is saved, if the sinner is justified, if the condemned is acquitted, it is most clear that it must be upon the basis of an atonement that should not compromise the righteousness of the Divine government, but should so harmonize all the attributes of God, so meet all the claims of justice and holiness and truth, as shall enable Mercy to walk upon the high battlements of his grace, waving her olive-branch of peace in view of a revolted and guilty world. Such an expedient has been devised, such a basis has been provided, such an atonement has been made. We now approach nearer to the subject before us.

The term is forensic—employed in judicial affairs, transacted in a court of judicature. We find an illustration of this in God's Word:—" If there be a controversy between men, and they come into judgment, that the judge may judge them, then they shall *justify* the righteous, and condemn the wicked."† It is clear from this passage that the word stands opposed to a state of condemnation, and in this sense it is employed in the text under consideration. To justify, in its proper and fullest sense, is to release from all condemnation. Now it is important that we do not mix up this doctrine, as the Church of Rome has done, with other and kindred doctrines. We must clearly distinguish it from that of sanctifi-

* Hab. i. 13.　　　† Deut. xxv. 1.

cation. Closely connected as they are, they yet
entirely differ. The one is a change of state, the
other a change of condition. By the one we pass
from guilt to righteousness, by the other we pass
from sin to holiness. In justification we are brought
near to God; in sanctification we are made like God.
The one places us before him in a condition of
non-condemnation; the other transforms us into his
image. Yet the Church of Rome blends the two
states together, and in her formularies teaches an
imputed sanctification, just as the Bible teaches an
imputed justification. It is to be distinguished, too,
from *pardon*. Justification is a higher act. By the
act of pardon we are saved from hell; but by the
decree of justification, we are brought to heaven.
The one discharges the soul from punishment; the
other places in its hand a title-deed to glory. But
the main question relates to the method of God's
justification. And this is a point of vital moment.

The Lord Jesus Christ is emphatically the justification of all the predestined and called people of God.
"By him all that believe are justified from all things."
"Being justified freely by his grace, through the
redemption that is in Christ Jesus." The antecedent
step was to place himself in the exact position of his
church. In order to do this, it was necessary that he
should be made under the law; for as the Son of
God, he was above the law, and could not therefore
be amenable to its precept. But when he became
the Son of man, it was as though the sovereign of a

vast empire had relinquished his regal character for the condition of the subject. He, who was superior to all law, by his mysterious incarnation placed himself under the law. He who was the King of Glory, became by his advent the meanest of subjects. "When the fulness of the time was come, God sent forth his Son, made of a woman, made under the law, to redeem them that were under the law." * What a stoop was this! What a descending of the Son of God from the height of his glory! The King of kings, the Lord of lords, consenting to be brought under his own law, a subject to himself, the law-Giver becoming the law-Fulfiller. Having thus humbled himself, he was prepared, as the sacrificial Lamb, to take up and bear away the sins of his people. The prophecy that predicted that he should " bear their iniquities," and that he should "justify many," received in him its literal and fullest accomplishment. Thus upon Jesus were laid all the iniquities, and with the iniquities the entire curse, and added to the curse, the full penalty belonging to the Church of God. This personal and close contact with sin affected not his moral nature ; for that was essentially sinless, and could receive no possible taint from his bearing our iniquity. He was accounted "accursed," even as was Israel's goat, when upon its head Aaron laid the sins of the people ; but as that imputation of sin could not render the animal to whom it was transferred morally guilty, though by the law treated as such, so the

* Gal. iv. 4. 5.

bearing of sin by Christ could not for a single instant compromise his personal sanctity. With what distinctness has the Spirit revealed, and with what strictness has he guarded, the perfect sinlessness of the atoning Saviour! "He hath made him to be sin for us, *who knew no sin,* that we might be made the righteousness of God in him." Oh, blessed declaration to those who not only see the sin that dwelleth in them, but who trace the defilement of sn in their holiest things, and who lean alone for pardon upon the sacrifice of the spotless Lamb of God! To them, how encouraging and consolatory the assurance that there is a sinless One who, coming between a holy God and their souls, is accepted in their stead, and in whom they are looked upon as righteous! And this is God's method of justification. By a change of place with the Church, Christ becomes the "Lord our Righteousness," and we are "made the righteousness of God in him." There is the transfer of sin to the innocent, and in return, there is the transfer of righteousness to the guilty. In this method of justification no violence whatever is done to the moral government of God. So far from a shade obscuring its glory, that glory beams forth with an effulgence which must have remained for ever veiled, but for the redemption of man by Christ. God never appears so like himself as when he sits in judgment upon the person of a sinner, and determines his standing before him upon the ground of that satisfaction to his law rendered by the Son of God in the room and stead of the guilty. Then does he appear infinitely holy, yet infinitely gracious; infinitely just, yet infinitely merciful. Love, as if it had long been panting for an outlet, now leaps forth and embraces the sinner; while justice, holiness, and truth gaze upon the wondrous spectacle with infinite complacence and delight. And shall we not pause and bestow a thought of admiration and gratitude upon him, who was constrained to stand in our place of degradation and woe, that we might stand in his place of righteousness and glory? What wondrous love! What stupendous grace! that he should have been willing to have taken upon him our sin, and curse, and woe. The exchange to him how humiliating! He could only raise us, by himself stooping. He could only emancipate us, by wearing our chain. He could only deliver us from death, by himself dying. He could only invest us with the spotless robe of his pure righteousness, by wrapping around himself the leprous mantle of our sin and curse. Oh, how precious ought he to be to every believing heart! What affection, what service, what sacrifice, what devotion, he deserves at our hands! Lord, incline my heart to yield itself supremely to thee!

But in what way does this great blessing of justification become ours? In other words, what is the instrument by which the sinner is justified? The answer is at hand. "Being justified freely by his grace, through the redemption which is in Christ Jesus: whom God hath set forth to be a propitiation

through faith in his blood."* Faith, and faith alone, makes this righteousness of God ours. " By him all that *believe* are justified." And why is it solely and exclusively by faith? The answer is again at hand: " Therefore it is of faith, that it might be by *grace*."†
Were justification through any other medium than by believing, then the perfect *freeness* of the blessing would not be secured. The expressions are, " Justified *freely* by his grace;" that is, gratuitously—absolutely for nothing. Not only was God in no sense whatever bound to justify the sinner; but the sovereignty ot his law, as well as the sovereignty of his love, alike demanded that, in extending to the sinner the greatest boon of his government, he should do so upon no other principle than as a perfect act of grace on the part of the Giver, and as a perfect gratuity on the part of the recipient—having " nothing to pay." Therefore, whatever is associated with faith in the matter of the sinner's justification—whether it be Baptism, or any other rite, or any work or condition performed by the creature—renders the act entirely void and of none effect. The justification of the believing sinner is as *free* as the God of love and grace can make it.

Yet more: Faith is not only the instrument by which we receive a free grace justification, but it harmonizes the outward act of God with the inward feelings of the believing heart. Thus in justification the heart of the Justifier and the heart of the

* Romans iii. 23, 24.   † Romans iv. 16.

justified beat in the most perfect and holy unison.
It is not a stupendous act on the part of God meeting no response on the part of man. Oh no! the
believer's heart flows out in gratitude after God's
heart, travelling towards him in the mightiness and
majesty of its saving love; and thus both meet in
Christ, the one Mediator between God and man.
Here the believer is conscious of a vital union with
his justifying Lord. He feels he is one with Christ.
The righteousness wrought out, is by faith wrought
in, and that faith is the uniting grace of a real,
personal union between the justified soul, and a
risen, living Saviour. " He that is joined to the
Lord is one Spirit." Oh close and blessed union!
Justified by God, accepted in Christ, condemnation
there cannot be. I stand in the Divine presence as
Joshua stood before the Lord, or as the woman stood
before the Saviour, charged, accused, guilty; but I
am in the presence of him who, though now he sits
upon the throne as my Judge, once hung upon the
cross as my Saviour. And, investing me with his
own spotless robe, he proceeds to pronounce the sentence—" No CONDEMNATION !" " These things write
I unto you that your *joy* may be *full.*"

In conclusion, while this subject, as we thus see,
lays the basis of the deepest joy, it is equally pro-
motive of the highest *holiness*. Some have thought
that a link were wanting in the chain of truth we are
contemplating, because no specific mention is made of

sanctification. But this is not really the case. The apostle does not deem it necessary to say that, he "whom God justifies he also *sanctifies*," simply because in the preceding verse he had already in the strongest manner affirmed that God's people were predestinated to be conformed to the image of his Son. And what were this but the very highest order of sanctification? No sinner can be pardoned and justified without the implantation in his soul by the Holy Spirit of the germ of holiness; so that the "path of the just is as the shining light, that shineth more and more unto the perfect day." Fully and freely, and for ever justified, oh, how powerful the motive to yield ourselves unto God! "I beseech you therefore, brethren, by the mercies of God, that ye present your bodies a living sacrifice, holy, acceptable unto God, which is your reasonable service."

We must learn to discriminate between our justified state, and the existence of indwelling sin. The one does not necessarily involve the present annihilation of the other. And by not clearly discerning the difference, many of God's people are exposed to great distress of mind. Let us, to illustrate the case, suppose an act of free pardon transmitted from the sovereign to a condemned criminal, slowly sinking beneath the ravages of a fatal disease. He passes out of his cell, delivered indeed from a humiliating and painful death, but bearing with him a hidden worm that feeds at the very root of the vital principle. Thus is it with the justified. They have "no condemnation " written as with beams of light upon their tranquil brow. Yet they bear about within their souls a moral disease, which shall not cease to work and distress until they lay down the body of sin and death, and wake up perfected in the likeness of their Lord.

CHAPTER XXIX.

ETERNAL GLORIFICATION.

"And whom he justified them he also glorified."
ROMANS viii. 30.

SUCH is the last in the regular sequence of truths
which, in the unfolding of this verse, we have been
contemplating. It would appear that there are two
links in this marvellous chain,—the purpose of God,
and its final consummation; both so remote and invisible as to bring the mind to a calm, unquestioning
belief in certain doctrines of God's Word which may
more properly belong to the "*deep* things of God."
But whilst the two extremes of this chain of truths
must for the present be left invisibly locked in God's
hand, we have endeavoured to convince the perplexed
and inquiring reader that there are certain intermediate and visible links upon which, if he lay hold,
he shall be saved, though all the rest remains wrapt in
the profoundest mystery—like its Divine Author,
dwelling in lone and unapproachable grandeur. It
is not essential to our salvation, that we lift the veil
of that awful mystery, and penetrate the depths of a

past predestination, and a future glory; but it *is* essential to our salvation that we are called of God, and that by God we are justified. We may arrive at heaven without fathoming the awful profound of the one extreme, and with but twilight views of the magnificence spreading over all the other; but we cannot get to heaven without the Spirit's grace, and Christ's righteousness. Grasp in faith, and receive into your heart, these two central and essential truths, and they will by-and-by lift you into a sunnier region, where all the rest will stand forth, clear and transparent, bathed in the noontide splendour of heaven's own glory.

Before we show in what the future glorification of the saints will consist, and trace the influence of this truth upon the present life, it may be proper to speak of the *certainty* of the fact, that he who justifies his people will also assuredly glorify them. Final and eternal glorification is the grand end and consummation of all God's purposes of love towards his Church; and we may therefore expect that this truth should be revealed in his word with a distinctness and clearness commensurate with its importance and greatness. Nor will this expectation be disappointed,—for around no single fact of the Bible does there gather a larger accumulation of demonstrative evidence than that of the certain glorification of all who are " accepted in the Beloved."

We find some clear revealings of this truth in the Old Testament writings. To a comparatively obscure saint of God, yet honoured to be the parent of one of Israel's mightiest prophets—the mother of Samuel—a striking view of the saint's future exaltation was given: "He raiseth up the poor out of the dust, and lifteth up the beggar from the dunghill, to set them among princes, and *to make them inherit the throne of glory*."* See how this same truth beamed in upon the troubled mind of Asaph, diffusing over his perplexed and perturbed spirit, the lustre and serenity of a sunlight calmness: "Thou shalt guide me with thy counsel, and *afterwards receive me to glory*."† "Afterward—when life's storms are over, and its perils are passed, and its voyage is closed, and its work is finished—after having done and suffered thy holy will here on earth —thou wilt receive me to glory." Passing by other unfoldings of the future glory of the saints in the Old Testament, let us glance at a few proofs found in the writings of the New Testament. The apostle, referring to his own experience, says, "I endure all things for the elect's sakes, that they may obtain the salvation which is in Christ Jesus *with eternal glory*."‡ Thus clear is it, that the salvation secured to us by Christ is inseparable from future glory; so that he who is saved now, evidencing the truth of his salvation by his holy life, is saved for ever—"Salvation in Christ Jesus, *with* eternal glory." We find, too, that future glory is connected with present calling. "That they which are called might receive the promise of eternal inheritance."* Oh, what a high calling, then, is ours! Called to be saints now, and called to glory hereafter. Glory is also secured by our justification. "For if when we were enemies we were reconciled to God by the death of his Son, much more being reconciled, we shall be saved by his life."† But the inferential evidence of the certain glorification of the saints is not less conclusive. Their union with the Lord Jesus secures it. "Christ in you, the *hope of glory*." "When Christ who is our life shall appear, then shall we also appear *with him in glory*." Christ dwelling in us is our heaven below, and to dwell with Christ will be our heaven above. And thus our vital union to Christ, secures our eternal glorification with Christ. If Christ is emphatically our life, then we must be where our life is. This, too, was his prayer. "Father, I will that they also, whom thou hast given me, be with me where I am; that they may *behold my glory*."‡ And what are the various tracings of the Spirit's work but the foreshadowings of the coming glory in the soul? "The Lord will give grace and glory." The two are inseparable. They are indeed essential parts of each other. Grace is the germ of glory, glory is the full-blown flower of grace. Grace is the first degree of glory—glory is the highest degree of grace. And what are the saints of God but the precious "vessels of mercy afore *prepared unto glory?*" Purified from all alloy, refined from all imperfection,

* Heb. ix. 15.	† Rom. v. 10.	‡ John xvii. 24.

those vessels of silver and gold are arranged, each in its appointed place, in the Father's house, filled to overflowing with its glory. The essential relation of *grace* and *glory* is one of the most animating and consolatory truths upon which the Christian mind can repose. Musing in mournful recollection of the loved ones who have gently broken from our embrace and disappeared within the parted veil, does the painful doubt at times cross the mind as to their safety? Do you wonder, as you yearn for a surer evidence, whether Christ was with them in the shadowy valley, and whether they are now with Christ in the regions of light and glory beyond it? See here the evidence. Did you discern the *faintest* dawn of heavenly light in the soul? Did you descry the *tenderest* buddings of grace in the heart? Did you mark any of the *first-fruits* of the Spirit as exhibited in the life? Was it a hand that tremblingly touched the border, an eye that dimly beheld the cross, a heart that mourned, and wept, and loved at the Saviour's feet? Then, sorrow not—they are safe in glory! The *least* measure of grace, the *smallest* degree of faith, will have brought them there. O yes! all whom God justifies, he glorifies. Once invested with the righteousness of Christ, they are robed for the wedding, and at the marriage-supper of the Lamb they shall most assuredly appear. And now, what are some of the elements of the future and eternal glory of the saints? On this subject there has been much vain speculation; but

there need not be, since the outline of heaven's
happiness and employments is so distinctly drawn in
the Word of God. To this outline let us briefly
refer.

The expansion and perfection of the intellectual
faculties will result in a consequent *enlargement and
perfection of knowledge.* This is no inferior element
of the future happiness of the redeemed. All that
is gracious and sanctifying in the soul of the believer
has its basis in a certain degree of spiritual knowledge. The mind is the medium through which the
first communications of the Spirit are received. A
knowledge of ourselves has led to a knowledge of
Christ; and a knowledge of Christ has laid the
foundation of all the joy, and peace, and hope, the
soul has experienced. And as our spiritual knowledge increases—the mind becoming more and more
informed in Divine truth—there is a corresponding
and proportioned increase of the blessing which an
experimental acquaintance with the truth yields.
Now, if this be so here, what must it be in the
glorified state? Think we not that it will greatly
augment the happiness and deepen the glory of the
saints in heaven, that in their enlarged mental
capacity, in the fullest development of their intellectual powers, they shall be enabled to take a
wider range of thought? That they shall compass a
greater knowledge of God, and see infinitely more of
the glory, and drink infinitely deeper of the love, of
Christ, than the most exalted angel in heaven?

What, if in the present school of God—often the school of deep trial—as we advance from truth to truth, knowing more of Jesus, and increasing in the knowledge of God, we grow more holy and more happy; our peace flowing like a river, and our righteousness as the waves of the sea; our confidence in God strengthening, and our affections entwining more fondly and closely around the Saviour—What, we ask, will be the glory deepening around us when all the present obstructions and impediments to our advancement in spiritual knowledge are removed, and our intellectual faculties, then unclouded and un-fettered, expand their long-folded wings, and sweep an infinite circle of knowledge—knowing even as we are known? If our progress in spiritual knowledge is an accession to our happiness here, what hereafter will be the happiness rushing into our glorified souls through the medium of an enlarged mind, vast as its range of thought, and pure and transparent as the atmosphere in which it floats? Deem it not, then, O expectant of heaven, an inferior element of the glory that awaits you, that your intellectual enjoy-ment, perfect in its nature, shall ever be augmenting in its degree. "Then shall the righteous shine forth as the sun in the kingdom of their Father."

But a still higher element will be, *the perfect holiness* of the glorified. The very utterance of the thought seems to awaken music in the soul. Seeing Christ as he is, and knowing him as we are known, we also shall be *like* him. Perfected in holiness! Oh, what a conception! what a thought! No more elements of evil working like leaven in the soul. No more traces and fetters of corruption. No more evil heart of unbelief, perpetually departing from God. No more desperate depravity. No more sin warring within, and no more temptation assailing from without. All is perfect holiness now! The outline of the Divine image is complete, for the believer has awakened in the finished likeness of his Lord. The spirit of the just man is made perfect. Oh, is there not enough in this anticipation to make us long to be there? What now shades your spirit, and embitters your joy, and suffuses your eyes with tears, and inflicts the keenest pang? Not adversity, nor sickness, nor changed affection, nor blighted hopes, nor the shaded landscape of life, nor the hollow falling of the earth as the grave closes from your view the heart's fond treasure. Oh, no, not these! *It is the sin that dwelleth in us!* Extirpate all sin, and you have erased all sorrow. Complete the grace, and you have perfected the glory. You then have chased all sadness from the heart, and have dried all tears from the eye. That glory will be the glory of unsullied purity. Nothing of sin remains save its recollection, and that recollection but heightens our conception of the preciousness of the blood that shall have effaced every stain, and of the greatness and sovereignty of that grace which shall have brought us there. " Let the saints be joyful in glory," for their battle with sin is over. " These are they which follow the Lamb whithersoever he goeth. These were redeemed from among men, being the firstfruits unto God and to the Lamb. And in their mouth was found no guile: for they are *without fault* before the throne of God."*

The absence of all evil will be another feature of the coming glory. Take the long catalogue of ills we suffer here—the cares that corrode, the anxieties that agitate, the sorrows that depress, the bereavements that wound, the diseases that waste, the temptations that assail—in a word, whatever pains a sensitive mind, or wounds a confiding spirit; the rudeness of some, the coldness of others, the unfaithfulness and heartlessness of yet more ; and as you trace the sad list, think of glory as the place where not one shall enter. All, *all* are entirely and eternally absent. "God shall wipe away all tears from their eyes ; and there shall be no more death, neither sorrow, nor crying, neither shall there be any more pain: *for the former things are passed away.*" †

The presence of all good will take the place of the absence of all evil. And in the foreground of this picture of glory we place the full, unclouded vision of Jesus. Oh, this is the Sun that will bathe all other objects in its beams. We see him now through faith's telescope, and how lovely does he appear ! Distant and dim as is the vision, yet so overpowering is its brightness as for a moment to eclipse every other object. How near he is brought to us, and how close we feel to him ! Encircled and absorbed by his presence, all other beings seem an intrusion, and all other joys an impertinence. Reposing upon his bosom, how sweetly sounds his voice, and how winning his language, " Oh, my dove, thou art in the clefts of the rock, in the secret places of the stairs: let me see thy countenance, let me hear thy voice; for sweet is thy voice, and thy countenance is comely." These are happy moments. But oh, how transient and how brief their stay! Some earthly vapour floats athwart our glass, and the bright and blissful vision is gone—veiled in clouds, it has disappeared from our view! But not lost is that vision. Not withdrawn is that Object. As stars that hide themselves awhile, then appear again in brighter, richer lustre, so will return each view we have had of Christ. The eye that has once caught a view of the Saviour shall never lose sight of him for ever. Long and dreary nights may intervene; the vision may tarry as though it would never come again, yet those nights shall pass away, and that vision shall return and " we shall see him as he is." And oh, if the distant and fitful glimpses of the glorified Christ are now so ravishing, what will the ecstatic and overpowering effect of the full unclouded vision be, when we shall see him face to face!

With this unveiled sight of the glorified Redeemer, will be associated the *certain reunion and perfected communion of all the glorified saints*. We are far from placing this feature of glory in an obscure corner of our picture of heavenly happiness. A source of so much pure and hallowed enjoyment now, surely will not be wanting, nor be less limited hereafter. It is a high enjoyment of earth—that of sanctified relationships and sacred friendships. The intercourse of renewed intellect, the union of genial minds, and the fellowship of fond and sympathizing hearts, God sometimes kindly vouchsafes, to smooth and brighten our rough and darksome path to the grave. And yet even were this all wanting, Jesus were enough to illumine the gloom, and people the solitude of the desert we traverse. But death interposes and sunders these precious ties. And are they sundered for ever? Oh, no! We shall meet again all from whom in faith and hope we parted—whom we loved in Jesus—and who in Jesus have fallen asleep. "For we believe that through the grace of our Lord Jesus Christ we shall be saved even as they." Heartbreaking as was the separation, it was not final, nor will it be long. The time-piece we wear upon our persons reminds us at each second that the period of our reunion is nearing. Yes! we shall meet them again in closer, fonder, purer friendship. They wait and watch our coming. Think not that they forget us: that cannot be. Thinking of us, they love us still. The affection they cherished for us here, death did not chill; they bore that affection with them from the earthly to the heavenly home, and now, purified and expanded, it glows and clings with an intensity unknown, unfelt before. Heavenly thought is immortal. Holy love never dies. Meeting, we

shall know them again; and knowing, we shall rush
into their warm embrace, and sever from them—
never! "I would not have you to be ignorant,
brethren, concerning them which are asleep, that ye
sorrow not, even as others which have no hope. For
if we believe that Jesus died and rose again, even so
them also which sleep in Jesus will God bring with
him." * Oh, what a soothing, sanctifying thought—
what a heaven-attracting hope is this! Applied to
the *holy* dead, how touching and how true the beautiful sentiments of the poet, himself now mingling
with the beings of the spirit-land:—

> " Is it not sweet to think hereafter,
>   When the spirit leaves this sphere,
>   Love, with deathless wings, shall waft her
>   To those she long hath mourned for here?
>
> " Hearts from which 'twas death to sever;
>   Eyes, this world can ne'er restore;
>   There, as warm, as bright as ever,
>   Shall meet us, and be lost no more!
>
> " When wearily we wander, asking
>   Of earth and heaven, where are they,
>   Beneath whose smile we once lay basking,
>   Blest, and thinking bliss would stay?
>
> " Hope still lifts her radiant finger,
>   Pointing to the eternal home,
>   Upon whose portal still they linger,
>   Looking back for us to come.
>
> " Alas, alas! doth hope deceive us—
>   Shall friendship, love, shall all those ties
>   That bind a moment, and then leave us,
>   Be found again where nothing dies?

* 1 Thess. iv. 13, 14.

" Oh, if no other hope were given,
  To keep our hearts from wrong or stain,
Who would not seek to reach a heaven,
  Where all we love shall live again ? "

We cannot consent to dismiss this contemplation
of the coming glory, without an allusion to the
Scripture teaching in reference to what has been
termed the *degrees of glory*. It is but little that
is said upon the subject, yet that little is interesting
and instructive; and we should remember that no
truth of God's mind, however obscurely revealed,
ought to be overlooked. The Apostle thus figuratively advances the idea, " One star *differeth* from
another star in glory." But in what will this
disproportion of glory consist? We cannot adopt
the idea of some, that it will be according to the
difference of gift; that the scale of heavenly happiness will be the measure of mental endowment; that
Newton, the great philosopher, for example, with his
gigantic intellect and vast resources, will necessarily
be more richly replenished with glory than another
of more limited acquirements and less mental capacity.
This would resolve the happiness of the heavenly
world mainly into the purely intellectual rather than
the purely spiritual, of which we believe it to consist.
If there are degrees of glory—and we see no reason
to question the fact—we believe that those degrees
will be graduated, not by the strength or capacity
of the intellect, but according to the measure and
standard of *holiness* which the believer attained in

this life. If, as we have shown, glory is the perfection of grace, then it follows, that proportioned to the degree of grace here, will be the degree of glory hereafter. It must be borne in mind that God is not merely an intellectual, he is also a spiritual Being. As an intellectual Being, the unfallen angels, creatures of mightier intellect than we, must be supposed to form the most lofty conceptions of his greatness and grandeur. But will it be supposed that an angel's mind can form such a conception of the Divine glory, as the recovered, renewed, and sanctified soul of fallen man? Will not that mind that has been brought into closer contact, and union, and sympathy with the will, the heart, and the perfections of God, know more of God, drink in deeper views of the glory of God, than the mind of the angel who in his study of redemption could but bend over the Mercy Seat, his wings encircled, desiring to look within its awful mysteries? If the great and grand perfection of God be his *holiness*, then the more clearly I approximate to that holiness, the more deeply must I partake of the glory of God, and the higher must be my degree of glory. It is acquaintance with, and conformity to, God's moral, and not his intellectual being, that will constitute the highest source of our happiness in heaven. That our enlarged intellectual capacity will be a vast inlet to expanded views of God, we do not dispute; but it will be the conformity of our moral nature to his that will constitute and augment our perceptions of glory.

If it be not thus, that the spiritual and not the
mental will form the standard of our happiness in
the glorified state, how is it that the astronomer
whose mind had been overwhelmed with the wisdom
and grandeur of God in creation, could descend
from his observatory with an oath upon his lips?
Yet such is known to have been the fact. Imágine
that mind suddenly transported to heaven, and
placed in the immediate and glorified presence of
that God whose works of nature it had been contemplating, and yet whose holy name it had pro-
faned;—if the argument be true that the amount
of glory will be proportioned to the mental capacity
of the glorified, then it follows that that 'undevout
astronomer' would be more capable, even with an
unrenewed intellect, of understanding and knowing
God than the unlettered Christian, whose intellect
was of the most dwarfish capacity, but who yet
spiritually knew God and Jesus Christ whom he had
sent. Were we asked to pass through the Church of
God, and from its various communions select the
individual whom we should regard as the richest heir
of glory, whose degree of happiness would, perhaps,
transcend that of the glorified philosopher, we should,
it may be, find him the inmate of some obscure hut,
dwelling amidst lonely poverty, sickness, and neglect;
and yet holding communion with God, so filial, so
endearing, and so close, as to present to our eye his
soul's uplifted and soaring pinions, " as the wings
of a dove covered with silver, and her feathers with

yellow gold." We should go to him whose heart
thus breathing after holiness, whose spirit thus im-
bibing more and more of the mind of Christ, who
in this lowly and suffering school was learning
more deeply of God, and what God is, and who
thus was gathering around him the beams of that
glory whose unclouded visions were so soon to burst
upon his view,—and we would unhesitatingly point
to him as the man whose degree of glory will be
transcendently great—grace enriching and encircling
him with more glory than gift. Do you, my reader,
desire to be a star of the first magnitude and lustre
in heaven? then aim after a high degree of grace
on earth. "There is not," says the Saviour, "a
greater than John the Baptist; notwithstanding, he
that is least in the kingdom of heaven is greater than
he." The nearer your present walk with God, the
nearer will be your future proximity to God. The
closer your resemblance to Christ, the deeper your
holiness, the more spiritual and heavenly-minded
you become on earth, be assured of this, the higher
and the more resplendent will be your glory in
heaven. As the ungodly man is treasuring up wrath
against the day of wrath, and is growing more and
more meet for hell—so the godly man is laying up
glory against the day of glory, and is growing more
and more meet for heaven. We need not speculate
and surmise about the future. Let the child of
God be careful as to his degrees towards meetness
for glory, and he may calmly and safely leave his

degrees of glory to the period when that glory shall be revealed.

But we must not overlook, in this outline of the coming glory, the *glorified body* of the saints. The first resurrection will give back this 'vile body' so changed that it shall be 'fashioned like unto Christ's glorious body.' We have two examples of what this "glorious body" of our Lord is. The first was at his transfiguration, when the "fashion of his countenance was altered, and his face did shine as the sun, and his raiment was white as the light." The second was when he appeared to John, in Patmos, arrayed in such glory that the apostle says, "When I saw him I fell at his feet as dead." Fashioned like unto Christ's glorious body will be the glorified bodies of the saints. No deformity, no wrinkle, no defect whatever, shall mar its beauty. "It is sown in corruption; it is raised in incorruption: it is sown in dishonour; it is raised in glory: it is sown in weakness; it is raised in power: it is sown a natural body; it is raised a spiritual body. And as we have borne the image of the earthy, we shall also bear the image of the heavenly."* "We shall be like him, for we shall see him as he is."

What, in conclusion, ought to be the practical influence of this animating subject? Should it not, in the first place, urge us with all diligence to "make our calling and election sure?" With all affectionate earnestness, we would exhort the reader to seek to be

* 1 Cor. xv. 42, 43, 44, 49.

assured of his standing in Christ. Are you called?
Are you justified? Do you know that God loves
you? Has the great change taken place? Have you,
in a word, passed from death unto life? Postpone
not these questions to a dying bed. Answer them
now.

And is not the anticipation of the coming glory
most sanctifying? Ought it not to have so powerful
an influence upon our minds as to lessen the value of
the things that are seen and temporal, and enhance
the value of those things which are unseen and
eternal? We are at present in a state of nonage—
children under tutors and governors. But ere long
we shall attain our full age, and shall be put in
possession of our inheritance. And because we are
children, we are apt to think as children, and speak
as children, and act as children—magnifying things
that are really small, while diminishing those that are
really great. Oh, how little, mean, and despicable
will, by-and-by, appear the things that now awaken
so much thought, and create so much interest!
Present sorrows and joys, hopes and disappointments, gains and losses—will all have passed away,
leaving not a ripple upon the ocean they once agitated,
nor a footprint upon the sands they once traversed.
"Men forget what they were in their youth, or at
best only partially remember it; it is hard even for
those whose memories are strongest and liveliest to
put themselves exactly into the same position in
which they stood as boys; they can scarcely fancy

that there was once a time when they cared so much for pleasures and troubles which now seem so trifling. And it may be, that if we rise hereafter to angels' stature; if wisdom be ours such as we dream not of; if being counted worthy to know God as he is, the poorness of all created pleasures shall be revealed to us, flashing upon our uncreated spirits like light—it may be that we shall then feel it as hard to fancy how we could have cared for what we now deem most important; how twenty years, more or less, taken from this span of our earthly life; how being parted for a few years, more or less, from those dear friends with whom we are now united for ever—how this could have seemed of any importance to beings born for immortality. It is quite reasonable to suppose that the interests of manhood will hereafter appear to us just as insignificant, I ought rather to say ten thousand times more so, than the interests of our boyish years seem to us now."* Why, then, allow our white garments to trail upon the earth? If glory is before us, and so near, why so slow in our advance to meet it? Why so little of its present possession in our souls? Why do we allow the "bright and Morning Star" to sink so often below the horizon of our faith? Why, my soul, so slow to arrive at heaven, with heaven so full in view? Oh, to press our pillow at night, composed to slumber with this sweet reflection —" Lord, if I open my eyes no more upon the rising sun, I shall open them upon that risen sun that never

* Arnold.

sets—awaking in thy likeness." Oh, to be looking
for, and hastening unto, the coming of the Lord,
that blessed hope, that glorious epiphany of the
church, which shall complete, perfect, and consummate the glorification of the saints.

How should the prospect of certain glory stimulate
us to individual exertion for Christ! What a motive
to labour! With a whole eternity of rest, how little
should we think of present toil and fatigue for the
Saviour! Shall we, then, be indolent in our Master's
cause? Shall we, in selfishness, wrap our graces as a
mantle around us, and indolently bury our talents in
the earth? Shall we withhold our property from the
Lord, complaining that the calls of Christian benevolence are so many, the demands so pressing, and the
objects so numerous? Oh, no! It cannot, it must
not be. Let us live for Christ—labour for Christ—
suffer for Christ—and, if needs be, die for Christ—
since we shall, ere long and for ever, be glorified
with Christ. And who can paint that glory? "So
much as moments are exceeded by eternity, and the
sighing of a man by the joys of an angel, and a
salutary frown by the light of God's countenance,
a few frowns by the infinite and eternal hallelujahs,
so much are the sorrows of the godly to be under-
valued in respect of what is deposited for them in
the treasures of eternity. Their sorrows can die;
but so cannot their joys. And if the blessed martyrs and confessors were asked concerning their past
sufferings and their present rest, and the joys of

their certain expectation, you should hear them glory in nothing but in the mercies of God, and in the cross of the Lord Jesus. Every chain is a ray of light, and every prison is a palace, and every loss is the purchase of a kingdom, and every affront in the cause of God is an eternal honour, and every day of sorrow is a thousand years of comfort, multiplied with a never-ceasing numeration—days without nights, joys without sorrow, sanctity without sin, charity without stain, possession without fear, society without envyings, communication of joys without lessening; and they shall dwell in a blessed country, where an enemy never entered, and from whence a friend never went away."*

* Jeremy Taylor.

CHAPTER XXX.

GOD IS FOR US.

" What shall we then say to these things ? If God be for us, who
can be against us ?"—ROMANS viii. 31.

THE Apostle had concluded the sublime argument
which, with so much consecutiveness of reasoning,
and power of language, he had been pursuing. And
now he comes to the inference logically deducible
from the whole. "What shall we say to these things ?
To what conclusion shall we arrive, touching the
power of the gospel to succour and console us in all
our assaults and sufferings?" Then, proceeding to
answer his own question, he resolves the blessed results of the entire argument into a single, animating,
and comprehensive one—GOD IS FOR US! "If God
be for us, who can be against us?" The question
supposes the existence of a combined and powerful
hostility to the Christian. Let this, briefly, be our
first point of consideration.

To establish this fact, no lengthened proof is necessary. The Bible declares it—observation confirms it

—and experience demonstrates it. There is, in fact, no possible form of evil — no machinations of the power of darkness—not a single one of the noxious principles indigenous to our fallen nature, which is not in direct and deadly antagonism to the best interests of the child of God. The believer may be compared to an individual who has thrown off allegiance to his king, has disowned his country, and refuses obedience to its laws, yet continues to dwell in the land he has renounced, and hard by the sovereign he has forsworn. The grace of God has called us out of the world; yet the providence of God has sent us into the world. We may, therefore, expect nothing but hostility from the god of this world, and hatred from the world itself. From these two sources, as from another, to which we may presently advert, strong opposition proceeds. There is much of mystery connected with the subject of satanic agency which we may never entirely comprehend. With a power and a ubiquity differing from Divine omnipotence and omnipresence in nothing but their reality, he sways a fearful sceptre; and is everywhere, and at the same moment, accurately acquainted with every circumstance of our history, and, it would appear, with each hidden thought of the human heart. Satan is against us. All his force —all his wisdom—all his malice—all his subtlety and skill—and all his myrmidons, are exerted and marshalled in tremendous opposition to the interests of the child of God. Let the histories of David, and

Job, and Joshua, and Paul, yea, of our Lord himself,
testify to the truth of this. The *world*, too, is against
us. It will never forgive the act by which we broke
from its thraldom, renounced its sway, relinquished
its pleasures, and resigned its friendship. Nor can
it forget that the godly, self-denying, unearthly life
of the Christian, is a constant and solemn rebuke of
its worldliness, its irreligion, and its folly: "Ye are
not of the world, therefore the world hateth you."
Sometimes veiling its opposition and concealing its
malignity beneath smiles and flattery, it seeks to
win back the votary it has lost. And when this effort
proves unavailing, it changes its course, and, with
venomed tongue, and sleepless zeal, and malignant
hatred, seeks, by detraction and falsehood, to malign,
and wound, and injure the sons of God. How
touching the words of Jesus addressed to each disciple—"If the world hate you, ye know that it hated
me before it hated you. If ye were of the world,
the world would love his own; but because ye are
not of the world, but I have chosen you out of the
world, therefore the world hateth you."* But there
is yet another source of opposition to the Christian.
We utter but a home truth and a self-evident one,
when we add to these forms of hostility—*that of our
own hearts!* And after all that we have said, our
most powerful and treacherous foe is this one which
we cherish in our bosom. Oh, yes! the sin that
dwelleth in us—"a heart deceitful above all things,

* John xv. 18, 19.

and desperately wicked "—the body of corruption and death which we bear about with us forms a source of opposition to our holiness and furtherance in the Divine life, as continuous and powerful, as it is humbling and distressing to our renewed nature. Truly, " we wrestle not against flesh and blood, but against principalities, against powers, against the rulers of the darkness of this world, against spiritual wickedness in high places." * With this mighty phalanx opposed to him, is it not a marvel that any child of God should ever maintain his stand, and at last arrive at heaven? But the wonder ceases when our eye lights upon these words, "If God be for us, who can be against us?" To this great and consoling truth let us now direct our attention.

We shall find, on examination, great prominence given to this fact—God on the side of the Christian —in his holy word. It was with this assurance that Jehovah calmed the fears and strengthened the faith of his servant Abraham. It was a period of intense anxiety with the patriarch. He had just achieved a signal victory in his battle with the kings, from whose power he had generously and valorously rescued his nephew, Lot. It was natural to expect that the nations whose armies he had defeated, and whose sovereigns he had slain, should collect their scattered forces, and, with renewed strength and a fresh onset, descend upon him with overwhelming force. Just at this juncture, when trouble was near,

* EPH. vi. 12.

all anxious, and fearful, and trembling as he was, God appeared to his servant, and soothed him with these words—"Fear not, Abram: *I am thy shield, and thy exceeding great reward."* And all that God was to Abram he is to all those who have like precious faith with him. Christian, assailed and fearful! JEHOVAH is thy "shield, and thy exceeding great reward." Then, fear not! I ask not what your trouble is, what form of opposition assails you. I meet you,—be your peril, be your trembling, be your anxiety, what it may,—with this fact, "If God be for us, who can be against us?" And God *is* for you! Oh, but believe it, and all shall be perfect peace! His Divine shield is ever around you, and before you can be injured, that shield itself must be broken. This, too, was the truth with which God stayed the faith of Isaac. "And the Lord appeared unto him by night, and said, I am the God of Abraham thy father: fear not, *for I am with thee.*"† To the godly children of Christian, perhaps glorified parents, how peculiarly appropriate and precious are these words! It is an argument and a plea of no little power with God when a tried and needy Christian is led to pray, "Thou wast the God of my parents, my father's God, faithful and loving. And since thou didst say to thy servant, 'I am the God of Abraham thy father, fear not,' I am emboldened in this time of necessity and fear to cast myself upon the same love, and faithfulness, and

* Gen. xv. 1.   † Gen. xxvi. 24.

power. 'Oh, turn unto me, and have mercy upon me; give thy strength unto thy servant, and save the son of thy handmaid.'" God's dealings with the prophet Elisha afford another striking illustration of the same precious truth, that he is on the side of his people. Alarmed at the overshadowing forces of the Syrian hosts, the servant of the prophet exclaims, "Alas, my master! how shall we do?" And he answered, "Fear not: for they that be with us are more than they that be with them." * Ah, yes! chariots of fire encircle every believer; and, best of all, the LORD is in his chariot, "riding upon the heavens in their help, and in his excellency on the sky." It was in view of this same truth that David encouraged himself. "The LORD is my light and my salvation; whom shall I fear? The LORD is the strength of my life; of whom shall I be afraid?" † And when God was about to send Jeremiah into his vineyard, what was the truth with which he strengthened his hesitating faith?—"Thou therefore gird up thy loins, and arise, and speak unto them all that I command thee . . . . they shall fight against thee, but they shall not prevail against thee; *for I am with thee,* saith the LORD, to deliver thee." ‡ And when Paul repaired to Corinth, and was met by much opposition and blasphemy in his mission of testifying to the Jews that Jesus was the Christ, it was with this same blessed assurance —God on the side of the Christian—that his faith

* 2 Kings vi. 15, 16.   † Psa. xxvii. 1.   ‡ Jer. i. 17, 19.

was strengthened and his spirit comforted. "Then spake the Lord to Paul in the night by a vision, Be not afraid, but speak, and hold not thy peace; *for I am with thee,* and no man shall set on thee to hurt thee." * It was the Lord Jesus, who, in all the tenderness of his love, thus appeared to soothe and animate his servant. And since he is the "same yesterday, to-day, and for ever," he is prepared to comfort our trembling hearts with the same blessed assurance—"I am with thee." And what were his last words to his Church, still vibrating on the ear, "Lo! *I am with you alway;* even unto the end!"

God must be on the side of his people, since he has, in an everlasting covenant, made himself over to be their God. In an especial manner, and in the highest degree, he is the God of his people. In the most comprehensive meaning of the words, he is *for us.* His love is for us—his perfections are for us—his covenant is for us—his government, extending over all the world, and his power over all flesh, is for us. There is nothing in God, nothing in his dealings, nothing in his providences, but what is on the side of his people. Enshrined in his heart, engraved on his hand, kept as the apple of his eye, God forms a mighty bulwark for his Church. "As the mountains are round about Jerusalem, so the Lord is round about his people from henceforth even for ever." In Christ Jesus, holiness, justice, and truth, unite with mercy, grace, and love, in weaving

* Acts xviii. 9, 10.

an invincible shield around each believer. There is not a purpose of his mind, nor a feeling of his heart, nor an event of his providence, nor an act of his government, that is not pledged to the happiness, and security, and well-being of his people. What Joshua said to the children of Israel, trembling to encounter the giants of Anak, may be truly said to every believer in view of his foes, " The Lord is with us, fear them not."

Not the Father only, but the *Son of God*, is also on our side. Has he not amply proved it? Who, when there was no eye to pity, and no arm to save, undertook our cause, and embarked all his grace and glory in our salvation? Who slew our great Goliath, and rescued us from Pharaoh, discharged our debt, and released us from prison? Who extinguished the fires of our hell, and kindled the glories of our heaven? Who did all this by the sacrifice of himself? Oh, it was Jesus! Need we further proof that he is for us? Who appears on our behalf within the veil? Who sits for us as a priest upon his throne? Whose blood, first shed on Calvary, now sprinkles the Mercy Seat? Who pleads, and argues, and intercedes, and prays for us in the high court of heaven? Whose human sympathy flows down in one continuous stream from that abode of glory, blending with our every trial, and suffering, and sorrow? Who is ever near to thwart our foes, and to pluck our feet from the snare of the fowler? Oh, it is Christ! And there is not a moment of time, nor a circumstance of life, in which he does not show himself strong in behalf of his people.

And so of the *Holy Spirit.* Who quickened us when we were dead in trespasses and in sins? Who taught us when we were ignorant, enlightened us when we were dark, comforted us when we were distressed; and when wounded, and bleeding, and ready to die, led us, all oppressed with guilt and sorrow as we were, to Jesus? Who inspired the first pulsation of life, and lighted the first spark of love, and created the first ray of hope, in our soul, and dried the first tear of godly grief from our eye? Oh, it was the Eternal Spirit, and he, too, is for us. Survey the record of your own history, dear reader. What a chequered life yours, perhaps, has been! How dotted the map of your journeyings, how many-coloured the stones that have paved your path, how varied and blended the hues that compose the picture of your life! And yet, God constructed that map, and God laid those stones, and God pencilled and painted that picture. God went before you, and God is with you, and God is for you. He was in the dark cloud that enshrouded all with gloom, and he was in the sunshine that gilded all with beauty. " I will sing of *mercy* and of *judgment :* unto thee, O Lord, will I sing." And who has carried forward the work of grace in our souls—checking our feet, restoring our wanderings, holding up our goings, raising us when we had fallen, and establishing our feet more firmly upon the rock? And who has befriended us when men rose up against us? Who has healed all our diseases, and has filled our mouths with good things, so that our youth has been renewed like the eagle's? It was the Lord who was on our side, and not one good thing of all that he has promised has failed.

It may, then, well be asked, "Who can be against us?" With such a Father, such a Friend, and such a Comforter, who can urge a successful hostility to the saints of God? God himself cannot be against us, even when the clouds of his providence appear the most louring, and his strokes are felt to be the most severe. "Though he slay me, yet will I trust in him." The law cannot be against him; for the Law-fulfiller has, by his obedience, magnified and made it honourable. Divine justice cannot be against us,—for Jesus has, in our stead, met its demands, and his resurrection is a full discharge of all its claims. Nor sin, nor Satan, nor men, nor suffering, nor death, can be really or successfully against us,—since the condemnation of sin is removed, and Satan is vanquished, and the ungodly are restrained, and suffering works for good, and the sting of death is taken away. "If God be for us, *who* can be against us?" With such a Being on our side, whom shall we fear? We will fear nothing but the disobedience that grieves, and the sin that offends him. Fearing this, we need fear nothing else. "God is our refuge and strength, a very present help in trouble. Therefore will not we fear." Listen once more to his wondrous words,

"Thou art my servant. I have called thee, and not cast thee away. Fear thou not; for I am with thee: be not dismayed; for I am thy God: I will strengthen thee; yea, I will help thee; yea, I will uphold thee with the right hand of my righteousness."*

The subject, if most consolatory to the Christian, is, in its converse, a solemn one to the *unregenerate*. It is an awful thing *not* to have God for us. And if God is not for us, there is no neutral course: he must be *against* us. And God is against you, my unconverted reader. So long as you are in an irreconciled state, not only God, but every creature of God, is at war with you. The whole creation is an armoury of destructive agencies to a soul out of Christ. All are messengers of death to a Christless sinner. Yes, God is *against* you! Mistake not the blessings of his providence for the smiles of his grace. The hand that prospers your worldly schemes, that drops its mercies so profusely around your path, yet holds its drawn sword of vengeance above your head. Not a night do you compose yourself to rest at peace with God through Christ Jesus. And are you prepared for the consequences? Have you thought of them, weighed them, deprecated them? Look at them now! When your sorrow comes—as come it will—God will mock; when your calamity approaches, he will laugh; when

* Isa. xli. 10.

you stretch forth your hand, he will withdraw his, so long stretched out to you in vain.* Who will then befriend you? Not an angel or a saint but will tune his harp to the holiness and the justice of your condemnation. Alas! there is no appeal from the decision of the Judge, there is no hiding-place from his indignation, no cessation of his wrath. "It is a fearful thing to fall into the hands of the living God." And yet that God loves sinners, gave his Son to die for sinners, is willing to receive sinners, and is gracious, full of compassion, and ready to forgive sinners. Let the goodness of God, then, lead you to repentance.

Would we always have God for us? then let us aim to be for God. God deals with us his creatures by an equitable rule. "The ways of the Lord are equal." "If you walk contrary unto me, then will I walk contrary unto you."† Is not God for you? Has he not always, since he manifested himself to you as your covenant God, been on your side? Has he ever been a wilderness to you, a land of darkness? Has he, in any instance, been unkind, unfriendly, unfaithful? Never. Then be for God,—decidedly, wholly, uncompromisingly for God. Your heart for God, your talents for God, your rank for God, your property for God, your influence for God, your *all* for God,—a holy, unreserved consecration to him, all whose love, all whose grace, all whose perfec-

* Prov. i. 24—31. † Lev. xxvi. 27, 28.

tions, all whose heaven of glory is for you. "Yield
yourselves unto God as those that are alive from
the dead." Trembling Christian! God is on your
side. And, "if God be for us, who can be against
us?"

CHAPTER XXXI.

THE GIFT OF GOD'S SON, THE GUARANTEE OF ALL OTHER BLESSING.

"He that spared not his own Son, but delivered him up for us all, how shall he not with him also freely give us all things?"

ROMANS viii. 32.

EACH successive application which the Apostle makes of the great doctrine he had been so ably discussing, serves but more fully to unfold the glory and sweetness of the truth. We can scarcely light upon a passage in this brilliant and consolatory chapter, so rich and comprehensive as the present. Our admiration is divided between the vastness of the truth it contains, and the exquisite grace and appropriateness with which it is introduced. It was just the truth needed to give repose and enlargement to the mind, after threading its way through the mazes—lucid, though profound—of God's predestinating purpose and plan. As if anticipating the cold, impassive view of God, which some might be disposed to cherish, Paul introduces a fact which would at once dispel the false conception, vindicate the Divine character, and exhibit it in all the glow and effulgence of its infinite benevolence and love. There can be nothing contracted or frigid in the disposition of that Being who, from the fathomless depths of his nature, gave so costly a proof of his love as his Son. He must be love, if this is the manifestation of love. You have, it may be, deemed him partial and cold—you have thought him distant and repelling—you have settled down with the crude and gloomy notion, that because your lot was unchangeably fixed, believe as you may, and act as you will, it is of little purpose; and thus all your thoughts and efforts after salvation have become impeded and paralyzed, and you have resigned yourself to sinful, sullen despair. But lo! a truth bursts upon your mind, developing a new idea, and presenting to your view a new portrait of God,—thus changing the whole current of your thoughts and feelings respecting him. "He that spared not his own Son, but delivered him up for us all." "What a wondrous declaration!" you exclaim; "this surely is not that Being whom my conceptions pictured to my view so frigid, contracted, and arbitrary. He spared not his own Son! Is this true? Then, there is love in God; then, there is salvation in God; then, there is hope in God. I had thought him cold, unjust, and austere. But lo! he appears wearing the character of love—breathing the spirit of love—displaying the acts of love—and laying at my feet

the most costly and precious boon of his love.   O
God, bow my heart before this love of thine, unspeakable!"

"His own Son."   We are here met with a great
and glorious truth,—the Sonship of our Lord.
There may be much of mystery connected with it;
nevertheless it is a revealed doctrine, and as such,
we believe and are sure that it is true.   With what
clearness did Christ himself propound this doctrine
to the cavilling Jews!   "Jesus answered them, My
Father worketh hitherto, and I work.   Therefore,
the Jews sought the more to kill him, because he
not only had broken the Sabbath, but said also that
God was his Father, making himself equal with
God."*   Now it must be borne in mind that this
declaration of his Sonship involves also a declaration of *equality* in all respects with the Father.   So
the Jews evidently understood it.   In a far different,
because in a far higher and diviner sense, the Lord
Jesus is declared to be the Son of God than believers,
who are also denominated the "sons of God."   The
passage before us makes this distinction.   "His *own*
Son," a mode of expression peculiar to the essential
relation of Christ to God.   Just as a father would
distinguish, by the same phraseology, his own son
from the son he had adopted; so God distinguished
his Eternal and Essential Son from his adopted sons.
Christ is elsewhere called the "only-begotten Son
of God," that is, the only one claiming so close an

* John v. 17, 18.

affinity with the Father. And can the essential equality of the Son with the Father be more distinctly declared than in the quotation which the apostle makes from one of the Messianic Psalms, and applies it, as it originally was, to the Eternal Son of God: "Unto which of the angels said he at any time, Thou art my Son, this day have I begotten thee? And again, I will be to him a Father, and he shall be to me a Son? And again, when he bringeth in the first-begotten into the world, he saith, And let all the angels of God worship him."* And if all the angels of God are commanded to *worship* him, surely then our Lord spake no blasphemy when he "made himself *equal with God.*"

God "*spared not* his own Son." Expressive words! Knowing what redemption required—justice, stern and inexorable, demanding full satisfaction—the law, rigid and unbending, demanding perfect obedience—he withheld not the only sacrifice that could meet the case. "He *spared* not his own Son." He did not relax aught of the requirement, nor abate aught of the suffering. Oh no! the utmost payment was exacted, and the last drop of the cup was drained. Had there been the least relaxing of the law's stringency, or the slightest curtailment of the law's penalty, then there had been no salvation for us. And all this was the unveiling of love. To spare his people, he spared not his Son.

* Heb. i. 5, 6.

"Delivered him up for us all." If any other expression were necessary to deepen our sense of the vastness of his love, we have it here. Who delivered up Jesus to die? Not Judas, for money; not Pilate, for fear; not the Jews, for envy;—but the Father, for love! "Him being delivered by the determinate counsel and foreknowledge of God, ye have taken, and by wicked hands have crucified and slain."* In this great transaction we lose sight of his betrayers, and his accusers, and his murderers, and we see only the Father travailing in the greatness of his love to his family. And to what was he delivered? To the hands of wicked men,—God's "darling to the power of the dogs." To poverty and want, to contempt and infamy, to grief and sorrow, to unparalleled suffering, and a most ignominious death. "It pleased the LORD to bruise him, he hath put him to grief." And for whom was he thus delivered up? "For us all;" for the church purchased with his own blood. For all in that church he has an equal love, and for all he paid an equal price. Oh, deem not yourself—poor, unlettered, and afflicted as you may be—less an object of the Father's love, and less the purchase of the Saviour's merits. Oh, blessed, comforting truth—"For *us* all!" For you, who are tempted to interpret your afflictions as signals of wrath, and your sins as seals of condemnation, and your poverty as marks of neglect, and your seasons of darkness as tokens of desertion, and your

* Acts ii. 23.

doubts and fears as evidences of a false hope and of self-deception; for you, dear saint of God, Jesus was delivered up.

And now let us consider this unspeakable gift of God as the guarantee of all other blessing.

"How shall he not with him freely give us all things?" How beautiful and conclusive the reasoning of the Apostle! Arguing from the greater to the less, he proceeds to assure the believer of God's readiness freely to bestow all needful blessing. To this he stood pledged. The gift of his own Son, so freely and unreservedly bestowed, was the security and the channel of every other mercy. When God gave his Son, the reconciliation had not actually been effected, justice had received no satisfaction, and the broken law no repair. Thus, "God commended his love towards us, in that, *while we were yet sinners*, Christ died for us."* If, then, when we were enemies, we were reconciled to God by the death of his Son, much more, being reconciled, will he freely give us all things. "All things!" How comprehensive the grant! "According as his Divine power hath given unto us *all things* that pertain unto life and godliness." † Holding the security in the hand of faith, you may repair to your Heavenly Father, and ask for all that you need. So to speak, God has bound himself to withhold no good thing from you. He is pledged, and from that pledge he will never recede, to grant you all you need. What is your

* Rom. v. 8.　　　　　　† 2 Pet. i. 3.

demand? Is it the Spirit to seal, to sanctify, to comfort you? Then draw near and ask the gift. "For if ye who are evil know how to give good things to your children, how much more shall your Heavenly Father give the Holy Spirit to them that ask him?" Is it *pardon?* Then ask it. He who provided the sacrifice for sin, will he not freely bestow the forgiveness of sin? Is it *grace?* Having given you the Reservoir of grace, is he not as willing and "able to make *all* grace abound toward you, that ye, always having all sufficiency in all things, may abound to eyerv good work?"* Is it *comfort?* Having given you the "Consolation of Israel," will he not prove to you the "God of all comfort?" Is your necessity *temporal?* Are your circumstances adverse? Filled with forebodings of approaching difficulty, the cruse of oil and the barrel of meal wasting, are you anxious and fearful? Take your temporal need to God. What! will he bestow the higher blessings of grace, and withhold the inferior ones of providence? Never! And can you press to your believing heart the priceless, precious, unspeakable gift of his Son, and yet cherish in that heart the gloomy, misgiving, thought of God's unwillingness and inability to supply *all* your need?

"Freely give." God's gifts are both rich and gratuitous. He always bestows more, never less, than we ask. It would seem as though he could not open his hand to a poor comer, but it overflowed

* 2 Cor. ix. 8.

with a bounty worthy of himself. Here are met all the objections to our coming which spring from our unworthiness, unfruitfulness, and unfaithfulness. Having nothing to pay, nothing in return is required. "Without money, and without price." Free as the sun-light—free as the balmy air—free as the mountain stream—*free* as the heart of God can make it, is every blessing which he bestows. "He that SPARED NOT HIS OWN SON, BUT DELIVERED HIM UP FOR US ALL, HOW SHALL HE NOT WITH HIM ALSO FREELY GIVE US ALL THINGS?"

CHAPTER XXXII.

THE BELIEVER'S CHALLENGE.

"Who shall lay any thing to the charge of God's elect? It is
God that justifieth."—ROMANS viii. 33.

THE Apostle recurs again to the great proposition
with which he started—no condemnation in Christ
Jesus,—the evidence of which had so richly accumulated in his course, as to justify this, the keynote
of the triumph with which he conducts his brilliant
argument to a close. It is impossible not to perceive
that his spirit kindles with the inspiration of his
theme, until from the pinnacle on which he now
stood, he seems to have caught an expanded view,
and to reflect the first beams, of that heaven of glory
from which he had so lately descended.

"God's elect." It was important that the Apostle
should distinctly specify who the persons were against
whom no accusation could justly be alleged. And
what terms could he employ more expressive of their
character and relation than this? It involves two
ideas—God's choice, of a people beloved. The term
occurs in other places. "But for the *elect's* sake

these days shall be shortened."* "According to the faith of God's *elect*."† "*Elect* according to the foreknowledge of God the Father."‡ "His own *elect*."§ It is quite clear, then, that those on whose behalf this challenge is made, are a people who, like their Lord and Master, are "chosen of God and precious." Now, scriptural as this doctrine is, it cannot be concealed that many anxious minds have made it a stumbling-stone at the very threshold of their spiritual career. The great mistake has been the making the doctrine of election the starting-point of their conversion, rather than a point to be reached at a subsequent and distant part of their religious course. With God it doubtless is the starting-point, if we may suppose a beginning with him who has no beginning—but not with man. We have in a previous chapter shown that our calling of God by the Spirit is the premise, and that our election of God by his love is the conclusion. Thus reasoning, as logicians term it, *à posteriori*, without having looked into the mysterious volume of the Divine decrees, the Apostle, addressing the converted Thessalonians, could boldly say, "Knowing, brethren beloved, your election of God." And how did he know it? From their faith, their knowledge, their reception of the truth, and its transforming effects on their character. Adopt this mode of reasoning as yours, and you will no longer complain that the doctrine of election is a perplexing truth, casting its

* Matt. xxiv. 22. † Tit. i. 1. ‡ 1 Pet. i. 2. § Luke xviii. 7.

deep and gloomy shadow upon your path to the cross. In your spiritual voyage your *calling by grace* is like an isthmus standing between two eternities; the past, in which God has chosen his people; and the future, in which he will glorify them. Reach this middle point and you are safe.

"It is God that justifieth." We believe that by many this cardinal doctrine of God's justification is but imperfectly understood, and but indistinctly seen in its results. The lofty position of security in which it places the believer, the liberty, peace, and hope into which it brings him, are points dim and obscure in the spiritual vision of many. We also believe that much of the weak, sickly Christianity of numbers is traceable, in a great measure, to the crude and gloomy conceptions they form of God, produced by not clearly seeing the interest which he felt, and the initiatory part which he took, in the great matter of our justification. Let our faith but trace the act of our justification to God, and we have placed ourselves upon a vantage-ground of the boldest defiance to all our enemies. Survey the truth in this light for a moment. Against whom have you sinned? Adopting David's confession, you exclaim, "Against thee, and thee only have I sinned." Having sinned against God, from God, then, you looked for the condemnation. You had violated his law, and from the lips of the Lawgiver you waited the sentence. When, lo! he declares himself on your side. Descending, as from his tribunal, he comes and stands in your place, and avows himself your Justifier. "It is GOD that justifieth." Upon you, a culprit, trembling at his bar, he throws his own righteousness, "which is unto all, and upon all them that believe;" and from that moment you are justified. Shall we, then, be indifferent to the part the Father took in the great question of our acceptance? Shall we cherish the shy and suspicious thought of God as if he looked coldly at us, and felt that, in pleading for his mercy, we were infringing upon his righteousness? Oh, no! Away with such thoughts of God! He it is who pronounces the act of your acquittal, and from his lips sound the glorious words, "No CONDEMNATION!" "It is God that justifieth."

We are now prepared for the challenge based upon this truth. "Who shall lay anything to the charge of God's elect?" Who in heaven; who on earth; who in hell? God will not; sin cannot; Satan dare not. Who? If there be in this wide universe an accuser of those whom God has justified, let him appear. There is none! Every mouth is closed. "*Who* shall lay *any thing* to the charge of God's elect?" If there remain a sin unpardoned, a stain uneffaced, a precept unkept, by the Mediator of his church, let it appear. But there is none! The work of Christ is honourable and glorious. It is a finished work. And on the basis of this complete Atonement, God, while he remains just, is the justifier of him that believeth. Oh, embrace this truth, ye who, in bitterness of soul, are self-accused and self-condemned before God! Satan could accuse, and the world could accuse, and the saints could accuse, but more severe and true than all, is the self-accusation which lays your mouth in the dust, in the deepest, lowliest contrition. Yet, as a poor sinner, looking to Jesus, resting in Jesus, accepted in Jesus, who shall lay anything legally to your charge, since it is God—the God against whom you have sinned—who himself becomes your Justifier? May you not with all lowliness, yet with all holy boldness, challenge every foe, in the prophetic words of Christ himself—" He is near that justifieth me: who will contend with me? "

This truth is an elevating, because a deeply sanctifying one. It exalts the principles, and these, in their turn, exalt the practice of the Christian. Oh! the thought, that it is God who justifies us at an expense to himself so vast, by a sacrifice to himself so precious, surely is sufficiently powerful to give the greatest intensity to our pantings, and fervency to our prayers, for conformity to the Divine image. Deep sorrows, and sore trials, and fiery temptations, we may have, and must have, if we ever enter the kingdom; but, what is sorrow, and what is trial, and what is temptation, if they work but in us the fruits of righteousness, meeten us more perfectly for heaven, and waft us nearer to our eternal home? Press, in humble faith, this precious truth to your heart, for God has forgiven all, and has cancelled all, and has forgotten all, and is your God for ever and ever.

" No weapon that is formed against thee shall prosper : and every tongue that shall rise against thee in judgment thou shalt condemn. This is the heritage of the servants of the LORD, and their right-eousness is of me, saith the Lord."*

* Isa. liv. 17.

CHAPTER XXXIII.

THE BELIEVER'S TRIUMPH.

" Who is he that condemneth ?   It is Christ that died, yea rather,
that is risen again, who is even at the right hand of God,
who also maketh intercession for us."—ROMANS viii. 34.

WE have remarked that the soul of the Apostle
rose with the sublimity of his theme.   It was impossible not to perceive, as we followed him in his
masterly and conclusive argument, how his mighty
mind kindled with fresh rapture, as each successive
step conducted him towards its magnificent climax.
It may truly be said to be the "mighty work of a
mind acting in all the dignity of independent greatness, and fired and elevated by a principle no less
commanding than the love of Jesus." He had
thrown down the undaunted challenge, unaccepted,
and now he breathes the final triumph—" Who is he
that condemneth ? " Let us briefly follow him in the
different parts of the mediatorial work of Christ,
which he exhibits in the passage, as constituting the
ground of the believer's triumph.

" It is Christ that died." Upon this fact we have

somewhat descanted elsewhere, in explaining the doctrine of the believer's justification. The object of the writer in introducing it again, was to confirm the Christian's exemption from condemnation, on the broad basis of Christ's mediation. This event formed the first of all the subsequent steps in the working out of the great plan of the Church's redemption. To this, as its centre, every line of truth converged. It was as a suffering Messiah, as an atoning High Priest, as a crucified Saviour, as a Conqueror, returning from the battle-field with garments rolled in blood, that the Son of God was revealed to the eye of the Old Testament saints. They were taught by every type, and by every prophecy, to look to the "Lamb *slain* from the foundation of the world." Christ must die. Death had entered our world, and death—the death of the Prince of Life—only could expel it. This event formed the deepest valley of our Lord's humiliation. It was the dark background—the sombre shading of the picture of his life, around which gathered the light and glory of all the subsequent parts of his history. But in what character did Christ die? Not as a Martyr, nor as a Model, but as a Substitute. His death was substitutionary. "God hath not appointed us to wrath, but to obtain salvation by our Lord Jesus Christ, *who died for us*."* This great truth, the Apostle, we find in another place, appropriating to himself. "The Son of God who loved me and gave himself *for* me."†

* 1 Thess. v. 9, 10. † Gal. ii. 20.

Here was the personal application of a general truth. And this is the privilege of faith. There breathes not a babe in Christ, who may not lay his hand upon this glorious truth—" Christ gave himself for *me*." Contemplate now, the conclusiveness of this reasoning for the non-condemnation of the believer. Since Christ bore our sins, and was condemned in our place; since by his expiatory death the claims of Divine justice are answered, and the holiness of the Divine law is maintained, who can condemn those for whom he died? Oh, what security is this for the believer in Jesus! Standing beneath the shadow of the cross, the weakest saint can confront his deadliest foe; and every accusation alleged, and every sentence of condemnation uttered, he can meet, by pointing to Him who died. In that one fact he sees the great debt cancelled, the entire curse removed, the grand indictment quashed—and "No condemnation to them that are in Christ Jesus," are words written as in letters of living light upon the cross.

"Yea rather, that is risen again." This is the second part of the mediation of Christ, which the Apostle assigns as a reason why none can condemn the believer. It would seem by the word "rather" that we are taught to look upon this fact of our Lord's life as supplying a still stronger affirmation of the great truth he was establishing. A few observations may make this appear. The atoning work of Christ was in itself a finished work. It supplied all that the case demanded. Nothing could possibly add to its perfection. "I have *finished* the work which thou gavest me to do." But we wanted the proof. We required that evidence of the reality and acceptance of the Atonement which would render our faith in it a rational and intelligent act. The proof lay with him who was "pleased to bruise him and put him to grief." If God were satisfied, then the guilty, trembling sinner may confidently and safely repose on the work of the Saviour. The fact of the resurrection was therefore essential to give reality to the Atonement, and hope to man. Had he not returned in triumph from the grave, the sanctity of his precepts, the sublimity of his teachings, the lustre of his example, and the sympathies awakened by the story of his death, might have attracted, charmed, and subdued us, but all expectation of redemption by his blood would have been a mockery and a delusion. But, "This Jesus hath God raised up." And grounded on this fact the believer's acquittal is complete. When he bowed his head and gave up the ghost, the sentence of condemnation was reversed; but when he burst the bonds of death, and appeared in the character of a Victor, the believer's justification was for ever sealed. "For if when we were enemies we were reconciled to God by the death of his Son, much more, being reconciled, shall we be saved *by his life.*" Here, then, lies the great security of the believer. "Delivered for our offences, he rose again for our justification." Planting his foot of faith upon the vacant tomb of his living Redeemer, the Christian can exclaim, " Who is he that condemneth ? it is Christ that died, yea *rather, that is risen again.*" Oh, to feel the power of his resurrection in our souls ! Oh, to rise with him in all the reality and glory of this his new-born life, our minds, our affections, our aspirations, our hopes all quickened, and ascending with our living Lord. " Because I live, ye shall live also."

" Who is even at the right hand of God." The exaltation of Christ was a necessary part of his mediatorial work. It entered essentially into the further continuance of that work in heaven—the scene of the intercessory part of the High Priest's office. "The right hand of God" is a phrase expressive of power and dignity. "When he had by himself purged our sins, sat down on the right hand of the Majesty on high."* "Who is gone into heaven, and is on the right hand of God; angels, and authorities, and powers, being made subject unto him."† What stronger assurance has the believer that no impeachment against him can be successful, than this ? His Saviour, his Advocate, his best Friend, is at the right hand of the Father, advanced to the highest post of honour and power in heaven.

> " There sits our Saviour crowned with light,
>   Clothed in a body like our own."

All power and dominion are his. The revolutions of the planets, and the destinies of empires, his hand

* Heb. i. 3.   † 1 Pet. iii. 22.

guides. The government is upon his shoulders; and for the well-being, security, and triumph of his Church, power over all flesh, and dominion over all worlds, is placed in his hands. Who, then, can condemn? Jesus is at the right hand of God, and the principalities and powers of all worlds are subject to his authority. Fear not, therefore, O, believer! Your Head and Redeemer is alive to frustrate every purpose, to resist every plot, and to silence every tongue that would condemn you.

" Who also maketh intercession for us." To what a beautiful climax does the Apostle conduct his argument! The exaltation of Jesus in heaven is associated with the dearest interests of his people on earth. Joseph was forgotten when Pharaoh lifted up the head of the chief butler. But our Lord, amidst the honours and splendours to which God hath highly exalted him, still remembers his brethren in bonds, and maketh intercession for them. How expressive is the type of our Lord's present engagement on behalf of his people! " And he (Aaron) shall take a censer full of burning coals of fire from off the altar before the Lord, and his hands full of sweet incense beaten small, and bring it within the vail: and he shall put the incense upon the fire before the LORD, that the cloud of the incense may cover the mercy seat that is upon the testimony."* The passing of Aaron into the holy of holies, was the shadowing forth of our Lord's entrance into

* Lev. xvi. 12, 13.

heaven. The blood sprinkled at the mercy seat was the presentation of the great Atonement within the vail. And the incense overshadowing with its fragrant cloud the mercy seat, thus touched with blood, was the figure of the ceaseless intercession of our Great High Priest in the Holiest. "For Christ is not entered into the holy places made with hands, which are the figures of the true: but into heaven itself, now to appear in the presence of God for us."* It is an individual, an anticipative, and a present intercession. It embraces all the personal wants of each believer, it precedes each temptation and each trial, and at the moment that the sympathy and the prayers of the Saviour are the most called for, and are felt to be the most soothing, it bears the saint and his sorrow on its bosom before the throne. Just at a crisis of his history, at a juncture, perhaps, the most critical in his life; and when the heart, oppressed with its emotions, cannot breathe a prayer, Jesus is remembering him, sympathizing with him, and interceding for him. Oh, who can fully describe the blessings that flow through the intercession of the Son of God? The love, the sympathy, the forethought, the carefulness, the minute interest in all our concerns, are blessings beyond description. Tried, tempted believer! Jesus maketh intercession for you. Your case is not unknown to him. Your sorrow is not hidden from him. Your name is on his heart. Your burden is

* Heb. ix. 24.

on his shoulder; and because he not only *has* prayed for you, but prays for you *now*, your faith shall not fail. Your great accuser may stand at your right hand to condemn you, but your great Advocate stands at the right hand of God to plead for you. And greater is he that is for you, than all that are against you.

Behold the ground of the believer's triumph! What has he to fear? "Who is he that condemneth?" The mediatorial work of Christ shuts every mouth, meets every accusation, and ignores every indictment that can be brought against those for whom he died, rose again, ascended up on high, and makes intercession. Oh, what a glorious triumph does Christ secure to the weakest saint who stands in faith upon this rock! "There is therefore now NO CONDEMNATION to them that are in Christ Jesus."

CHAPTER XXXIV.

MORE THAN CONQUERORS.

"Who shall separate us from the love of Christ? shall tribulation,
or distress, or persecution, or famine, or nakedness, or peril,
or sword? As it is written, For thy sake we are killed all
the day long; we are accounted as sheep for the slaughter.
Nay, in all these things we are more than conquerors through
him that loved us."—ROMANS viii. 35, 36, 37.

THE Apostle here enumerates certain things which,
to the obscure eye of faith, and to the yet obscurer
eye of sense, would appear to make against the best
interests of the Christian, regarded either as evidences
of a waning of Christ's love to him, or as calculated
to produce such a result. He proposes an inquiry—
the purport of which we reserve for the consideration
of the closing chapter of this work—and then proceeds to give the reply. That reply sets the question
entirely at rest. He argues that, so far from the
things which he enumerates shaking the constancy of
Christ's love, perilling the safety of the Christian, or
shading the lustre of his renown, they but developed
the Saviour's affection to him more strongly, con-

firmed the fact of his security, and entwined fresh
and more verdant laurels around his brow. "Nay,
in all these things we are more than conquerors
through him that loved us."

We are first invited to contemplate the Christian
in the character of a 'Conqueror.' The battle we have,
at some length, already considered. We have seen it
to consist of a moral conflict, with inward and outward enemies, all leagued in terrible force against the
soul. To this is added—what, indeed, was most
peculiar to the early Church—a war of external
suffering, in which penury, persecution, and martyrdom constituted the dark and essential elements.
Now it will be instructive to observe in what way
Christ provides for the holy warrior's passage through
this fiery contest. It will be perceived that it is
not by flight, but by battle; not by retreat, but by
advance; not by shunning, but by facing the foe.
The Captain of their salvation might have withdrawn
his people from the field, and conducted them to heaven
without the hazard of a conflict. But not so. He
will lead them to glory, but it shall be by the path of
glory. They shall carve their way to the crown by
the achievements of the sword. They shall have pri-
vation, and distress, and suffering, of every kind; yet
while beneath the pressure, and in the very heat of
the battle, victory shall crown their arms, and a glorious triumph shall deepen the splendour of their
victory. And what spiritual eye does not clearly see,
that in conducting his people across the battle-field,

the Lord wins to himself more renown than though he had led them to their eternal rest with entire exemption from conflict and distress? But, in what sense are we conquerors? Just in that sense in which the Holy Ghost obtains the victory. It is not the believer himself who conquers; it is the Divine Spirit within the believer. No movement is seen, no tactics are observed, no war-cry is heard, and yet there is passing within the soul a more important battle, and there is secured a more brilliant victory, than ever the pen of the historian recorded. In the first place, there is the conquest of *faith*. Where do the annals of war present such a succession of victories so brilliant, achieved by a weapon so single and simple, as is recorded in the eleventh chapter of the Epistle to the Hebrews? And what was the grace that won those spiritual and glorious victories? It was the grace of *faith!* "This is the victory that overcometh the world, even your faith."* Faith in the truth of God's word—faith in the veracity of God's character —faith in the might, and skill, and wisdom, of our Commander and Leader—faith eyeing the prize, gives the victory to the Christian combatant, and secures the glory to the Captain of his salvation. And then there is the triumph of *patience*. "That ye be not slothful, but followers of them who through faith and *patience* inherit the promises." "And so, after he had *patiently* endured, he obtained the promise."† Oh, is it no real victory of the Holy Ghost in the

* 1 John v. 4. † Heb. vi. 12, 15.

believer, when beneath the pressure of great affliction, passing through a discipline the most painful and humiliating, the suffering Christian is enabled to cry, "Though he slay me yet will I trust in him?"* "The cup which my Father hath given me, shall I not drink it?"† "Not my will but thine be done!" Suffering child of God, "let *patience* have her perfect work, that ye may be perfect and entire, wanting nothing." ‡ And, then, there is the conquest of *joy*. "And ye became followers of us, and of the Lord, having received the word in much affliction, with *joy* of the Holy Ghost."§ "My brethren, count it all *joy* when ye fall into divers temptations,"‖ or trials. Why is trial an occasion of joy? Because it is the triumph of the Holy Ghost in the soul. And does not Christ say, "Ye shall be sorrowful, but your sorrow shall be turned into *joy?*" ¶ And who but Jesus can turn our sorrow into joy?—not only assuaging our griefs, alleviating our sufferings, and tempering the furnace-flame, but actually making our deepest, darkest sorrows, the occasion of the deepest gladness, praise, and thanksgiving. "Thou hast turned for me my mourning into dancing: thou hast put off my sackcloth, and girded me with gladness; to the end that my glory [my tongue] may sing praise to thee, and not be silent."** Oh, yes! it is a glorious victory of the Holy Ghost, the Comforter, in the

---

* Job xiii. 15.   † John xviii. 11.   ‡ James i. 4.
§ 1 Thess. i. 6.   ‖ James i. 2.   ¶ John xvi. 20.
** Psa. xxx. 11, 12.

soul, when it can enable the believer to adopt the words of the suffering Apostle, " I am filled with comfort, I am *exceeding joyful in all our tribulation.*"* Suffering reader! Jesus knows how to turn *your* sorrow into joy. Confide your grief to him, and he will cause it sweetly to sing.

" More than conquerors." The original word will admit a stronger rendering than our translators have allowed it. The same word is in another place rendered, *a far more and exceeding* and eternal weight of glory." So that in the present instance it might be translated, "*far more exceeding* conquerors." The phrase seems to imply that it is more than a mere victory which the believer gains. A battle may be won at a great loss to the conqueror. A great leader may fall at the head of his troops. The flower of an army may be destroyed, and the best blood of a nation's pride may be shed. But the Christian conquers with no such loss. Nothing whatever essential to his well-being is perilled. His armour, riveted upon his soul by the Holy Spirit, he cannot lose. His life, hid with Christ in God, cannot be endangered. His Leader and Commander, once dead, is alive and dieth no more. Nothing valuable and precious shall he lose. There is not a grace in his soul but shall come out of the battle with sin, and Satan, and the world, purer and brighter for the conflict. The more thoroughly the Lord brings our graces into exercise,

* 2 Cor. vii. 4.

the more fully shall they be developed, and the more mightily shall they be invigorated. Not a grain of grace shall perish in the winnowing, not a particle of faith shall be consumed in the refining. Losing nothing, he gains everything! He returns from the battle laden with the spoils of a glorious victory —"*more* than a conqueror." All his resources are augmented by the result. His armour is brighter, his sword is keener, his courage is more dauntless, for the conflict. Every grace of the Spirit is matured. Faith is strengthened—love is expanded —experience is deepened—knowledge is increased. He comes forth from the trial holier and more valorous than when he entered it. His weakness has taught him wherein his strength lieth. His necessity has made him better acquainted with Christ's fulness. His peril has shown him who taught his hands to war and his fingers to fight, and whose shield covered his head in the day of battle. He is "*more* than conqueror"—he is *triumphant!*

"Through him that loved us." Here is the great secret of our victory, the source of our triumph. Behold the mystery explained, how a weak, timid believer, often starting at his own shadow, is yet "more than a conqueror" over his many and mighty foes. To Christ who loved him, who gave himself for him, who died in his stead, and lives to intercede on his behalf, the glory of the triumph is ascribed. And this is the song he chants, "Thanks be to God which giveth us the victory *through our Lord Jesus Christ.*" Through the conquest which he himself obtained, through the grace which he imparts, through the strength which he inspires, through the intercession which he presents, in all our " tribulation, and distress, and persecution, and famine, and nakedness, and peril, and sword " we are " more than conquerors." Accounted though we are as "sheep for the slaughter," yet our Great Shepherd, Himself slain for the sheep, guides his flock, and has declared that no one shall pluck them out of his hand. We are more than conquerors through his grace who loved us in the very circumstances that threaten to overwhelm. Fear not, then, the darkest cloud, nor the proudest waves, nor the deepest wants, —in these very things you shall, through Christ, prove triumphant. Nor shrink from the battle with the " last enemy." Death received a death-wound when Christ died. You face a conquered foe. He stands at your side a crownless king, and waving a broken sceptre. Your death shall be another victory over the believer's last foe. Planting your foot of faith upon his prostrate neck, you shall spring into glory, more than a conqueror, through him that loved you. Thus passing to glory in triumph, you shall go to swell the ranks of the " noble army of martyrs "—those Christian heroes of whom it is recorded, " THEY OVERCAME HIM BY THE BLOOD OF THE LAMB."

CHAPTER XXXV.

NO SEPARATION FROM CHRIST JESUS.

"For I am persuaded that neither death, nor life, nor principalities, nor powers, nor things present, nor things to come, nor height, nor depth, nor any other creature, shall be able to separate us from the love of God which is in Christ Jesus our Lord."—ROMANS viii. 38, 39.

THIS sublime chapter having opened with a strong declaration of no condemnation in Christ Jesus, it was meet that it should close with a declaration equally strong, of no separation from Christ Jesus. In passing through its rich and precious contents, our feelings have resembled those of a tourist coursing his way over an extended and magnificent landscape of varied feature and of exquisite loveliness. We have surveyed the scenery of the Christian life, from almost every point of observation, and in all its variety of form, beauty of colouring, and harmony of design. And now, having reached the loftiest summit of Christian hope, with a rapid survey of the radiant and far-reaching prospect stretching out before the eye, we will conduct our reflections to a close. It is a delightful and animating theme with which the chapter terminates. The last object it presents to the eye is JESUS. The last accents that linger on the ear, are of the love of JESUS. Jesus was the beginning, and Jesus is the ending—and Jesus, in his personal glory, in his mediatorial work, in his inexhaustible fulness, in the close and tender relations which he sustains to his people, forms the sum and substance of all that intervenes between these two extremes—no condemnation, and no separation. The central figure is Christ. He is the Magnet which attracts all the affections awakened by these great and glowing truths; and he is the object around which the truths themselves closely, exclusively, and indissolubly entwine. Christ is the Alpha and the Omega —the beginning and the end—yea, Christ is all and in all. Be he all in all to our hearts!

It is of great moment that we have a clear apprehension of the Apostle's leading idea in these concluding verses. He refers to a love from which there is no separation. Of whose love does he speak? The believer's love to Christ? On the contrary—it is Christ's love to the believer. And this view of the subject makes all the difference in its influence upon our minds. What true satisfaction and real consolation, at least how small its measure, can the believer derive from a contemplation of his love to Christ? It is true, when sensible of its glow, and conscious of its power, he cannot but rejoice in any evidence, the smallest, of the work of the Holy Ghost in his soul.

Yet this is not the legitimate ground of his confidence, nor the proper source of his comfort. *It is Christ's love to him !* And this is just the truth the Christian mind needs for its repose. To whom did Paul originally address this letter? To the saints of the early and suffering age of the Christian Church. And this truth—Christ's love to his people—would be just the truth calculated to comfort, and strengthen, and animate them. To have declared that nothing should prevail to induce them to forsake Christ, would have been but poor consolation to individuals who had witnessed many a fearful apostasy from Christ in others, and who had often detected the working of the same principle in themselves. Calling to mind the strong asseveration of Peter, "Lord, though all should forsake thee yet will I not," and remembering how their Master was denied by one, and betrayed by another, and forsaken by all his disciples, their hearts would fail them. But let the Apostle allure their minds from a contemplation of their love to Christ, to a contemplation of Christ's love to them, assuring them, upon the strongest grounds, that whatever sufferings they should endure, or by whatever temptations they should be assailed, nothing should prevail to sever them from their interest in the reality, sympathy, and constancy of that love, and he has at once brought them to the most perfect repose. The affection, then, of which the Apostle speaks, is the love of God which is in Christ Jesus.

The love of Christ! such is our precious theme!

Of it can we ever weary? Its greatness can we ever know? Its plenitude can we fully contain? Never. Its depths cannot be fathomed, its dimensions cannot be measured. It passeth knowledge. All that Jesus did for his Church was but the unfolding and expression of his love. Travelling to Bethlehem—I see love incarnate. Tracking his steps as he went about doing good—I see love labouring. Visiting the house of Bethany—I see love sympathizing. Standing by the grave of Lazarus—I see love weeping. Entering the gloomy precincts of Gethsemane—I see love sorrowing. Passing on to Calvary—I see love suffering, and bleeding, and expiring. The whole scene of his life is but an unfolding of the deep, and awful, and precious mystery of redeeming love.

The love of the Father! Such, too, is our theme; and it is proper that with this truth the chapter should close. "The love of God which is in Christ Jesus our Lord." The love of the Father is seen in giving us Christ, in choosing us in Christ, and in blessing us in him with all spiritual blessings. Indeed, the love of the Father is the fountain of all covenant and redemption mercy to the church. It is that river the streams whereof make glad the city of God. How anxious was Jesus to vindicate the love of the Father from all the suspicions and fears of his disciples! "I say not unto you, that I will pray the Father for you, for the Father Himself loveth you." "God so loved the world that he gave his only-begotten Son." To this love we must trace all the

blessings which flow to us through the channel of the
cross. It is the love of God, exhibited, *manifested*,
and seen in Christ Jesus. Christ being, not the
originator, but the gift of his love; not the cause,
but the exponent of it. Oh, to see a perfect equality
in the Father's love with the Son's love! Then shall
we be led to trace all his sweet mercies, and all his
providential dealings, however trying, painful, and
mysterious, to the *heart* of God; thus resolving all
into that from whence all alike flow—everlasting and
unchangeable LOVE.

Now it is from this love there is no separation.
"Who shall separate us from the love of Christ?"
The Apostle had challenged accusation from every foe,
and condemnation from every quarter; but no accuser
rose, and no condemnation was pronounced. Standing on the broad basis of Christ's finished work, and
of God's full justification, his head was now lifted up
in triumph above all his enemies round about. But
it is possible that though in the believer's heart there
is no fear of impeachment, there yet may exist the
latent one of *separation*. The aggregate dealings of
God with his church, and his individual dealings with
his saints, may at times present the appearance of an
alienated affection, or a lessened sympathy. The age
in which this epistle was penned, was fruitful of suffering to the church of God. And if any period or any
circumstances of her history boded a severance of the
bond which bound her to Christ, that was the period,
and those were the circumstances. But with a con-

fidence based upon the glorious truth on which he had been descanting—the security of the Church of God in Christ—and with a persuasion inspired by the closer realization of the glory about to burst upon her view —with the most dauntless courage he exclaims—" I am *persuaded* that neither death, nor life, nor angels, nor principalities, nor powers, nor things present, nor things to come, nor height, nor depth, nor any other creature, shall be able to separate us from the love of God, which is in Christ Jesus our Lord." Let us briefly glance at each of these things which may threaten, but which cannot succeed in separating us from the love of God, and from our union with Christ.

The passage commences with "death." That there is a separating power in death, is a truth too evident and too affecting to deny. It separates the soul from the body, and man from all the pursuits and attractions of earth. " His breath goeth forth, in that very day his thoughts perish." All his thoughts of ambition—his thoughts of advancement—his thoughts of a vain and Pharisaical religion—all perish in that day. What a mournful sublimity is there in this vivid description of the separating power of death over the creature! What a separating power, too, has it, as felt in the chasms it creates in human relationships! Who has not lost a friend, a second self, by the ruthless hand of death? What bright home has not been darkened, what loving heart has not been saddened, by its visitations? It separates us from the husband of our youth—from the wife of our bosom—from the child of our affections—from the friend and companion of our earlier and riper years. It comes and breaks the link that bound us so fondly and so closely to the being, whose affection, sympathy, and intercourse seemed essential elements of our being, whose life we were wont to regard as a part of our very existence. But there is one thing from which death cannot separate us—the love of God which is in Christ Jesus, and all the blessings which that love bestows. Death separate us! Nay; death unites us the more closely to those blessings, by bringing us into their more full and permanent possession. Death imparts a realization and a permanence to all the splendid and holy anticipation of the Christian. The happiest moment of his life is its last. All the glory and blessing of his existence cluster and brighten around that solemn crisis of his being. Then it is he feels how precious the privilege, and how great the distinction of being a believer in Jesus. And the day that darkens his eye to all earthly scenes, opens it upon the untold, and unimaginable, and ever-increasing glories of eternity. It is the birth-day of his immortality. Then, Christian, fear not death! It cannot separate you from the Father's love, nor can it, while it tears you from an earthly bosom, wrench you from Christ's. You shall have in death, it may be, a brighter, sweeter manifestation of his love than you ever experienced in life. Jesus, the Conqueror of death, will approach and place beneath you his almighty arms, and your head upon his loving bosom. Thus encircled and pillowed, you "shall not see death," but passing through its gloomy portal shall only realize that you had actually died, from the consciousness of the joy and glory into which death had ushered you. "Nor life." The hope of life is meant. The Apostle wrote, as we have re-marked, in a peculiarly suffering era of the church— an age of fiery persecution for the Gospel's sake. Under these circumstances, life was not unfrequently offered on condition of renouncing the Gospel, and denying the Saviour. This was a strong temptation to apostasy. When in full view of the rack, the cross, the stake, life—precious life, with all its sweet attraction and fond ties—was offered, and which a simple renunciation of the cross, and a single embrace of the crucifix, would purchase back; to some, weak in faith, such a temptation might be well nigh irresistible. But it shall not succeed in separating the suffering Christian from the love of Christ. Nor shall anything connected with life—its trials, its vicissitudes, or its temptations—dissever us from God's affection. Thus both life and death shall but con-firm us in the assurance of our inalienable interest in the love of God: "For whether we live, we live unto the Lord; and whether we die, we die unto the Lord; whether we live therefore, or die, we are the Lord's."*   "Nor angels, nor principalities,

* Rom. xiv. 8.

nor powers." Of course, not good angels, but evil spirits, are here meant. And these include, not demons merely, but all evil agencies—men of the world—human governments—civil powers—all that is hostile to the spiritual interests of Christ's truth and kingdom. Such are often found either powerful engines of spiritual persecutions themselves, or else by indifference and connivance, sympathizing with, and abetting the high-handed persecutor. But no human or superhuman power shall prevail to impair the interest of God's saints in his love. Have they in a single instance done so? Has God ever forsaken his people, when the Evil Spirit has stirred up ungodly men and despotic governments to rob them of their rights, to fetter their consciences, to imprison or to slay their persons? No, never! Secure in his love, no floods of enmity, no sword of persecution, shall ever displace the church of Christ. The day of her triumph over all her enemies is fast speeding on. A splendid day will that be. Her home had often been the fastness of the rock —the solitude of the mountain—the depth of the cave—the midnight gloom of the dungeon. She had often prophesied in sackcloth and in blood; at one time avowing her faith from the rack, and at another confessing the name of Jesus from amidst the flames. But the day of her triumph and glory draws nigh. Then shall her enemies come bending unto her, and shall lick the dust of her feet. Who shall lay anything then to her charge? Silenced and condemned, all her foes shall retire to their terrible doom, leav-

ing her enshrined in all the glory of the CHURCH
TRIUMPHANT. "Things present." Things temporary and transient, be they sad or joyous, pleasant
or painful. Indwelling sin, temporary trial, occasional temptations, the momentary suspensions of
God's realized love,—none of these, or any other
things present, shall separate them from Christ.
"Things to come." What human foresight can
predict the future of the earthly history of the child
of God? What human hand can uplift the veil that
conceals the events that shall yet transpire in his
history ere he reaches that perfect world where there
will be no future, but one eternal present? Oh, what
goodness hides it from our view! But be that future
what it may, shady or sunny, stormy or serene, God
will stand fast to his covenant with his Church,
and Christ to his union with his people. Things
to come, be they more terrible than things that are
past, or that are now, shall not touch their interest
in the Lord's love. "Nor height." No elevation
to which he may advance them, no height of rank,
or wealth, or honour, or influence, or usefulness,
shall peril their place in his love. Thus it was the
Lord advanced Moses, and David, and Joseph, and
Gideon; but in their elevation to worldly distinction, power, and affluence, they were kept walking
humbly with God—and this was the secret of their
safety. "The Lord God is my strength, and he
will make my feet like hind's feet, and he will make
me to walk upon mine high places."* "Nor depth."

* Hab. iii. 19.

Oh, how deep those depths may be! From the loftiest height to the lowest depth of adversity, God can bring his servant, yet love him still with an unchanged and deathless affection. But no depth of soul-distress, no depth of poverty, or suffering, or humiliation, shall disturb the repose or peril the security of a believing soul in the love of God. "Nor any other creature." If there be any other thing or being in the wide universe that wears a threatening or unkindly aspect towards the Christian, Divine power shall restrain its force, saying to the proud waves, "Thus far shalt thou come, and no farther." And thus all the billows, amidst which the Ark has for ages been tossed, shall but bear it gently and triumphantly onward to the Mount of God. On that mount, beloved, where now are gathering all who have the Father's name written on their foreheads, we, too, through grace, shall stand eternally extolling the LAMB, through Him, who—because he died,—there is for us NO CONDEMNATION from Divine justice,—and through Him, who—because he lives,—there is for us NO SEPARATION from Divine love.

> "Oh, when my God, my glory, brings
>   His white and holy train
> Unto those clear and living springs
>   Where comes no stain:
> "Where all is light, and flowers, and fruit,
>   And joy, and rest,
> Make me amongst them, 'tis my suit!
>   The last one and the least."